Summer's Stars

J.W. CRONICAN

PublishAmerica
Baltimore

ISBN: 1-4241-1531-0
PUBLISHED BY PUBLISHAMERICA, LLLP
www.publishamerica.com
Baltimore

Printed in the United States of America

DEDICATION

This book is dedicated with affection first to Mr. And Mrs. Rich Alday. I can only hope that my words are able to illustrate for you how much Ambrose meant to me and how special the time I was able to spend with him still is to me.

Secondly, to the boys with whom I share these memories. Few days go by that I don't have some thought of you and those wonderful, summer days.

This book is also dedicated to Hoddy. I think of you daily. Thank you for believing in me, everyday of my life.

ACKNOWLEDGMENTS

This book would never have been completed without help from many. Often times I doubt they even know of their contributions.

Thank you to my family for all their help through too many tough times.

To my best friends Craig and Kristi for all their support.

To all the players I have ever had the privilege of coaching, particularly those in the years 2003-2005. You help to remind me of why I keep going.

To Avery Elizabeth, the thought of her smile inspires me every day.

Prologue

I could feel the warmth of the golden, spring sun on the back of my neck as a gentle breeze rustle the leaves of two giant Cottonwood trees nearby. The sky, a faint, mid-morning blue without a cloud in sight as I took in my surroundings. Familiar, but foreign surroundings for I hadn't been back here in years.

A six-field complex of youth baseball and softball fields, filled with the sounds of youth. A game played on each field while all around more teams prepared for their turn. Parents and friends looked on or in some cases, couldn't look as their child came to bat or took the mound to pitch. Six fields of emerald green spotted with all the colors of the rainbow disguised as uniforms. Perfect lines of reddish-brown fit tightly against the green with single, white, chalk lines drew even more pictures on the ground.

I stepped to the top of a set of wooden bleachers next to the biggest field. The field used for ages thirteen to fifteen. Just as had been the case when I was young, the paint on these bleachers had peeled off due to weather and only spots remained. I smiled, thinking of how much had changed and really, so little. I had grown up playing baseball on these same fields, under the same pale blue sky, the same friends and passions. Guessing, I'd say even the same dreams.

The fields seemed to be in better shape now, still laid out the same. Chain link fencing which surrounded each field still bowed from the continuous pounding of balls into their middles. What used to be a huge dirt parking lot on the south end now was a strip mall. I used to fall down getting out of my Mom's car in that parking lot, partly due to my own clumsiness and partly to make sure my uniform was dirty. The concession stand, a small two-story shack in my time, was now a three story building used not only for concessions but meetings and equipment as well. Trees, not much taller than myself when my father and others when I was nine years old were now fully established shade makers being taken advantage of in the New

Mexico sun. Thinking back, I could remember the cool March morning and the smell of my Father's coffee as he and several other Fathers planted those trees, constantly having to tell my friends and I to go play catch as to stay out of their way.

A sharp *"ping"* brought me back from my daydream, as one of the players launched a ball into the sky, leaving no doubt for all who were watching, where the ball would land. Everywhere I looked, waves of memories washed over my mind, leaving behind nothing but smiles in their wake. Out of the corner of my eye, I caught glimpse of something flying above, flags or rather pennants. Red and blue lettering against white cloth, all three colors faded by the passage of time. A huge smile crossed my face as I read what each had to say. Years and age groups, recorded on the pennants, representing City, State and other championships won by different teams in different years. Twenty-seven I counted, knowing there were a few missing, quite a testament to the talent and types of young athletes to have come through this league. I couldn't help but see the largest of these trophies, a World Championship banner, won by the twelve-year-old girls softball team in 1984. Then I made sure of the seven championships I had been a part of, two as a player and five as a coach. All were there, snapping occasionally as the breeze shook the dust out of them.

If someone had been watching me, I'm certain they would have thought me to be crazy. Here I sat, head craned backward, smiling as if I were stir-crazy at a group of banners flapping in a breeze. Paying no attention what so ever to the games going on around me. The games weren't the reason I was here. Neither were the flags really. Honestly, I was probably there for some self-therapy or perhaps to exercise some demons. Maybe I was there just to remember and smile again.

I stepped off the bleachers to walk around the complex. Something else should have been there, something else I had been a part of. I was sure it wasn't important to the people there today but it was very important to me. Where was it? Could it have been moved, forgotten? Finally, I found it, a simple, engraved, marble block. A small monument to a fallen friend. No one at the park seemed to notice it. Maybe they had seen it before, read it and moved on. Most wouldn't have known the young man for whom it had been made but I did.

That small block represented so many memories. Memories of friendships forged and lives touched. It was symbolic of a period of time that a group of young men and myself would never nor could never forget. My life had changed because of it. I'm sure theirs had too.

Chapter 1

Three twelve-year-old boys sat across from each other as if they were big time businessmen discussing the merger of two companies. A rectangle table covered with a red checkerboard tablecloth, paper plates and half eaten pizza served as their conference room.

Todd, a toe headed blonde, spoke with the most emotion and fervor. His blue eyes turned dark as he relived the final moments of a baseball game earlier that day. Dirt still hid among the few freckles on his young face. He was most upset at the fact that he couldn't really understand what had gone wrong.

Three hours prior, Todd, Kris and Tim had taken the field with a team of All-Stars representing the Little League they played at. The team was comprised mostly of friends they were quite close to and had grown up with. A great deal of hype had accompanied this team, as often happens in the legends of Little League baseball, about how this was the best group of players ever to come through the league. They would certainly be the team to represent the United States in the Little League World Series. This was hype that had followed this group around from their nine-year-old season. A burden? Not to these boys. They never seemed to be bothered by it. Then again, they had never really lived up to it either.

As eleven year olds, this same group of boys, together for the most part had only reached the quarter finals of the City tournament. To go on to the World Series a team had to win City, State, Regional and a Divisional tournament. Now here in their twelve-year-old season they had another problem, one loss. Each part of this Nation wide tournament is a double elimination. These boys had already lost once. Something was missing from this team but no one knew what it was. They were far too talented to be beaten. It must have been the weather or field conditions. Perhaps it was poor officiating. Coaching? Who knew? It just didn't make sense.

Sure as the sun comes up in the East, the boys had lost again. With the help of a young man new to New Mexico, the team from across the North East Heights had defeated Todd's team by a score of five to three.

Todd fumed as he talked with Tim and Kris, both of whom were as unhappy as Todd just not as capable of expressing what they felt. Probably because Todd's father had been a High School baseball coach, Todd knew how to go about letting those around him know what he thought.

Frustration turned to sorrow or maybe it was just exhaustion. The three boys slumped against the table as a few more teammates sat down to pizza, soda and spirited conversation. It was nothing new to this group.

Most of the boys had known one another from the first day of Kindergarten. Some of them had even known one another before that. There were fourteen players on the team, all were friends but nine of them were more than that. Kindred spirits, maybe? Soul mates? It was hard to say why but there was a definite closeness about this group. They were always together. Not just one or two of them but rather five or six were always together and whoever wasn't with the larger part of the group was probably with the other boys and they would all meet up at some point. All nine lived within walking distance of each other. They went to school together, played each season's sport together often they even called one another's parents Mom and Dad. They were, in a way, brothers. Looking out for the others while knowing they would be looked out for as well.

Each one had their own personality or some characteristic, which allowed their individuality to stand out, but knowing one meant knowing them all. As they had grown, certain talents became obvious. One might be better at basketball or perhaps football. Grades might have been higher on one report card than another, though none of the boys ever struggled in school. Shy, outgoing, or comedian no matter what was different about these boys one common thread was undeniable. Baseball. They all loved playing baseball. Each boy thrived at the game; maybe one was better than another but not by much. The game was theirs and they would play it with or against one another.

As the boys sat watching Todd hold court, the fourteen-fifteen year old team came into the restaurant. It was a common place for teams to come. They had just won the City championship, having come in to celebrate. The twelve year olds watched with a bit of jealousy as the older boys strolled in, smiles on their dirt and eye black covered faces. The last person to enter the room with the team was the coach, Coach John. Most of the boys in the league knew the twenty two year old coach, as he had grown up in the same neighborhood, played in the same Little League and graduated from the same High School these boys would be attending. In fact, he had played for Todd's father while in High School. Todd had even been the over confident, borderline brat of a batboy for the Varsity team. John's personality was infectious and easy to get along with, though many could also say he was a bit on the arrogant side. Most who would say that of course were other coaches who couldn't beat him but even John admitted he could use a lesson or two in humility. Quietly admitted, that is. Then again, what twenty something doesn't have a bit of hubris? The world is a plaything and youth is invincible, just ask one.

He was tall, standing six feet three or so, dark blonde hair with blue, gray eyes. A late bloomer, he was just then coming into his looks and for the outward appearance of cocky, he struggled with himself inside. His smile allowed people to feel comfortable around him, particularly children. "A twelve year old hiding inside a twenty something body" is the way he described himself. Having left college to pursue his dream of playing baseball, John had put himself in a bad position. No baseball, no college, no direction. His lack of direction had brought him back to his hometown of Albuquerque, which in turn, had brought him back to baseball. Getting on the staff of his former High School, John had gotten to know some of the boys he now coached. A falling out with the head coach spited John enough to want to coach the boys his way, which meant coaching them in the summer at this Little League. It couldn't have worked out better. At least that was how it appeared.

The twelve year olds waved Coach John over to ask how they had won. They always enjoyed hearing John's stories. No matter how many days, months or years had passed, it seemed John never forgot a detail. He spoke with such passion and with such theatrical mannerisms, each story seemed like a production. This story had his team down by three runs with only two innings to go. Two home runs and a game saving play had put them in the championship. A championship won with a no hitter. The boys ate it up. They loved it and inside they all wanted the same for themselves. It was of course, Todd who said what everyone else was thinking. "Coach us next year." All the boys chirped in with their agreement as well.

It was something to think about. Actually, John had already been thinking about it. Todd's father had brought it up earlier in the summer and together they had looked at the pieces. John told the boys it could happen but for now he had to focus on the team he had then going to the State part of the tournament. Pizza and sodas all around, a light seemed to appear at the end of the tunnel.

Chapter 2

The sound of birds chirping could still be heard over the steady pattern of rain falling against the roof as John sat just inside his door looking outward. An afternoon summer shower was always a favorite of his, whether it was a time to nap or relax, the rush of water as cars passed by or the almost hypnotic sound of the storm always made him feel good. The scent of the air after the rain in particular brought back memories of summers past.

He had always believed that his ability to remember, in the greatest of detail, past events whether they were his or events he witnessed was a curse rather than a blessing. All his life he had lived in the moment, able to enjoy what was going on while some people missed it. That part was all good and well, the problem came after, when he remembered and wanted so desperately to be back in that moment. Maybe it was a fear of growing up, having to take on responsibility. Maybe it was the wanting for more moments, like those he had enjoyed while younger, to come around. Whatever it was, whenever it happened, something was lost. Somewhere along the way, John had lost his ability to enjoy life. No more laughter, no more smiles.

That isn't to say he never did either of these things anymore. He could smile and laugh. He did have fun but it was never freely. Every time, it seemed he had to take just a second to think about whether he would look ridiculous or if someone would think him immature.

John had always been able to laugh or cut up with the boys like anyone else but now he couldn't. More often than not, he would blend in and be part of the group but never the one to lead the crowd or be seen at the front. Just blend in and not do anything that could be perceived as "stupid." Maybe it was an image he wanted to portray or maybe it was only a personality trait. Whichever or whatever it was, John didn't know when it happened and worse, why it happened.

The rain came harder. Sheets of rain crashed down, many of them shining as the sunlight to the West reflected off the drops. That sunlight vanished as the clouds blanketed the sky and it became obvious it would come down for some time. John became lost in his thought once again. Thinking back to his thirteen-year-old summer, he remembered it as the best summer of his life. He could say that without thinking twice. He had nothing to think about except baseball. It was his thirteen year old year as far as baseball was concerned but really was only twelve as his birthday fell in September, putting him up a year in baseball and in school. He would start High School in the fall, that idea contributing to the excitement of the time and he didn't care about girls or driving just yet so there was nothing to think about but the game itself.

Along with seven of his good friends, he had been elected to the league's All Star team and for the first time in his life, baseball had become big. Big, meaning it wasn't just a game to play during the summer and watch on television. It was his game and he was good at it. It was obvious, through the summer, who would play at the next level and who would not. The game was easy, it was fun but that summer, the other side of baseball, the bonding and special moments had been clear. Maybe this had been the last year he smiled without thinking.

The All Star team John played on had some potential. As twelve year olds they had finished second in the city tournament and could have finished first. This year, they had a good luck charm, a toy car, a "hot wheels" car, modeled after a popular television show at the time had been found by one of the players. Before each game, John and his teammates would touch the car for luck. As fate would have it, there was enough luck in that car to take the team to Arizona for the divisional part of the All Star tournament. It was the most amazing time in his life. Playing at a level of baseball he had never experienced but moreover, spending time bonding with his friends. Even his father had made an effort above and beyond anything John had seen before. While in Phoenix, his father had flown down to watch and took John out to dinner after a tough loss. It wasn't much; except for the fact the two of them weren't really close. At least in John's eyes. With one simple act, it had become clear to John that his father did care about him and the two days the spent were as big a part of making the summer special as any. Those were moments John could remember forever and he did.

It was at that moment, the moment he came out of his daydream, John knew he would coach and why he would do so. Briefly, he realized he was smiling. Of course he was. No one was looking; there would be no judgment. Still, he was unhappy inside, he had always been unhappy inside, and it was just that no one had ever known.

John sat in his doorway the rest of the evening, listening to the rain and embracing the dark. Darkness meant that no one could see him. That was important, that no one see "him." The less people who knew him, the less people he could disappoint.

Chapter 3

The season wouldn't begin for another five months or so; still the boys would talk endlessly about the summer to come. They would play catch or go to batting cages to work out their frustrations of having to wait so long. All of the boys played football and would also be playing basketball and yet here they were working so hard at baseball.

The leaves had begun to turn, a brilliant array of yellows and oranges. Nothing to rival the East coast of course, still a thing of beauty as the sun would hang just above the horizon around four in the afternoon, a gentle wind, with gust of haste would blow from the west. The Sandias, a mountain range looming over the city of Albuquerque, named for the color the would turn at sunset, did just that, taking on the color of watermelon against the blue sky. Wisps of clouds allowed for oranges to become yellows and reds to become pinks, as the sun would set. Many people think of the Southwest as all pine trees and ground brush, not so. The huge Cottonwood trees would shed their leaves, as do the small groups of Aspens, which can be seen around the city. With the mild weather, Albuquerque's fall would be hard pressed to pass up.

This fall brought about another change for the boys, probably the most important change of all. Another young man, one whom all the boys knew by name and a few a little better, was moving into the neighborhood. His name was Ambrose.

Ambrose had moved to Albuquerque a year and a half earlier, from Arizona. His father had been a Junior College baseball coach there and had accepted the head job at the university there in town. Not knowing a great deal about the city and where the best place for a young boy, athletically inclined might be, the family had moved into a part of the city nearby but not quite in the school district the boys were already in. Now having a better idea and having had some contact with boys such as Kris and Todd, Ambrose's family was moving into the neighborhood.

Ambrose's skin was a dark brown; his family was of Hispanic descent, though one could easily mistake that for Native American. His huge, dark eyes made the features of his face soften, with a smile no one could help but become accustomed to. Ambrose lived for baseball. He played all the other sports but baseball was his passion. Growing up with a father who coached in the College ranks tends to keep a young boy's attention on the sport but Ambrose would have thought baseball all day everyday even if his father didn't coach. A few years earlier, before their move to Albuquerque, Ambrose's father had been a coach on the United States Olympic team. It was only a test sport that year but had gone on to win the Gold medal. Ambrose had been the batboy for that team. A great deal of his knowledge and passion for the game had come during that time. When he played the game, those traits were easy to see.

It had been Ambrose's former team, which had knocked the boys out of the twelve-year-old tourney. Ambrose had done his part to put them out as he had hit a home run. So all the boys knew him by name, the damage he had done in that game and by Ambrose's most distinguishing feature, a huge head. Not in an egocentric way but really, his head was already a size eight at twelve years old. When 'Brose, as the boys came to call him, began the school year, he immediately fit in. It was as if he had been part of the group since day one. Everyone accepted him, everyone except Tim that is.

From the first time Tim had stepped onto a ball field wearing his yellow, Los Angeles Lakers tennis shoes, he was the best player, plain and simple. He was the fastest, tallest, hardest thrower, best hitter. In fact, no matter the sport, he was the best athlete. A wonder, really as neither of his parents were particularly gifted in athletics and certainly didn't know anything about the game of baseball. He was a tall, slender, olive skinned young man. A great smile and even at the young age of twelve, it was obvious he would be a heartbreaker. Striking features reminiscent of James Dean, and the attitude to go with them. Tim's demeanor was continually questioned, as he was often quiet and aloof. He seemed to quietly observe all that went on around him, never saying too much or speaking without thinking through what he intended to say. To an outsider, Tim came of as arrogant, to his friends, Tim was just Tim.

The day it became clear Ambrose would be moving in, Tim's appearances seemed to lessen. It didn't seem as if he were avoiding the group nor Ambrose, he just wasn't around nearly as much as he once was. Maybe it was due to more time being spent with John, with whom he had definitely found a bond or perhaps he just wanted to give 'Brose some latitude as he became the new player on campus. No one knew for certain, as his personality could attest, Tim was the only one who knew what Tim was thinking. Todd sensed that there was a tension which had come about when 'Brose showed up. He talked to his father and John as well, unsure if the addition would cause problems within the team or stir things for now but strengthen them in the end. Both men assured Todd that an eventual strength and even a greater bond with the team was sure to happen but for now, time would be needed.

Ambrose didn't play football that fall but did play basketball over the winter. It gave all the boys a chance to compete with him and get to know each other better. 'Brose said he liked basketball but only played to keep himself in shape for baseball. It became obvious during the first practice, exactly what the addition of Ambrose would mean to the group. During a three on three drill, he dove for a loose ball, knocked down two other players while rebounding a missed shot and gave his team a short, pointed talking too during a time out. The fathers who witnessed it could only smile and the players commented to themselves how "cool" he was for doing so. A friend, teammate and leader seemed to be emerging from this group. The winter wouldn't be welcome for long; spring and baseball were pushing forward.

Chapter 4

The day they had talked at the restaurant, Tim and John had a bond. John had been places with baseball that Tim wanted to go and Tim had talent, which needed to be fine-tuned. Tim bordered on being "uncoachable" while John loved to challenge him while allowing Tim to realize by himself how much the coach really knew. Day by day, the two grew closer, working on baseball, going to movies, just "hanging out." Occasionally, John would even baby-sit for Tim and his two younger siblings.

Though he would fight it, Tim couldn't get enough of the knowledge John had. He loved to hear stories about baseball tournaments and players John had seen or known. Tim would try to be sly while asking but John knew exactly what Tim was doing. He loved to share those things, as much as Tim wanted to know them. It was a father-son, coach-student, and brotherly type relationship all at once.

It was during this winter, one day as John looked after the three, that he asked Tim what his ultimate goal was in life. Was it sports? School? Family? Tim hemmed and hawed over several things but eventually shared that he truly wanted to go to the University of Miami to play baseball and from there play professionally. He liked basketball and wanted to pursue that avenue as long as possible but eventually baseball would be his ultimate goal.

Hearing Tim share his goals gave John, for the first time since he had stopped playing, a direction. A direction in which to focus, something, no someone on whom to focus other than himself. It had always been about him and his problems. His only other focus had been baseball, and then he "lost" that. Then, life became a blur. No direction, no sense of being. He hadn't been sure what the next step in life was going to be. Would it be business? Teaching? Maybe back to school.

As he sat listening to Tim expound upon his dreams, John remembered what it was like to have those dreams and even how it felt to get close. He had always wished someone in his life had been able to help him get there. This was his chance to be that person, to help someone or maybe many to achieve their goals. John hated the mistakes he had made in his life and knew fully well that, with some guidance, those mistakes would never have been made.

Each day, for a while, John had forced himself to find a reason to get himself out of bed in the morning. Sometimes, he even needed a reason to keep going. He would find simple reasons, a soon to be released movie or maybe a date with a young lady. Anything he could think of to continue on. Here was a living breathing reason well, really several of them, young men looking for the little things he had missed out on. Few things in life could be more important than that. Finally. Tim was higher on the list though. Somehow, someway, he would help Tim to achieve his goals and along the way learn to achieve his own. No one would ever know it but Tim, along with the other boys had saved John's life.

Chapter 5

A sheet of charcoal colored clouds, wisps of a lighter gray between, covered the Southwestern sky on a windy, cool March morning. Only a few leaves had been able to survive their early spring arrival, allowing little life to the trees of the foothills. The mountain, which loomed over the Northeast Heights, seemed dark against the colorless backdrop.

Little by little, in small groups mainly, reds, greens and yellows began arriving at the ballpark. Like a handful of jelly beans dropped on a tan carpet, the uniforms worn by hundreds of young boys covered the still hibernating grass.

It was tryout day for the league. Every player who had signed up was now given the opportunity to show their ability by making five throws, catching five fly balls, fielding five ground balls and swinging at, hopefully hitting five balls thrown at them by the most erratic pitching machine the league could find. It really wasn't much more than a reason for the players and Dad's to get together.

Most of the coaches were dad's, who had more free time than anyone else, allowing them to do this. Others were father's who either felt no one could do a good enough job at coaching his child that he had to do it or they were average athletically, but felt as if the had been wronged during their baseball youth and wanted to ensure their child didn't suffer the same injustice. They sat in the bleachers, lists of players in hand, looking on as the boys attempted to show their ability. Notes were scribbled, speed and strength assessed and these were the coaches who were there only because they felt obligated. The other type of coach would be that guy who dresses with the athletic look, shorts or sweats and a ball cap, reliving his days as a player or worse yet, the guy who really shouldn't try to wear that look but does anyway. His shorts too tight or pants too high, a whistle perhaps and dark colored tennis shoes. These were the men who would teach the next great ball player exactly how to play the game.

In reality, the coach has little, if anything to do with how far a player goes in the game. Not to say they were never a part of it, however it was more likely they just happened to be there. Most players make it due to pure athletic ability or perhaps a very good High School coach. They watch the game and have the ability to pick up subtleties or play it so often with such dedication that the game becomes a part of them. Little League dads rarely are the springboards.

John was there, though for no reason more than to try and "option" Tim and Ambrose to his team. Each team was allowed two "options," to allow coaches and assistant coaches to make sure their own children were on their team. A coach in John's situation however could manipulate the rule. He had no children playing, so in essence he could take the two best players in the league. *The rule at this league was later changed to avoid this situation just for John and another coach who had gone through the league in the same manner a few years prior.* John fully intended to use the rule to his benefit. Ambrose wasn't cooperative, not because he didn't want to but in order for the "option" to be legal, the player and parent had to sign a document. Ambrose had taken that weekend to travel with his father's collegiate team. He wasn't available. Undeterred, as always, John took the next best player, perhaps an equal physically, Bret.

Freckled to the point of not being able to see his nose, Bret was at an awkward stage in life. Thirteen years old, a small amount of hair was growing at the edges of his upper lip. Horn-rimmed coke bottle glasses magnified his eyes when he looked straight ahead. A shaggy mane of black hair covered his head. Bigger than all the boys, save

Tim, Bret was now just ahead of the curve but still strong and powerful for his age. On top of all his other attributes, Brett was left-handed.

The past two seasons, it had been the combination of Tim and Bret, which had dominated their age group. On the same team for both years, each would take turns pitching and hitting home runs, leaving a wake behind them, until the All-Star tournament. Bret would suddenly disappear come that stretch and no one could really understand why. Most said it was due to the fact his parents had divorced, unfavorably and when both parents came to watch a big game tournament like that, Bret would cave in under the pressure.

It was without hesitation that Tim and his father signed over to play for John but Bret's father did what any good father would, he asked questions, to John and about him. He took half the morning to think about it then, after declining several other suitors, he agreed putting Tim and Bret together one more year. A game of "telephone" broke out, starting with the simple message of the two boys agreeing to play for John but getting back around before the end of an hour that the boys were being paid and Ambrose would be joining them. The gossip hotline of the Little League system.

As the weekend wound down, not one more player from the group of boys had been picked up by John. Not because he didn't want them, they simply weren't available. Kris, Kyle, Ambrose and CJ ended up on the same team, Mustangs. Brad, Todd and John G and Steve became Cardinals while Tim, Bret with John were Giants.

The first day of practice, as Tim played catch with Bret and John walked around the Giants explaining, in detail, the best way to throw the ball, the two boys gave each other a look of uncertainty about their team mates. John noticed their apprehension, then later overheard them talking about how bad some of the other boys were. How was it, the other teams had three or four really good players? John didn't worry or even flinch when Tim came out and said he was disappointed in the level of play for those on his team. He simply made a bet. If this team did not win the league's championship, Tim would get lunch on John and a trip to the sports clothes shop for a jersey of his choice. If they did win the league championship, Tim would have to buy John lunch. Walking away, John had to ask himself *"What was I thinking?"*

Chapter 6

Summer had taken hold. The last day of school, with the water balloons, shaving cream fights and lockers emptied onto the floor, signified it. Long mornings, sleeping until noon, waking up long enough to walk from bedroom to couch and fall asleep again. This would be the teen-aged summer. One hundred degree days, cooled down by short afternoon rain showers then wonderful, just right evenings would be the New Mexico summer. The boys liked to combine both.

While evenings were devoted to baseball, the boys would use every minute of the day to do what they wanted. Most days it was known everyone slept until at least ten. Some days it was earlier, most days it was later. Walk to someone else's house, Todd or Tim's, play video games, dress, then head out. Lunch at Dion's Pizza, or Hogan's Heroes for a slice or a sub. Then to the ballpark to play a game of home run derby. Those games would last forty-five minutes to an hour for the heat would wear on anybody before too long. The walk home was split in two by the Seven-Eleven where the boys would stop for an Icee, usually of the "suicide" flavor, all the fountain flavors combined. The boys of summer took on new meaning. Many people don't like the heat of summer, these boys though, looked for days when the thermometer would reach one hundred. It was almost as if it wasn't a summer day until the century mark was broken.

Games were heating up as well. Not in a controversial sense but rather in skill and the level of play the boys were achieving. Ambrose was gaining popularity with everyone he came in contact with, John had established himself as the coach everyone wanted to play for and Tim was looking to make some money as it looked like he would be buying lunch after all, as it was more than three quarters of the way done with the season and the Giants had lost only once. John had known that having the two most dominant pitchers would give him an opportunity to win every game so all he needed was a little help from the other players. Each game it seemed to be somebody different. Tim or Bret would pitch and to that point, one of the other eleven players would have a game allowing the team to have success. One of those boys was Justin.

Justin was slightly built, looking as if a stiff breeze might blow him to Arizona. Eighty-five pounds dripping wet and fully clothed if he was lucky. By his actions, it was easy to see, baseball was not his sport of choice, and in fact sports in general weren't his choice. He made one out of two practices, maybe. More often than not, it was one out of three. Still, John found it in his good nature to allow the young man to play his share of time in every game. After eighteen of them, with only two to go, Justin still did not have a hit. He hadn't even hit a ball that looked like it might be a hit. He hadn't even been on base by walk or error. Not a single smile or hint of joy had snuck across his freckled face during that summer. Baseball was not Justin's friend.

It was that eighteenth game when baseball became fun. Why so many generations of fathers and sons shared and loved the game. The Giants led by two runs in the bottom of the sixth inning with Tim on the mound. The game should have been easy from that point but as the game often does, something funny happened. For no reason at all, Tim lost his control, deciding it was easier to throw harder and harder rather than letting up and composing himself. A couple of walks, a hit and an error the Giants trailed by one. As far as positioning and place in the league, the result wouldn't matter but hearing the cheers and gasps as the score changed, most of the spectators from other fields had come over to see what was going on. Tim's implosion finally ended, bringing the Giants to bat in their half of the last inning. They needed a run to keep going but the last three hitters in the line up were due to hit. Justin was one of them.

It never fails. If a good team allows a team, not as good as themselves, to be in a game, that team will find a way to win. It seemed as if the Giants had done just that. The first two batters in the inning hit hard line drives, one at the first baseman, and the other at the third baseman. *Murphy's Law, whatever can happen, will happen.* Only one out left, Justin was the batter.

The crowd had grown to a substantial size. What had been parents and siblings now included the two teams due to play the following game, most of the onlookers of the nearby twelve-year-old game and the administration of the league. A third of the crowd watched only for the sake of watching, another third watched to see if John could convince his team to pull out a win. The final third hoped simply for the arrogant twenty three year old to lose so they could gloat. John was a good person but he definitely carried himself with the cocksureness of most twenty three year olds, invincible and always right.

John knew this as he gazed into the crowd of khaki shorts and colored t-shirts. It was out of his hands now though. The players play the game and a coach can only do so much. This wasn't the time for so much. Justin crept into the box one foot at a time. You'd have thought there was a trap door waiting to open by the timid steps he took to get his footing. For a moment, the tension was spelled as pitches one and two sailed high for two balls. The following pitch centered the plate for strike one and again with strike two. Justin stepped out of the box to look down at his coach. John just clapped his hands, gave him a wink and turned away. *Not a chance in the world*

Once again, Justin stepped in, still looking for that trap door. The pitcher toed the rubber as the umpire settled down behind the catcher. Baseball's greatest match-up, only one of the participants really didn't want to be there.

The young boy in blue wound up and hurled the ball toward home plate. Justin's eyes squinted as he gathered all the strength in his eighty-five pounds soaking wet body and swung his aluminum bat. To everyone's amazement, the bat struck the ball or perhaps it was the other way around. It wasn't the sound of wood on leather but the ping was undeniable. Those who were watching closely might have been able to see that the bat actually stopped its momentum forward and went backward as contact was made. Still, it was enough to send the ball upward on a looping trajectory in the direction of first base.

The fans in the bleachers rose to their feet, straining to not only see if the ball might actually reach the ground safely but also in effort to somehow help the ball to do so. Everything seemed to suddenly go into slow motion, the ball in flight, the first baseman back pedaling to get the ball and Justin, still standing in the batter's box hand on the bill of his helmet, lifting it slightly to better see the ball. It struck him just then, to run toward first in case the ball did touch ground.

John could see from his angle the ball would drop safely. He shook his head in a sort of, pleasant disbelief. *You play this game long enough and you'll see everything.*

Sure enough, the ball drifted gently over the outstretched glove of the boy playing first base, probably six to eight inches. The boy fell to his knees as his body was stretched to its limit in his effort. The ball was moving so slowly, you could almost count the stitches on it as it turned only two or three revolutions on it's short journey. As everything came back to full speed, the ball landed gently on the green grass of the outfield, nestling on the top of it, not even having enough speed to push the blades down.

Justin reached first safely for the first time all summer. Probably the first time ever. The fans remained standing and clapped heartily. Teammates rose from the bench to hang on the chain link fence of the dugout, rattling it and cheering furiously. Though Justin's parents were not on good terms, the stood among the crowd, hugging one another, forgetting their differences for a single moment to remember the joy of being parents. Tears rolled down both their cheeks. John swallowed hard to clear whatever it was beginning to choke him up as well. He clapped and hollered over to Justin to remind him of what to do next.

The slight, red haired, freckled faced boy lifted the bill of his helmet again in order to see. For the first time, John saw a smile on the boy's face, a genuine smile for a moment that would not be forgotten.

The next batter hit a fly ball to the shortstop, ending the inning and the game. The Giants had lost. It didn't matter. Every person who participated or watched that game had been reminded why we play these games. Why baseball is the wonderful past time that it is. A young boy and his teammates had just had a moment together and there is the magic of the game.

Chapter 7

Two weeks earlier, after a Saturday game, each team was required to vote for five members from their team to be put onto a ballot. That ballot would be used in the voting for that year's All Star team.

The All Star team and tournament itself was the reward for those who were recognized by the league as the "best" in their age group. For many, this was the only real part of the baseball season. For others, it was simply about the prestige. Unfortunately, this was also the ugliest side of youth baseball. Too many parents feel that their children have to make this team and go to unbelievable measures to ensure this honor for their kids. It can be a political nightmare. It can also be a popularity contest as it is the players themselves who do the majority of the voting. Sometimes the league itself feels that it must be recognized and have bragging rights around the city, thus administrators often "change" the voting rules to ensure the best team is gathered.

As for the players, every boy has dreams of making an All Star team, at least most boys. Certainly the boys whose life is baseball and those who want their future to include baseball. The eleven-twelve year old age group gets the most press, as it is the one age group that is televised at the end of the summer. Bottom of the last inning, standing at the plate in Williamsport, Pennsylvania, a home run to win the game is the most common dream.

The intention of the All Star tournament is a good one. It's basis coming from the past time itself. The voting of players, who have performed at a higher level, to a team that will compete against other All Star teams in the area and hopefully, the nation.

So many bad things have come from the best of intentions. Because of the manipulations of adults or the naivety of youth, the system became fouled up along the way, even if just a little.

Of course, Tim and Bret had made the ballot, along with three other members of the Giants. Also on the list were Ambrose, Kris, Kyle, Todd and all the other boys that hung around together. This Saturday, before the boys were able to sit down to barbeque with their parents, they had to first go to a secluded area of the park and vote for the final thirteen boys who would make up the league's All Star team. Each player on the team plus two coaches were permitted to vote. The first eight or nine were always easy; it was the final three or four that were difficult to choose.

Who only knows if the vote counts were on the up and up at this league, John could only hope that they were. He had made the team when he was twelve and thirteen, though he had always been part of the "in" crowd. For the most part, he had felt the voting then was as close at it could get to being right. His mom, on the other hand felt different. That was where he had learned that not all is as it seems nor is the world rainbows and roses.

Attitudes or at least opinions come from across the kitchen table. John had learned a great deal about people and the underhanded things they did from his mother. She never kept anything to herself, offering up very loud opinions on those involved in her and the family's lives. Somewhat of a conspiracy theorist at times, John's mom never held anything back and most of the time it was for the boys around John, not for her own son. That was a good lesson to learn, though the reality of life was sometimes hard to swallow.

During John's twelve year old season, actually during the All Star schedule, that his mom had made it very clear she did not enjoy the politics of baseball. While John was a starter on the team and on this particular day, had been the winning pitcher, his mom still saw fit to absolutely rip the coaches up one side and down the other for failing to play all the boys on the team, even at the expense of playing time for her own son. This of course, had not sat well with John but had put it squarely into his head that even though teams like this are more about winning then other times, everyone who is elected as part of the team should have some role to play in each game.

While he may not have like all the things he heard from his mother, John quickly understood they were the most valuable life lessons he could have received.

While the scenario played out in his mind, John finished his voting. He chose his thirteen and turned in his ballot. After, he watched the boys, not only from his team but the other teams as they did the same. Boys wore smiles both of assuredness and uncertainty as they turned in their folded paper. He remembered what it was like that week, waiting to hear your name called or rather hoping to hear it. The way his stomach would drop with each name that was called out before his. The faked smile he flashed to a friend when their name was called and he still waited. It was tough to get through but he remembered each time *what doesn't kill you only makes you stronger.*

He hoped that the boys who wouldn't hear their name that following Sunday would remember that and use it in their futures. It was heartbreaking to not make a team. He remembered that. John used that disappointment to make himself better and eventually be a success at every thing he put his mind to.

John finished up his ballot and turned it in. On his short stroll back to the barbeque he thought about his choices. The final four boys had been more difficult to choose than he had imagined. Still, he knew another lesson in life is that *life itself isn't fair.* Hopefully, those that made the team would be deserving and those who did not would be strong enough to move forward.

It was an amazing New Mexico summer afternoon. The blue sky was holding off the evening thunder boomers, which crept in from the west most days. If there were any breeze at all it was slight and only when necessary. There was no reason to think about it any longer. He had made his decisions as a coach and with no favorites in mind. That was all that could be expected of him. He had to keep reminding himself of that. John sat himself down to baked beans and fried chicken. The players from his team ran around playing games of tag and catch. Parents patted him on the back for the team's success. There should have been no reason for his mind to be elsewhere. Still, he reminded himself he had done all he could and with the best intentions. Why did he always have to remind himself of that?

It would be announced the following weekend, after the championship games had been completed, who had been chosen to represent the league in all the age groups. After each team had been announced, the players from that team then chose the coach. In some cases, the team that won the championship had a coach, players or parents didn't like. When a parent doesn't like a coach, the children know it. *Attitudes come from across the kitchen table.* So occasionally it worked better to have the team vote. There was little, if any, doubt that John would be chosen by the boys. It was only a matter of time. The question was which fourteen boys would be chosen. It would weigh on the coach's mind for the entire week and probably beyond that. It had become obvious to him that it wasn't about the baseball but the boys themselves. That was a good thing. The only problem was in John's mind; he continually had to remind himself that he was doing good things.

Chapter 8

Tim awoke to the sun tickling his nose, Todd, to the smell of coffee. Each boy awoke to something different but all with the same feeling, excitement, anticipation, and anxiety. It was championship Saturday at Roadrunner Little League. Championship Saturday meant two things, big baseball games and more importantly, the announcement of the All Star team.

Though there was no championship game in the thirteen year old age group, as the Giants had won the thing out right, there was a game in all the other divisions so there would be no announcements until after all the games had been completed. Then, the President of the league would present each age group with their trophies, followed by the announcement of that age groups All Star team.

Because of all those happenings, the announcement wouldn't be made until somewhere between four and five in the afternoon. That didn't matter. The grounds of the league would be filled from morning on with every boy and girl who had any thought of being elected to the team running around trying to control their excitement. There were many who had no illusions of grandeur who simply wanted to be around, to hang out with those who would be making the team.

Parents, not only fathers as one might think, but moms as well, walking the grounds with their chests puffed out, talking about how good their child was or how, whichever coach was selected would best use that child. Some might see the day as it was, a beautiful sun soaked summer afternoon, filled with the laughs and shrieks of children truly enjoying themselves. Their minds set only on whatever game they were playing or subject the discussed until the outside thought sneaked into their mind and briefly dreaming about what might be. Others might only see the parents and their politicking.

Choose your battles. It was something John had heard many times in many situations. He wasn't able to do so. There was no doubt in his mind, to that point in life, he had made too many mistakes, too many poorly thought out decisions and always had an excuse for things when they went wrong. He had been allowed to do so by watching others make excuses. In just thirty minutes spent standing by a field watching the game in progress, he heard more times than he could count, parents and children alike, making excuses why they or their children might not make an All Star team. His life had been filled with excuses, it still was. He didn't remember his parents making them. In fact, he knew his mother was never one to make them. He had heard all summer from Todd, Tim and Kris, why the team had lost the year before. Nobody ever seemed to be at fault.

John wanted to pull each one of the children he heard, those with a reason already made up for why their name wouldn't be called, a reason he was certain had come from the parents, and tell that young person that it wasn't OK, it wasn't alright to have an excuse. He wanted to turn to the parent he overheard and tell them how wrong they were for making excuses for their children. All he could do was walk away, gritting his teeth or mumbling to himself. No longer would he make excuses for his mistakes. He would take ownership of them. He realized there would be more mistakes in his life but no more excuses for them. He said this to himself and really wanted to mean it but he knew better. Unless something drastic or Earth shattering happened in his life, he would be inclined to continue to make excuses. No matter though, he would make it a point in his coaching that excuses would no longer be acceptable. Maybe if he preached it enough it would become part of his life as well.

As the championship games were finishing up, more and more people gathered at the park. By four-thirty, the only game left was the fourteen-fifteen year old game on the largest field in the middle of the complex. Uniforms of all colors sat packed together tightly on the wooden bleachers. On the soft, dusty, brown dirt stood parent, player and coaches alike five and sometimes six rows deep, all waiting to hear the long anticipated announcement. John stood near the fence, not so much as he wanted to be there in the front row as much as the swarms of people who had arrived after had trapped him there. Through the afternoon, players and parents had asked if he knew who would be on the team. It seemed as if they thought he might have so much pull as to choose the team himself. It was humorous. Not only did John not have any more say in the team than his one vote, he didn't know if any of the boys he voted for would make the team.

After explaining this to for the fifth time that afternoon, John turned his gaze from the field to the one building standing in the middle of the complex. It was a two-story, chocolate brown, adobe style building, used for both equipment storage and concessions. A large, wooden sign, painted with red, white and blue lettering. Across the top, the words "Roadrunner Little League Home of the World Champions" stood out in bright blue. A twelve-year-old softball All Star team had won the world championship. John's best friend, Craig had a younger sister who had played on that team. Here, in the sea of people, waiting to hear who would play for that summer, John's thought's drifted back to the summer when he and Craig had driven halfway to Gallup, New Mexico just to get the reception needed to listen to the broadcast of the championship game. On a day so much like this very one, two friends lay on the hood of an old, silver station wagon, shirts off, tanning in the desert sun while listening above the static as Craig's little sister hit a bases loaded triple effectively winning the game and the championship. It was an amazing feeling, John had thought, to play in such a game but also to share it with his best friend. After the game, the boys had laid there, still on the hood of the wagon known as the "Silver Bullet" talking about how great it was and the achievements they would have during their High School years. Day became night but the boys remained, the conversation turning to life and death as well as the infinite beyond. Looking up into the billions of stars, the two friends solved the problems of the world.

An ovation from the crowd, signaling the end of the game brought the now twenty three year old back to Saturday. A friend of John's and also a coach at the High School coached the winning team. Like John, he had no children and coached merely for the love of the game and like John; it was obvious he would coach that age group through the All Star tournament. It was a farewell of sorts, as that coach had been with that group of boys from their eleven-year-old season. Similar to this group, the boys of that age group were close and played the game very well.

It was then that John was struck by something. The older age group had four or five boys who were friends but it was more like two or three pairs of boys got along well but it was the pairs that were close. The same had been true of his own age group. Two or three were friends and got along with the others on the team. The group John was preparing to coach were different. They all were best friends, not just two or three and the pairs or trios got along, they were all close. If you saw two or three of them together, which was rare as more often there were nine or ten together, it was never the same two or three and if there were only two or three you could bet that more would show up shortly. There was never any jealousy when one friend was with another as can happen even in the closest of friends. It was odd but in the most wonderful of ways. How special would it be to be part of a group in which all eight or nine or ten people were best of friends?

Sure there were three or four that seemed more suited to be with one another. Brad, Matt, Steve and Jason all had a sense of humor which meshed, so much in fact there rarely was a minute passed without some sort of joke or a laugh shared. Many times at their own expense as the four were prone to clumsiness and often "Keystone cop" like shenanigans.

Tim, Kyle and Kris were more reserved but never closed, while Todd went from cut up to quiet as he moved within the group without a steady profile. C.J. and Jon were unsure of their place in the group, whether to be the center or just a part but never put to the side by the others but rather embraced as just one more side of the object.

Now there was Ambrose. The other boys had been together, in most cases, from kindergarten but Ambrose had just moved here and yet it was this young man who seemed to be the leader, the one person in this group of handsome, intelligent and popular group of boys that everyone, including the boys themselves seemed to gravitate to. It wasn't because of an excess of personality nor was it because of an overbearing personality; it was in fact, because he didn't have either. He was simply himself. In a world when everybody wants to or tries to be someone they aren't to gain acceptance or favor, Ambrose chose only to be himself. It was that simplicity which drew people to him.

John spotted Ambrose in the crowd. He sat with, to no surprise, the other ten boys at the top of the bleachers. They were laughing enjoying themselves as if they had no worries in the world. They probably didn't. Most of them would be on the team, if not all of them and even if they weren't they would be all right; it wouldn't be the end of the world. They had strong constitutions and support systems. No, they probably didn't have any worries.

It took a while but the President finally quieted the crowd. He started by giving the trophies for first and second place to the younger age groups, then softball. After each trophy presentation, the All Star announcement was made. Already, tears had to be wiped from children when the team had been announced and their name not called. It was the same for each age group both boys and girls. It was difficult to watch the children but the sympathy passed as John watched the parents throw small and in one case, a large fit. It was embarrassing really.

Before the fourteen-fifteen year old division could be announced, the thirteen year olds would take their turn. The Giants, led out by John and his two assistants, lined up down the third base line and were handed their first place trophies. The trophies were simple but nice, a gold, plastic ball player on top of a wooden block with a baseball diamond painted on it. They were then dismissed to return to the crowd.

Instead of leaving the field, John simply moved himself to the edge of the field, against the home dugout. There he could watch the players called out and see only the expressions of joy on the faces of those whose names were called. From this vantage point he wouldn't have to look upon the faces of the disappointed. John could be weak like that, not wanting to face a difficult moment but rather move away so as to not have to face it.

Alphabetically, the team was announced. Sure enough, each one of the boys was called. Ambrose, Brad, Matt, Kyle, C.J., Jon, Steve, Jason, Todd, Tim and Kris. Two other boys, a second Kyle and Chad were selected. They were friends but nowhere near as close as the rest of the group. The President instructed the boys to take a minute and select their coach. The boys huddled and whispered amongst themselves. Occasionally, one of their heads would pop up and look in John's direction as if to see whom it was they were discussing. As if they didn't know.

While they "debated" John looked toward the crowd. One of the boys John had coached all summer had not been selected. In John's eyes, he deserved to be there more than the other two boys and probably more than two of the boys from the group. His first instinct was to look away and not make eye contact. How would he be able to talk to a hurt boy about this? No excuses. He decided that not doing anything would be like making an excuse and he wouldn't do that. He gestured with his hand to wait for him until he could talk. The young man waited.

After a short session, the boys told their decision to the President. John was their selection and would be the All Star coach. John stepped into the huddle, told them where and when the practice would be and thanked them. It was a big deal to be chosen and he appreciated it. He knew this would be a great time but he had to deal with the young friend first.

He walked quickly over to the boy, thinking to himself how quickly the sun seems to lose its heat. It felt so cold at that moment as he neared the boy. He was surprised to see steadfastness in the boys face as he put his arm out to console the young man. Sure enough, as the coach began to speak, the boy's eyes welled up with tears. As he fought to keep them back, John put his other hand on his shoulder.

"I can't say I agree with the selection, but there is little I can do. If someone is to quit or cannot make the commitment, I can select another player." John talked in soft tones until he got to the point he'd been holding onto all day.

"You can take this as a failure or allow it to drive you in the future. What this does for you and your baseball is up to you."

The boy nodded but couldn't answer. He wiped his eyes across his forearm and thanked John for his words. The boy's mom did the same. None of what John had said was lip service. He meant it. Hopefully the boy would take the words to heart and never allow it to happen again. Only time would tell.

John climbed into his silver pick up truck. He had owned it since High School. The only thing in it he liked was his stereo system but today, he couldn't bring himself to even turn it on. He drove home in silence, his thoughts bouncing back and forth between who would play where and whether this was really a good thing. He couldn't decide. Driving home in silence, his mind bounced from subject to subject. Line ups, positions, the looks on those whose names were not called. His stomach turned. While he looked forward to this challenge and knew the majority of the time would be fun, he struggled with the fact he was part of the reward while there were many who were home, at that very moment wishing things were different or that something might change and allow them a small piece of the dream they had hoped for so greatly. He felt guilty for this. He had to remind himself that he had done nothing wrong.

His evening was spent doing much of the same. Sitting in the darkness of his living/bed room, the door open to the outside, listening to the sounds of night. This really wasn't different than any other night, sleepless and headache causing. By nature, he was an insomniac, had been for many years. He could spend all day thinking of absolutely nothing but put his head on a pillow at night, anything and everything would jump into his thoughts. Many nights he fought back those thoughts. Some were life affecting, money, job or relationship. Others meant nothing, what movie did he see with what person? He actually liked those thoughts better. At least he didn't have to decide anything. He struggled to make decisions. They always seemed to turn out wrong. He dreaded those types of sleepless nights. More than those, he dreaded the night where he thought about not going on. There were too many of those nights. At least tonight he had reason not to sleep.

Chapter 9

The boys, all of them including the one referred to as "coach" lounged in the soft grass of foul territory down the first base line. Tim picked the longest blade of grass he could find, twisted it between his fingers for a while, and then put it in his mouth as if he were planning on working the fields on a farm. Bret cleaned his glasses and Brad flipped his shoelace from one side of his shoe to the other. Most of the boys laid their legs out in front, propping themselves up with an elbow. Ambrose pulled his knees in to his chest and wrapped his arms around them. With the eight A.M. sun just beginning to heat the day, the young coach waxed poetic.

He spoke in varied tones, soft words, passionate rants and booming metaphors. He asked questions about why this group hadn't won before and what they wanted from the game, each other and from him. John's darkened jaw line, from a summer in the sun, tightened as he referred to his playing days and how he wished he had done something more or perhaps worked harder. They boys listened with more intent when their newly elected leader talked about no more excuses and how they would have the greatest time of their lives if they put in the effort and worked not only with one another but also for one another. What was originally supposed to be a short meeting explaining expectations and schedules, turned into thirty minutes of pomp and circumstance about the upcoming month and the boys bought into it, one hundred percent.

As they lay there in the grass, they discussed goals both team and individual. John didn't want the boys to think this was only a short-term project. He wanted them to have a vested interest in the team, each other and the future. As a team, they came up with a series of goals, one leading to the next. First, to learn to work hard, second, to win four games in a row and finally, to win a City Championship. These were followed by five more goals, to win State, Regionals, Divisionals, a World Series and finally, do it again when they were fifteen. As individuals, they were all surprised to hear what the others had to say. Brad wanted to be a lawyer, and Jason to go to West Point. Tim to play professional baseball, Todd wanted to go to the University of Notre Dame. What surprised John the most was Ambrose's goal. Expecting Ambrose to state his ambition of playing pro ball as Tim had, John was caught off guard when Ambrose said he wanted only to be successful in whatever direction he ended up, making his family as happy as his was then. It was a wonderful goal to be sure. It just didn't seem like one a thirteen-year-old boy; sitting with his friends on a baseball field would have at the time.

There was one week before the tournament was to begin. Several factors played to the team's favor. Half the games would be played at Roadrunner Little League, the boys' home field, the other half were to be played at West Mesa Little League. Also, the draw the team had received was laid out in such a way that the team should win two games before matching up with a formidable opponent. John made sure the boys knew this and heard it from him every practice.

Those practices were all about the fundamentals of baseball. John had seen the boys had talent and knew how to play the game but what the boys didn't have was a respect for the fundamentals, every little detail, from base running to pitch selection. The boys worked tirelessly on all the little things the coach could come up with. Twice a day, from eight in the morning to ten and again from five in the afternoon to whenever they finished. No matter how hard the coach wanted to work the boys, they were up to the challenge.

Challenge is what John put in front of the boys as often as he could.

He felt that the more often a person is challenged and learns how to face that challenge, whether they succeed or not, the better character that person would have. If he could challenge them, force them to face adversity, they wouldn't find excuses but rather they would find a way to win.

John wanted the boys tougher. It was the one thing he had always felt himself and the boys he had grown up with were not as good at as they should have or could have been was toughness, both mentally and physically. He discovered that at each new level, everybody was as good as he was or the teams were as good. Had he and his team mates been better about being tough, they would have achieved a greater level of success. So many athletes had come from that area of Albuquerque, the world in their hands. "The best ever to come through here." or "He's going to be paid to play someday." were phrases thrown about for many players for many years. Most of them went off to college or beyond with all the hype of a blockbuster movie only to return too soon with some excuse about politics or injury. "Big fish in a small pond" theory was never truer than in Albuquerque. It was far too easy to be a dominant athlete there but never achieves the next level for never having been pushed. That wouldn't happen to this group, not if this coach could help it.

One of the tools he used to implement his toughness rule was to not allow the boys to show any sign of being hurt. First, on the field, where if something was to go wrong, an error or strike out for instance, the boys were to show no sign of frustration. Simply, shake it off and make the next one. That wasn't difficult to convince the boys to do. What was harder was John's insistence that if a ball took a bad hop or a batter were beaned by a pitch, there would be no tears nor would the boys be allowed to rub it. Sure it hurt. John didn't try to convince them it didn't. What he wanted the boys to portray was the fact nothing would bother them. If something happened that might require rubbing, if something hurt, the boys were to grab a handful of dirt, rub it on the wound and move on. It was what baseball players did.

The boys spent most of the week sleeping over at each other houses, making sure they could all get to the morning practices on time. Between practices, the boys would walk to a nearby Burger King for a late breakfast or early lunch then head over a short distance to Tim or Todd's house where they would play video games and nap in the air conditioned coolness until it was time to walk back to practice.

These were the times John had thought about. Time spent bonding, becoming not only team mates but closer friends. This group was tight to begin with but only became tighter during this week. Ambrose led the way. On their walks, he would organize games where the object was to kick your rock into one of the other fella's rock, thereby allowing another kick to take the lead. First rock to the destination was the winner. He would tell stories of the time, three years earlier when he was the batboy for the first ever United States Olympic baseball team. His father was the catcher's coach for that team, allowing 'Brose the opportunity to be around that caliber of ball players and take in the atmosphere surrounding the team. He even had a video that had been made to celebrate the gold medal wane by that team. He would play it before every game to "pump" himself up. Of course, upon hearing about it, the boys insisted they be allowed to do the same. Tim may have been the best player in the group but it was without question, Ambrose was the leader.

John was tough, getting on the boys and pushing them to over achieve. Because of this, the coach made sure his assistants were his polar opposites. Bryce, a twenty two year old, red headed, Ritchie Cunningham looking man had grown up with John. In fact, they had been on the same team when they were twelve. He was quiet, soft spoken and a wizard with statistics. He hadn't been much more than a back up high school player but was a good friend and good coach. Dating back to when they were twelve, John had always felt he could trust Bryce.

Derry, was a favorite with the boys. Already in his mid sixties, Derry stood maybe five foot three, hunched over from a problem in his spine looking as if a stiff breeze would blow him over. He had coached baseball at Roadrunner for more than thirty years, starting while his boys were young, he had continued to coach long after they had grown. When John was fifteen, he had been on Derry's team with four of his closest friends. In all the time Derry had coached at that league, it was the first time he had ever won the championship. After John's group had moved on to High School, Derry decided to try a younger age group, moving down to twelve year olds. He found there too short an attention span and too much parental interference. Frustrated, he had gone back to coaching the fifteen year olds. When John began coaching a year earlier, he watched as Derry's team struggled as many of the same parents he had trouble with when the boys were twelve continued to complain and interfere with his coaching. It wasn't to say those parents didn't have a reason to speak up, Derry's coaching ideas were from a different time and very few of his players really improved but rather just were given the opportunity to play. Nonetheless, here was a man who loved the game of baseball and teaching that love to young men more than anything. He gave every bit of himself and his time with no reward except what he saw the boys take out of it.

At the end of that last season, the Board of Directors decided he wouldn't be given a team the following season. John knew this and had decided as soon as he took a team that Derry would be right there with him. At first, Derry declined, still believing he would be allowed to have his own team. It wasn't until the reality of not getting his own team, did Derry agree to help. It couldn't have worked better. Through the summer, the boys on the Giants had enjoyed him and now on this All Star team they absolutely loved him.

Being a dominant personality, John tended to do most everything himself. However, he felt an obligation to Derry to allow him to do something more than just throw soft toss to the boys. Every other morning, John had Derry hit ground balls to the boys. The problem with that was Derry being so small and weakened because of his condition, he could barely hit the ball through the infield grass. The first morning, all the infielders went along out of respect but after the second day, their frustration was obvious. Kris and Todd's body language, the kicking of dirt or throwing the ball into the ground as hard as possible said as much. Ambrose jogged over, put his hand over both their shoulders and told them to think of it as a way to work on slow rollers or a way to improve their footwork and quick hands. From that day forward, not a negative word came from the boys. They knew how much they mattered to him and he to them.

During the afternoon practices, the boys worked primarily on offense. John had become a fan of music during batting practice while in college so he incorporated it into his practices. For the last forty minutes or so, the boys hit in two cages with the two young coaches throwing, music blasting out of a "boom box." The cassette they were listening to, had been compiled by John filled with music he felt not only inspired but also calmed and focused an athlete as well. One of the songs, "Good Vibrations" was a fast moving, foot tapping type a song. About three quarters of the way through with the song, the line "If you ain't in it to win it, get the Hell out" came through loud and clear. Every day, John would make sure he stopped his throwing long enough to say or rather yell, the line along with the song. By the third afternoon, all the boys were singing along as well. After one of the practices, John showed the boys the underside of the bill of his cap. He had always written notes to himself or kept track of stats there. In this case, he had written the words, *in it to win it or get the #%&* out.* He didn't feel he would be a good role model to write the correct lyrics. He told the boys that would be their mantra, and then realized he had to explain that a mantra was a statement. A statement that summed up all they were about. Starting that day, after every practice, they would say that as a team. Before every game it would be the same thing. He asked only one thing. "If you don't believe it, don't say it." Every boy on the team said it. Every boy on the team believed it. They were in it to win it. The coach had convinced them of that.

Nothing gets to an athlete like the wait before and or between games. For football players, it takes an entire week of waiting before the opportunity comes to redeem or continue a roll. Baseball players have it a little better. In most cases, even in youth ball, the time between games is only a day or two. For this team, it had been in reality, a whole year. Yes, they had all just spent a summer playing games but not as *this* team. Not with *this* coach. Not with *these* friends. Inside, for Tim, Todd and Kris it had been their whole life. They were baseball players. This was everything they had ever waited for.

As practice came to an end that day, the coaches could feel the boys' tension. They talked about things other than baseball, hoping to loosen them up. John had Ambrose tell jokes and tried to tell one himself, thinking maybe the boys minds would relax. Nothing. If this kept up, the coach knew only bad things could happen. Rather than talk at them anymore, John decided to try and turn the tension to excitement. He told the boys there would be a team dinner, that night and every night before games where they would watch a movie, a movie that would motivate.

He chose one of the "Rocky" movies, a series about a down and out boxer who is given a shot at the World Championship. No person with any sense of competition or testosterone can watch the movie without getting excited to compete. The boys watched, moving in their seats, tensing and relaxing their bodies to the movie like little kids having to go to the bathroom. It was a great evening. The tension seemed to disappear and a team, a real team looked prepared to go compete together.

John watched his team interact with each other. He watched them caught up in the movie and how they talked after. This was truly a team and win or lose, they had something very special with one another. He knew he was in the company of greatness, maybe not individual but collectively. He was thankful to be a part of it.

Chapter 10

The day of their first game, Tim's parents asked John if he could watch all three of their children. Tim had a beautiful younger sister and a mischievous younger brother. They spent the morning playing video games, trivia and kick ball in the back yard. For lunch, they walked down the street to Dion's Pizza for a few slices and soda. The sun was already scorching, reaching over one hundred degrees by noon. No matter the heat, it was a well-spent summer day. That would have been true without the impending baseball game.

Baseball players are famous for being superstitious. The young coach was very much the same. As a player, he had dressed the same way for every game, socks, then sanitaries, stirrups, sliding shorts, sleeves, pants and finally jersey. He couldn't wear eye black, as he always played poorly when he did. There were many, many more. As a coach, to that point, all he had found was to write the line up with the same pen, in the same order. Often, along with his superstitions, John would look for signs. Signs that might give him insight as to whether it would be a good day for his team or bad. He believed there are signs every day, some which are obvious and some that are not. Some signs might not even be seen but they were there, if a person would simply look for them.

As John waited for Tim as he dressed for the game, he sat in the living room with the little brother watching the end of a movie. As the credits rolled and his mind thought about the game, across the bottom of the screen, the movie, which was to follow, was listed. It was a movie John had seen while on the road with his thirteen-year-old team. They had already won the State championship and were in Phoenix. The days were so hot; there could be no games until the evening. During the day, the coaches had taken them to the movies and this was one of them. It had nothing to do with baseball; in fact it was a science fiction movie.

John jumped out of his seat, hollering down the hallway to Tim's room. "We've had a sign!" Of course, Tim had no idea what he meant until he finished dressing and was able to come out and talk with his coach.

Whether it made any sense to the young man or not, he didn't say. The fact that John suddenly had supreme confidence was all Tim needed to have some of his own. While the team took batting practice for an hour prior to the game, Tim told the story to his teammates. Just as the coach's confidence had carried over to him, Tim's confidence carried over to his teammates. As the team entered the dug out to get loose for the game, something else came with them. John could feel it. It was a good thing.

All but one of the players felt good about the next few hours. Only Todd seemed preoccupied. John pulled him aside to see if anything was bothering him. Sure enough, Todd was nervous. *Nervous means that you aren't prepared.* It was a something the coaches had preached all week and John reiterated to Todd. This team was more than prepared so there was nothing at all to fear.

Todd sat down; his sparkling white uniform, covered with red pinstripes taking on it's first bit of dirt, from that which was on the wooden bench. He looked at John in a determined but shaken manner. He spoke the same. "This team has always been told how good we are and how we are supposed to win. We never have. I just don't want to fail again."

In just those few words, John could see how much this meant to Todd. He also knew that Todd had the pulse of this team. That was a good thing. This whole endeavor meant something to this group. Not just for the sake of winning but for one another, with one another. John's confidence went up again.

"All you can do Todd is your job. Take this feeling and use it on the field but only to a point where it keeps you playing hard. If every one of us does our job and plays with the passion I can see you will, this team will be just fine."

The toe head's freckled face smiled from ear to ear as he heard this. It became obvious to John at that point all the boy wanted was to be acknowledged for his eagerness to play. It would become a recurring theme.

Like clockwork, the afternoon clouds rolled in from the West, cooling the day. Parents and friends arrived, anxious to see if the results this year would be any different. Cleats tapped the ground and the boys popped their gloves, anxious to get started. With the game being held at Roadrunner, there would be a large crowd. It would be both beneficial and a detriment to the team. A comfort zone for the team and familiarity were the benefits, pressure to perform could potentially be a problem. John looked out at his team. They were just finishing their warm ups as Ambrose called them together. They huddled on a knee as a football team would, praying before a game. He had no idea if it was a prayer session or a knock, knock joke. It didn't much matter. If Ambrose had something to say, He could go ahead and say it.

As it was the first game of the tournament, before the game would start, the mandatory pageantry had to first be completed, the announcement of players and coaches, followed by the Little League pledge and the National Anthem. John would just as soon gotten on with the games as to go through all the formalities but it had always been this way. Instead of complaining, he used it as a time to judge who was ready to play, on both teams. The same pre-game rituals had taken place when he played and the year before as he had coached the fifteen-year-old team. He would stand at the back of the line, arms clasped behind his back and watch players. Often he could make his assessments quickly, allowing himself time to take in the beauty of the moment. For as long as he could remember, that time of day during that time of year was always his favorite time, a special time. The whole world seemed to slow down. The hustle and noise of the day seemed to disappear with the heat, leaving only the simple part of the day, the relaxing and enjoyable parts to remain. This was his Eden.

"Play ball!" As the National Anthem finished, both teams running to their dugouts, anxious to start the game. During this tournament, the coaches would meet with the umpires to discuss ground rules and flip a coin to determine who was to be the "home" team. John always looked to take "visitor" the first game of a tournament, knowing no matter how good a team might be, anxiousness or nervousness are human emotions and felt it was easier to hit than field when a player might be nervous. Winning the flip, the young, confident coach took "visitor" and the game was under way.

Sure enough, the North Valley Little League team was nervous, committing several errors in the first inning, allowing Roadrunner to score seven runs. Momentum and confidence quickly took their place beside John in the "visitor" dugout. Bryce could even feel it, commenting to John how relaxed the boys suddenly looked, feeling as if the game were already in hand.

Tim toed the rubber in the second half of the first inning, expecting to dominate. He left it in the fifth, having done just that. One thing Tim never lacked was confidence in his ability. Maybe it bordered on overconfidence and sometimes Tim felt it couldn't be his fault if the team didn't succeed, whatever the case Tim took the field every inning expecting success.

The only reason Tim left the mound in the fifth was the score. Roadrunner had completely demolished North Valley at that point, nineteen to one, and then finished the game twenty-one to one. John made sure not to pitch Tim too much and knew he would need other pitchers to get their time as well so as to be able to pitch if Tim, Ambrose or Brett struggled.

Joy had returned to *Mudville* or at least the happiness. All the doubts and fears the boys or parents had were now gone, for the moment at least. John had started the boys down the right path. Knowing it was a marathon not a sprint, he settled them down, taking away some of their excitement. He had learned from a former coach of his own, to let a team "have it" when they win and picking them up when they lose. He didn't so much as to let them have it as much as he reminded them of mistakes that could not happen again and flaws that needed to be fixed. In the end he let them know he was proud and the journey forward would be amazing.

The upcoming Saturday, two days from then, they would play again. One more step toward their first goal, the City Championship. There was a great deal to do in those two days. "Until tomorrow, enjoy tonight."

Chapter 11

John stared into the cab of his truck through the open window of the driver's side. The team had just finished practice and he had to get to work. On the seat lay a pile of brown mush. Mush really wasn't right but it was difficult to explain. It looked like a dog had somehow gotten into his truck and left a pile of "stuff." He thought about it for a moment. He hadn't seen a dog but he did always leave the window open, parking under the huge Cottonwood trees next to the field. It was possible for someone to put a dog inside or even possible, he thought, for a dog to jump inside. It was then he noticed, out of the corner of his eye, the team standing off to the side of the field. Ambrose stood at the front of the group.

Why, for any reason, had John even bothered to think of logical explanations for this problem? Of course, no one had put a dog in his truck, nor had a dog jumped inside. Why did he even think about those things? Ambrose loved to play these types of practical jokes. John reached inside the truck, to grab the gag gift, and toss it back to his player. Admittedly, there was that moment of truth, deciding whether Ambrose's joke was simply the "gift" itself or the fact the coach would reach in and grab it. Fortunately, it was simply a plastic toy. Only Ambrose could make John think twice. It was Ambrose's way.

The second game was less of a competition than the first. Other than the heat, which reached one hundred and three degrees, the day was lacking excitement, with a score of forty four to four. John knew the scores would make it seem he or his team were "rubbing it in" or "running it up" but neither was the case, by the second inning in this game, the starters came out and the substitutes in. He held runners and even had Bryce coach third base. It was simply a matter of one team being better than the other.

The third game was nothing like the first two. The opponent was Eastdale Little League, which in the years between John's playing days and his coaching had become the rival of Roadrunner. In fact, it had been this team, which had knocked Roadrunner out when they were eleven and won the tournament when they were twelve. While there was no tension that could be felt, there was a tentativeness in which the team went about its business. There was no pre-game joke, and Ambrose didn't pull the team aside to talk. The coaches just chalked it up to the fact he was that day's starting pitcher and he was focused. It turned out it was something else.

Ambrose threw the first two innings as if he were trying not to lose. It wasn't that he pitched badly but that he didn't go after it the way he had played in the previous two games. During the second inning, John took time to talk to Ambrose during the inning, letting him know it was time to lead by example and to take the game rather than to play it out. After the inning, he "went off" on the team, letting them know just how unhappy he was at their play. The score at the time was three to one in favor of Eastdale. By the top of the fifth inning, the score was eight to three Roadrunner, who went on to win ten to three.

From the point of John's conversation, 'Brose had pitched beautifully. The team had played as he pitched, just as the coach knew they would. Maybe they couldn't see it, maybe they didn't know it but this team would play as Ambrose did. Yes, Tim was the best player but Ambrose was the heart and soul. It takes each player to do their job and to pull for one another. No player is ever bigger than the team but Ambrose, he was the biggest part of this team. Perhaps he was what this group needed to complete them or maybe what John needed, someone to give him direction.

Having rolled through the first three games caused a stir in the Northeast Heights of Albuquerque. The team was living up to it's potential. The young, cocky coach was delivering on all he had promised. This team was going places.

It happens often on these journeys, a small or simple event can become the stuff of legend. At the very least, an event of mild excitement can be a moment that a person or group will remember forever. On the day of the championship, the team met as it always did, for batting practice at the school most of the boys attended. John would have his "boom box" blasting away music as he threw batting practice, Derry would work with the boys on soft toss. Bryce would meet the team at the ballpark for the game, routine to say the least.

As they finished batting practice, if the game was not at Roadrunner, the boys would play rock paper scissors or guess numbers to see who would ride to games with John. His truck was only a mini pick-up so at best, it would hold the coach and three players. The day of the City Championship, which was to be played at West Mesa Little League, Todd, Steve and Ambrose were the ones riding with the coach.

The ride would be about twenty-five minutes, to the West side of Albuquerque. John, being lost in his quest to find a career or even a job he enjoyed, often had trouble making enough money to pay bills let alone have the ability to pay for small necessities such as car maintenance, the price of being twenty something. As the foursome traveled down the four-lane road to the ballpark, Ambrose and John became engrossed in a conversation about signs and superstitions. Todd and Steve chimed in when they felt like it.

A sound like a gunshot echoed loudly as one of John's rear tires exploded against the hot black top of the road. He knew he should have replaced his tires as he could see the metal fibers showing through buy he couldn't afford it. Immediately, as a parent would do, the coach shot his arm across the chests of the three boys, pinning them against the seat. Using only his left hand to steer, John turned into the skid, and then moved slowly from the left lane to the right side of the road.

After they had stopped and John was certain they were clear of trouble, the three ball players and their coach climbed out of the truck to see what damage there had been. For safety's sake, only a blown tire was the problem, a spare could be put on and they'd be back on the road. The problem lied in the fact the coach and players had to be at the ballpark one hour before the game or there could be repercussions. John went to work as fast as possible to get the tire changed. Unfortunately, the tire was on the left side, which was next to traffic. To make sure of his own safety, John would have to take his time. Unknowing this pitfall was coming; John had been the last car in the caravan so no one from the team would be traveling this way. There seemed no way to get to the ballpark on time.

The three boys were having the time of their lives, while this went on. John noticed they looked like small circus folk, dressed in their white with red pinstripes, red belts and white hats with red bills. Cute, but not really looking like ball players. They stood on the side of the road, pretending to hitch hike, as young boys tend to think that is a cool thing to do.

Within minutes, a yellow taxicab slowed and pulled up behind John's disabled truck. A slightly built, shaggy haired Hispanic man, or rather boy, stepped out and offered his assistance. He said his fare was a lady who knew there was a ballpark near her home and that might be our destination. Sure enough, it was. The boys threw their bags and the equipment in the trunk and piled it on their laps as they all piled into the cab. Todd and Steve climbed into the back seat, John and Ambrose the front. The lady was pleasant enough, tired from a long day. The driver, looking not more than nineteen or twenty couldn't stop talking about baseball and the fact that his fare lived right next to our destination. What were the chances?

None of this seemed more than an inconvenience to John until Ambrose nudged him and pointed to the placard on the dash. There, below the driver's picture was his name, Angel. At a time the boys could use some help, an angel had come along to do just that. John smiled and nodded but never did get over the coincidence. He was into signs and superstitions but this was beyond any of that. The fact that Ambrose was the one to notice made it all the more surreal. The one person John had figured to have been sent specifically for this team noticed when a real Angel had been sent.

As he pulled the last bag from the trunk of the cab, John heard Bryce coming down from the field. "You have no idea how nervous I have been!" John knew Bryce would be panicking but couldn't help chuckling at him for it. He smiled, "Relax, I'm here. You'll never guess what just happened."

Bryce stood, rubbing his head as John told the story of the last half hour. It seemed almost unbelievable to him and he had been there. Many of the parents who had already arrived wanted all the details as well but there was no time. The coaches and players had to get on the field and start preparing. It was near game time and this was championship game time to boot. Even the usually calm coach could feel the excitement building.

The pre-game was good, Ambrose led the team in a talk, Bryce had calmed himself and it was time to flip for "home." There was no need to be nervous John felt as they were a far better team than there opponent, the home team West Mesa. He wanted to be the "home" team but lost the flip. They would hit first but as he told his players, got to be the team on the field when the championship was won.

"In it to win it!" the team yelled as they took the field. It had been that way for all three games to that point and would be so until they were done. The boys sprinted to their positions as if someone would steal it if they didn't. It was a trick John had learned in High School. Hustle everywhere, no matter the score and there will be a psychological edge over the opponent, Kris to shortstop, Todd to second, Brett to first. Ambrose to third, Brad was the catcher. Tim took the mound. John couldn't think of a better line up. Kyle stood in left field, Steve in center and Jason in right.

Right field was never settled, sometimes it was Jason or Chad or Kyle H. Usually C.J. and Chad were used, as runners late in the game and Jon would be the closer if needed. When John had taken the team, he had promised his mom he would play every player in every game. To that point, he had been true to his word. It was the reason a team was successful. Everyone had a job to do, everyone mattered, which is how teams win championships.

Out manned, out talented and plainly overmatched; the team from West Mesa took the game to Roadrunner without any fear of losing or intimidation. They're pitcher, a boy by the name of Justin, was a hard nosed, take the prize sort of kid whom his team mates believed in and would follow much the same as their opponents followed Ambrose. With Justin on the mound and a catcher who swung the bat as if it were large as a tree trunk, West Mesa jumped out to a two nothing lead and kept that lead through the fifth inning.

If not for Todd, making ten of the first fifteen outs with some slick fielding plays, Roadrunner might have been even farther behind. "Nails" as John had taken to calling Todd, because of his "tough as nails" attitude, kept the team up with his chatter and solid defensive plays.

In the sixth, Roadrunner was able to push across one run but still trailed two to one going into the seventh and final inning. By that point, John had taken Tim off the mound and replaced him with Bret, who was able to pitch out of trouble. A small sense of apprehension had crept into the "visitor" dugout. John's team had learned how to win but had not been faced with the challenge they had now.

As he walked across the field from first base side to third, the coach thought about this challenge. Would this team fall apart as they had in years past or would they overcome as he had been preaching since that day in the grass? Kris would be the first batter and the one to tell the story. If Ambrose was the vocal leader of the team, "Wilksey" was the leader on the field. His manner always remained calm no matter the situation but, if there were a time he might shut down, this would be it.

The left-handed hitter stepped into the box, digging his back foot in as a bull would in preparing to charge. A loose sway in his hips and rock of the bat, became a short, compact explosion of hips and hands as Kris swung at the first pitch.

With a sharp ping, as the ball struck the sweet spot of his aluminum bat, Wilksey shot the ball over the second baseman's head for a single. The boys in red came to life, jumping off the bench and rattling the fence. There was a chance to win this game and Kris had given it to them.

For all his gifts as a ball player, speed was not one of them. So, John replaced Kris with C.J., looking for speed on the bases. The rules would allow for Kris to re-enter the game so there wouldn't be a problem defensively if the game went to the bottom of the seventh inning. C.J. stretched as he stood at first base. This had been his job so far in the tournament but he had been picked of once already, so John's faith in him was guarded at best.

Tim was next to bat. John knew that Tim was swinging it well so getting C.J. into scoring position would probably be a run. A run was all they needed to tie and from there, the coach was confident they had more depth, which would allow them to finish off their over achieving foes. With two fingers, John tapped his forearm, his biceps followed by the bill of his cap. From there he touched his chest, thigh and arm again, followed again by the bill of his cap. On the first pitch, C.J. stole second, just as the coach had signaled, without a throw from the catcher.

The pitch had been called a ball, putting Tim ahead in the count one ball and no strikes. Tim stepped out of the batter's box, looking down at his coach as he had been taught. The coach held up his hand in the shape of a "C," signaling a game of "catch up." The game was meant to make a pitcher throw as many strikes as possible, allowing a batter to have the advantage. Tim acknowledged with a tip of his helmet and stepped back in. The game now dictated that Tim take pitches or not swing, until he had a strike. The following pitch came in outside. Ball two.

Now, if the game were played correctly, Tim would take the next pitch and hopefully take the count to three balls and no strikes. Sure enough, ball three.

At this point, ninety-nine out of one hundred coaches would have the batter take another pitch. With the game of "catch up" on all one hundred coaches would have Tim taking. Not John.

As Tim checked the coach for signals, John took both hands, grasped the bill of his cap in his fingers and slid them toward Tim, the signal for "green light." Green means go, as in swing if you like.

Tim looked a second longer to make sure he had it right. When he was certain, a smile crossed his lips, just enough for John to see but not allow the other team to know what was going on. The lanky thirteen-year-old dug back in and waited for the pitch.

C.J. took his lead from second, John bent over, holding the ends of his shorts as a winded basketball player might. The crowd quieted as the pitch sailed toward Tim and the heart of the plate.

There are moments in sports, which are timeless, Namath running off the field waving his number one finger, Jordan posing a second after his final memorable shot. Gibson limping around the bases, pumping his arm after his dramatic home run. For most people, these moments are watched but never lived. There are those times however, as children we are allowed to feel, if only briefly, what those moments are like.

Tim's swing was picture perfect. Short, quick and slightly down, then long and smooth as it finished. In between, it struck the ball in just a way as to create just a touch of under spin. As the ball drifted toward the left, center field fence, C.J. tagged up at second base, the team as well as their coach did all they could to "will" the ball over the fence and the crowd roared. With ten feet or so to spare, the ball left the field of play and Roadrunner led three to two.

The boys rushed out of the dugout, waiting to mob their teammate at home plate. C.J. arrived first, touching the plate as twelve hands slapped his helmet and swarmed him under. The greeting was twice as violent for Tim. He knew it was coming. Baseball has it's own set of rules, some of which make little or no sense at all. The one that says a player who hits a dramatic home run should be head slapped and pushed by a small mob is one that escapes even the purest of baseball people.

A sense of relief had taken over the team but it was quickly wiped away by the coaches reminding the boys of the fact the game was not over and still had a way to go. They could still score more this inning, which might be a good idea as the heart of the opponent's order was due to hit in the bottom of the inning.

Ambrose followed with a single only to be doubled up off the bat of Bret. Bret had struggled the entire tournament as far as hitting had gone. Kyle made the final out of the half inning, sending the game to the bottom of the last inning, Roadrunner three, West Mesa two.

Having made the promise to his mother that he would make sure every boy played in every game, had given John the idea of using Jon as his closer. A closer is a pitcher who throws hard enough that batters really struggle to hit. Jon didn't throw as hard as Tim but did throw harder than Bret. The coach felt like the difference of seeing Bret between Tim and Jon would be to his team's benefit. With that, Jon took the mound in his very first All Star pitching performance. Again, something most coaches wouldn't do.

John called Bryce over as he knelt next to the dugout entrance. "As long as he doesn't walk people, we'll be fine." He said to his assistant coach. The words hadn't even finished leaving his mouth when Jon's first pitch hit the batter square in the back. With a huge "thud" the ball hit and stopped, falling to the ground. Much like the coach's confidence in the young pitcher.

59

The very next pitch was greeted with a ping at it was hit sharply at Todd. The runner at first was running on the pitch, as it turned out, a good thing as Todd caught the ball and flipped it to Bret for a double play.

One out away but not out of the woods yet. The catcher, who had absolutely hammered Tim, was coming up, followed by the pitcher who swung the bat well in his own right. Without saying a word, John silently hoped for a ball to be hit at someone or at the very worst, walk the batter and hope for something better from the next one.

As he had done with the first pitch he had thrown, Jon hit the batter square in the back. In many cases, an opposing team might take exception to the pitcher's lack of control, especially when one team is predominantly white collar, Caucasian and the other blue collar, Hispanic. Jon was Hispanic and he had just put the tying run on base in the last inning. Instead of complaining, the fans practically patted him on the back. He was giving them all the help he could.

"Time!" John called, wanting to go to the mound and let loose on his young pitcher. Instead, as he trotted out he thought of the only joke he could. "Wanna hear a dirty joke?" He asked Jon as Brad arrived at the mound with the coach, his face dripping with sweat, dirt, now mud, streaking his face from a hard days work behind the plate. Jon could only look at his coach with a look like a deer in headlights. He nodded slowly. "Two white horses fell in the mud." John said, his timing perfect. Then he turned to Brad, "I guarantee they will be running on the first pitch, get rid of it as quickly as you can, good things will happen." Quickly, he walked back to the dugout, squeezing Bryce's shoulder as he knelt down again.

Sure enough, as Jon started to the plate, the runner at first started for second. John noticed he had a good jump but not great. If Brad could get rid of it cleanly, it would be close. The pitch was high and away, just as it should have been, allowing Brad to have a clear shot at the runner.

Kris waited until he was certain the batter wasn't swinging then broke toward the base. Todd did the same, and then ran toward shallow center field in order to back up.

Everything slowed down. Brad's throw looked good as John could almost count the stitches on the ball as slowly as it seemed to move. The runner began his slide, Kris stood, hunched over, glove extended as he waited for the ball to arrive. Knowing a ball in flight travels faster than reaching for a ball, he simply opened his glove as wide as possible and braced himself for the possibility of the runner colliding with him.

In a cloud of dust, the white leather or the ball disappeared into the brown leather of the shortstop's glove, a quick swipe and nothing was left except to wait for the umpire's call.

It came quickly, at least more quickly than anyone expected. Perhaps he wanted to get out of there or maybe it really was that good a play as Kris was already running toward Todd, hands raised triumphantly. He knew the call.

"Out!" As the umpire pumped his fist toward the ground to emphasize his point,

Instant pandemonium. Ambrose met Jon, Brad and Bret at the mound in an embrace that caused them to fall to the ground beginning the "dog pile." One by one, the boys piled on, creating a mound of sheer joy.

The parents and fans clapped passionately in the stands. Tears ran down more than a few cheeks. Not only mom's cheeks either.

John stood next to Bryce. His first instinct was to rush onto the field to join the boys. After one step, he held his ground. This was their time, not his. They needed to share the joy with each other and have a moment to remember forever. No, this time was theirs. His pleasure came in watching them.

As they unpiled from one another, the boy's uniforms were no longer white but the teeth, no longer hidden behind their lips shown whiter than ever. A pressure greater than a thousand pounds seemed to have lifted off the boys' collective shoulders. From that moment forward, they wouldn't have to win another game and it would be fine. Not because they had won a championship or because they had achieved their potential but because they had done so together. It was now theirs, forever.

As the sun neared the horizon to the West, the wisps of clouds turning gently to pastels of pinks and orange, the young coach stood with his team of newly crowned champions, a red, white and blue banner draped over his broad shoulders. He addressed both player and parent.

"This, guys, is only the first step in a long journey."

Chapter 12

Jason jumped forward, wrapping his arms around his tucked knees and leaned back to get as big a splash as possible. The water exploded onto the cement surrounding the pool, washing over the sandaled feet of Kris and Kyle's moms. It was a warm, star filled Southwestern evening, the sun had set but the light blue on the edge of the horizon tried to stave off the midnight blue trying to cover the sky. If people only knew the beauty the desert has to offer. It's there; one simply has to look for it.

John wanted to make sure all the families were on the same page for the State tournament three days away. In his twenty-three-year old, just out of college mind, this was the boy's time. It should be about the team and the game. He wanted the boys staying with the coaches and in their charge for any remainder of the season. This was the meeting where he would break that news to the parents.

He thought back again, to his thirteen-year-old season, while at the state tournament, he had stayed with his parents rather than in the rooms with all the other players. Not at his parent's request but rather because there were thirteen players and that broke down the rooms into groups of four. John's parents volunteered to keep him.

What he remembered most about that trip wasn't the fact they won the tournament or that he had played well, instead, John remembered the mornings, when he would hear stories about what went on in the rooms and all the fun his team mates were having. It was so difficult, wanting to be there with the group but always feeling as if he were the little brother, tagging along. That wasn't going to happen to any of these boys. They were too close to have any of them feel as if they weren't part of it.

As he spoke, standing in front of all thirteen dripping wet players, their mothers, who had never been away from their babies before listened, their cheeks warming with anger, John saw that this wasn't going well. Kyle's mom shook her head; Kris' shifted her weight impatiently. There was no way on God's green Earth that he was keeping the boys to himself.

He started with the argument that it wasn't a vacation but rather a baseball tournament. No good. He stated that there could be distractions that might hinder their play. Try again. The parents could look at this, as a time to be together, alone and still be able to watch the boys play, almost but not quite.

It wasn't until he told his story, how he had missed out when some of the fathers began to whisper in their wives ears. They too had felt like they had missed out. It would be a good thing for the boys. John could have it his way, for now.

Chapter 13

Cactus after cactus after tumbleweed flew by at sixty-five miles an hour. The endless sea of brown reflected off the window of the van John had borrowed for the trip. The sand of the desert was one shade, while the rocks, which hid from the heat of the sun under that sand, were another. Yucca plants randomly stood at attention, attempting to feel the breeze as cars went by on the highway. When that desperate attempt failed, their arms seemed to fall limp beside them. In defeat they slumped down, as did the rest of the desert agriculture. Destination, Roswell, home to the supposed crash site of an unidentified flying object many years before. Now it would be the weeklong home to Roadrunner Little League's thirteen-year-old All Star team.

The tournament itself was actually being held in Artesia, New Mexico, about thirty miles south of Roswell but there really was nowhere worth staying there. The team had chosen to make a drive every day but be comfortable, rather than stay somewhere in the tiny town.

John had been able to borrow a van from a family friend as to get the equipment and several players down to the tournament. Todd,

Tim and Kris had won whatever game of "odds and evens" or "rock, paper, scissors" in order to ride with their coach. It was great for about the first thirty miles, which was to say, until they were out of radio range of the "big" city. Then there was a small battle of wills over whose music they might listen to next. Todd and Kris enjoyed country music while Tim was into "rap" and "R and B." John settled things by saying they would start with Garth Brooks, but Tim's choice would be next. Tim pulled his usual shrug of indifference, then pulled his headphones up over his ears and listened to his own CD player.

The three listened, singing along with most of the songs until "The Dance" came up. It was then John noticed in the rear view mirror that Tim pulled one side off his ears in order to hear that song. It was amazing what stories could be told and the different types of people who would listen through music.

Conversation through the four-hour drive was mostly sports and continued steadily until about the three-hour mark, when the boys began to drift off to sleep. Kris had been in and out most of the trip to that point anyway. Apparently, he had always had trouble staying awake while traveling in a car. Not only on road trips either, he would fall asleep on the way to games from his house and that was only a ten minute trip.

It was during one his awake moments, while riding co-pilot with John when the van ended up behind Kris' family. Suddenly, from the driver's side of the car, CD's began flying out the window like Frisbees, five in all. While John stared in disbelief, Kris smiled wide as a Cheshire cat. "You know what that was about?" John asked his shortstop.

"Dad has always said we can listen to what we want but if we buy it and he finds it in his house, he'll throw it away. I'd say he found some of my brother's."

The two laughed for a while and told the story to the other's as they awoke. A short time later they arrived in Roswell. The streets were flooded for the team's arrival, literally. A downpour of monsoon-like proportions was beating down on the desert ground like a cow pissing on a flat rock. Already in his head, John was writing off the next day due to weather.

The vans pulled into the hotel parking lot with the boys falling out one by one, like clowns come out of the small car at a circus. Long and short arms alike, stretched to work out the four-hour drive. Some of the boys had slept the majority of the way and looked as if it were first light and they were waking up to greet the morning. The coaches hollered at them to get their bags, and gather as to hear their room assignments. There really was no point to who slept in whose room as the boys for one liked everyone the same and secondly, they would end up in one room the majority of the trip anyway.

Once they were organized, the boys were sent to their rooms to change and shower if they wanted. The tournament hosts had planned a barbeque at the fields, which the teams were to attend. It would be the team's only chance for dinner and timing wise, they were just about right. John also wanted to be there to size up the competition. There was nothing more fun than going to team gatherings before the tournaments to see what the competition looked like. Who had the "big boys," who was small, which teams carried themselves like players and who looked timid? Really, looks meant nothing but it still was a part of baseball that John had always enjoyed.

Due to the rain, what was supposed to be a twenty-minute drive turned into a forty-minute adventure. There were times when John couldn't see the lines of the road as the sheets of rain covered them. A jackrabbit jumped between the caravan at one point causing the second van full of boys to swerve. Still, the boys seemed to notice none of this as they were consumed with each other, just as the coach had foreseen. This trip wasn't about baseball to them; it was about being thirteen and having no worries in the world except when their voices would stop changing. It was a rite of passage into the next stage of their lives and they were making that step together.

Finally, the team arrived at the barbeque. It had been moved inside to a nearby church. Already, the five other teams, including a second team from Albuquerque, were eating their share of the pulled beef, baked beans and mashed potatoes. All the noise, from talking to chewing completely stopped as the boys walked into the room. Nothing more than a whisper could be heard as the boys made their way over to the "chow line." Having been weighed and measured, it seemed, the staring eyes went back to whatever it was they had been doing.

John turned to Bryce and smiled, "That is why I made sure we arrived late." as if he had caused the weather which had slowed them down. Really though, he had wanted to make an entrance. Sometimes, perception is everything.

The teams sat at long picnic style tables talking only between bites and most of the statements were muffled by the food in the player's mouths. Little, if any of the conversations were between players from different teams but mostly between each other. One coach did however; seem interested in all the teams. A slight build, typical of southern New Mexico, probably one hundred and forty pounds or so, wearing faded blue jeans and a maroon colored Polo style shirt. He had hair on the edges of his mouth, perhaps the beginning of a moustache or maybe just the way his grew. Without introducing himself, table-by-table, he invited himself to sit down and talk to the coaches of each team.

John nudged Bryce, as if the red headed coach hadn't seen this already. The man was headed to their table next.

"You are the team from the big city aren't you?" He asked in a mousy voice and heavy Hispanic accent.

"One of two." Bryce replied, speaking of the other district, which had been established that year. John simply nodded, taking another bite of his dinner.

"I'm the Bayard coach and we open with you tomorrow...if it stops raining." The coach stated triumphantly with slyness in his manner. "Got a fireballer?"

A "fireballer" is, in baseball terms, a pitcher who throws hard. In the Major Leagues, this would be someone who throws somewhere in the mid to upper nineties. For thirteen-year-old baseball, somewhere in the seventies would be considered a "fireballer." Tim was definitely one of those guys.

"Not really." John quickly replied, not allowing Bryce to give anything away. Not that he would have, at least not intentionally but the cocky coach wanted to give nothing away. "My guys all throw about the same. If they're on we have a chance if not we get beat."

None of that were true, of course. Tim, Bret, Kris and Ambrose all threw hard. All threw above average for their age. John simply didn't want to give away his hand. Coaching to him could be like a poker game. This was John's poker face.

"I do. So make sure your team gets their rest. They'll need it." Smiling as he spoke, the coach rose from the table and walked off. "Good luck."

The two young men said nothing as the man walked away. Bryce had known John since they were twelve years old. He knew that wouldn't sit well with his friend and if at all possible, John would make the coach eat his words. Bryce began to say something to John and then realized the coach was lost in thought for a moment. He could wait.

John was thinking about his friend Craig. Though they had graduated together, Craig had been a year older as far as youth sports had gone. Meaning, when John was twelve, Craig was thirteen and playing in the age group up from his friend. Craig's thirteen-year-old All Star team had also won the City tournament and gone to the State tournament. There they had run into a team from Bayard, which had two pitchers, the second of which had gone on to play minor league baseball. The first and John couldn't remember his name, had been this huge man-child which Craig had referred to as "leaving the field holding hands with his wife and kids" after the ball game. Of course, it wasn't true but what Craig had meant by that was how much bigger and older the boy had seemed. John also remembered his friend talking about how hard this boy had thrown the baseball. What if Bayard had another one of those types of guys? Then John smiled to himself. Craig's team had beaten them twice. Both pitchers had thrown and Roadrunner had won. In fact, the championship was won on a game ending triple play. Maybe this team had that sort of magic. It didn't matter. John had Tim and Ambrose both if need be. If anyone could beat those two, in the same game, then they deserved to win.

John's gaze came back allowing Bryce to ask his question. "What do you think?"

"He's right, we need to get our sleep." John said with a smile and a wink.

The coaches gathered the boys for the drive home. It would be an early morning as the game was scheduled for ten A.M. The rain was still coming down. John shook his head as he darted through the drops. It always seemed to be raining on him.

Chapter 14

Bret wiped the water from his glasses as he sat next to Ambrose at the back of Bryce's van. His jet-black hair dripped a few more drops onto the lenses before he could finish. His body was a little more filled out than his peers; though it was obvious he had plenty more growing to do. His face had a small acne problem and the hint of a moustache. An adult could tell this young man was in that awkward stage everyone goes through.

To that point in his baseball life, Bret had been dominant. Mostly due to his size but also the fact he was athletically gifted and coordinated for his size. Only Tim could compete with him on the baseball field for being the strongest player. However, when it came time for the All Star tournament, which he now was playing in for his third year, Bret simply disappeared. His towering, majestic home runs never came. His tailing fastball seemed to slow and straighten out instead of getting better. Most people who knew this young man thought it was a case of being too nice and not having the competitive fire to play "big" when it counted. While boys like Tim and Kris would take it to the next level, Bret would only be another player.

John had another theory. He knew a little about Bret's home life.

Having coached him through the summer, he also saw a side of Bret, which others might not. Bret was trying too hard.

Bret's parents had been divorced for two years. It wasn't good. The only time his parents were even near each other was at the kid's baseball games. During the summer it was easy as the two younger siblings played as well so the parents might be at different fields, not even near one another. During All Stars though, Bret was the only one playing and both parents were there. John believed that the boy had such a big heart and wanted to please both parents so badly, hoping that if he played well there would be nothing to talk or argue about except how well he had done and how happy they were for him that there wouldn't be any problems. Sometimes the weight was too much for Bret.

It was a long sniff from Bret that caught Ambrose's attention. Yes, it was wet and raining but not cold enough to cause a sniffle. Ambrose leaned forward and saw that Bret was weeping.

"You alright?" The sound seeming to almost come from out of the dark as the only time the boys could see one another's face was as they passed another car on the highway. 'Brose put his arm on Bret's knee.

"Just nervous." Bret replied, trying to make something up as fast as he could, not having expected to be caught in his pity party.

"Why be nervous? This game is fun and like John says, you should only be nervous if you're not prepared. We're more than prepared."

"I just don't want to let the team down again."

"Again? You've played fine so far."

"Not hitting." Bret mumbled

"Slumps happen dude. No big deal." Ambrose gave him a little fist to the thigh.

"Every year it's the same. All Stars comes and I can't hit. I can't. I can't. I can't!"

"Shhh." Ambrose put both hands over Bret's mouth. "Don't say that so loud. The baseball gods will hear you and then you're really done." 'Brose smiled, though Bret couldn't see it. "You know about the baseball gods right?"

"Nothing more than when John mentions them."

"Let me tell you a story."

Ambrose put his arm up and over his friend's shoulders. The whole ride home, Ambrose regaled Bret with stories about his baseball gods and other stories he had heard while traveling with his father on baseball trips. It happened that the two were sharing a bed in one of the two rooms Bryce was in charge of, so the story telling continued into the night. When Bret finally fell asleep, there was a smile and a sense of relief on his face.

The rain continued to beat down, making it easy for everyone to sleep. The soft, steady drizzle sounded like the sea crashing against the shoreline. The calming sound covered fourteen players, their parents but only one coach.

Chapter 15

The alarm blared, causing the coach to startle. How John hated to be woken that way. The red illuminated numbers read six-thirty. Rubbing his eyes, John allowed them to adjust to the dark before getting himself out of bed. The three players in his room, Kris, Todd and Tim never moved.

Sliding the thick curtain to the side, he looked out to see what the weather was like. A light sheet of clouds covered the sky, though it looked as if they would break as the sun warmed the air. No rain, though. Time to get things going.

Nothing feels better than the warm water of a high showerhead covering one's face and running down over their body. Baseball line ups, situations and the possibility of two games ran around in John's mind as he stood in the shower. He looked at his white, plastic disposable razor. As a player, he never shaved on game day, in his short coaching career some days he did others he did not. What would be the right one today?

Stepping from the shower, he wiped away the steam covered mirror to reveal that he had in fact, shaved. A quick comb through his hair, as he would have a hat on, and out he went to get the boys going.

There had been no call from the tournament director to delay the game so they had about two hours to get the boys up, fed and make the journey down to the ball park.

The coaches sat in a small courtyard outside the four rooms, waiting for the boys to get dressed. The team had two uniforms, the first were the "clown" uniforms as John called them, white with red pinstripes and a red waistband. The second were the same type of pants; only these had red belts, looking much better, and solid red jerseys. This morning they wore the "clowns" tonight, if they won, they would wear the others.

After a quick McDonald's breakfast, the vans were on their way to Artesia. Kris was asleep before leaving the city limits while C.J., Steve and Brad played their hand held video games. Bryce drove in one van while John drove the other. Sitting quietly behind the wheel, he went over the game in his head. There was a slight tension within the team that he could feel. Should he address it? Let it go? He noticed Ambrose in the rear view mirror. The boy popped his glove over and over, his fist causing the leather to sound off as they smacked together. The van was about five miles outside Artesia, Ambrose stopped playing with his glove and reached over the seat in front of him, putting both hands over Tim's shoulders. He didn't say a word but rubbed for a few seconds. He then turned to Brad and Steve next to him. Again, without a word, he held up his glove and nodded. As if they read his mind, the two teammates put away their games and looked forward.

C.J. never had been quite as aware of the subtleties of baseball and he didn't catch on at this point either. He continued to play his video game, giggling like a small boy and dancing in his seat. His teammates said nothing. When C.J. finally turned around to show the other boys his score he quickly caught on that it was time to focus.

Even during his playing days, John had never seen any player have the ability to focus his teammates without saying a word. It was the single most impressive thing he had ever witnessed and this from a thirteen-year-old boy.

Problem solved. The coach wouldn't even have to say a word to the team. He knew this group would focus the other van when they arrived and everything would take care of itself. If Kris would wake up that is.

As they piled out of the vans, the team could feel the unusual humidity in the air. For some of the boys, it was their first taste of humidity and made them feel almost sick to their stomachs. The coaches heard some of the boys complaining. Ambrose did as well.

"No excuses!" "We get to play ball and that's what were going to do. I don't want to hear about it again. Right coaches?"

John just smiled to what he was witnessing. "Right 'Brose." He noticed the absence of cars in the parking lot as he spoke.

Sure enough, upon walking into the ballpark, it was immediately obvious the game was delayed, as the field was muddy with standing water at first and third. Two men were pouring gasoline on the ground at shortstop and second base. John had seen this many times as a way to dry a field quickly as opposed to waiting for the sun to do it's job.

The director came out of a storage room in the third base dugout. He gave a questioning gesture toward the team as he walked toward them. "What are you doing here?"

Apparently, there was supposed to be a call made to the hotel to inform the team not to come down as the game had been postponed for two hours. No such call had been made.

In his youth, John hadn't learned tact in situations such as this so it was all he could do to control himself as he explained it was apparent to him that no call had been made purposely. Bryce also had to make sure he stood halfway between John and the director.

For years, through Little League and High School ball, John had seen how the smaller towns of New Mexico always had it in for the "big city boys" of Albuquerque. Hometown officiating, sub-standard facilities and intimidating fan behavior managed to find their way to every game in every sport. In the young coach's eyes, this was simply another attempt to shift the favor to the small town teams.

Artesia, New Mexico is in no way a hot bed for entertainment, particularly on a Saturday morning. There was nowhere for the team to go except back to the hotel. John decided against that, as it would be forty minutes in the van both ways and only an hour back at the hotel. Better to keep the boys outside in the humidity, hopefully acclimating them to it.

For the next hour and a half, the coaches and parents from Roadrunner Little League raked, shoveled and drug the field in an attempt to get it ready to play. The boys sat in the shade, playing games jokes and Ambrose told more stories about his experience with the Olympic team. Every so often, John looked over to the tree where the boys shaded themselves. Each time, Ambrose stood while the others sat as if he were the professor and they the students.

As the field became nearer to playable, the boys went off to take batting practice. Bryce noticed first, the drag in their step. No doubt the early morning plus humidity and heat was wearing on the boys. The two coaches decided to split the pitching between three or four as not to wear anybody out.

That decision turned out to be a good one, as the Bayard team did have a young man who threw hard but was wild. He walked four batters in the first and three more in the second. He worked so hard it was obvious he would wear himself out quickly. An early lead due to the wildness would allow for a cushion when the heat took it's toll and the boys from Roadrunner had a slight collapse. A final score of seven to four had the boys advancing to the second round where they would face the other Albuquerque team, who were also Ambrose's former team.

John wanted to explode on the boys for their poor effort, remembering a lesson he had learned from a former coach. *If you are going to get on a team, do it after they win. Try not to get on them after they lose.* He thought better of it though, knowing they had battled and had been in the sun for nearly six hours. The one bright side to all this was because of the rain, the second game, which was supposed to take place that night would be played the following day. It would be an early morning again but at least they could get home, have a good meal and relax.

As a reward for a supreme effort, John decided to take the boys to the fanciest place in Roswell, a Furr's Cafeteria. At least the boys could eat as much as they wanted.

Walking in, as it was about five o'clock, many of the customers were elderly couples. They watched the boys as they entered, very unsure of what to think. Obviously, teams had done this before and not acted in a way the residents of Roswell might have liked.

"I don't think they like to see baseball teams here." Bryce spoke aloud what John was thinking.

"They'll have to get used to it because these boys eat a lot and it's cheap to eat here." John replied. "Beside, our boys know how to behave."

His second statement was more uncertain than declarative. He knew they were good kids but boys could be boys. In his favor, he did have the boys showered and they had to wear a collared shirt. No hats allowed unless it was a fast food restaurant. *Look classy, think classy, you'll be classy.*

They made it through the dinner just as the coaches had hoped, without any problem except for C.J. going back for fourths which really wasn't a problem so much as just amazing that he could eat so much, Salisbury steak and chocolate cream pie at that.

Another fast night and early morning had the boys playing again the following day. The first day jitters gone and a rival who talked too much about Ambrose led the boys to play the type of game John had been waiting for. A thirteen-two waxing of 'Brose's former team and later in the day a seven-nothing game against the host team from Roswell gave the team a day off to wait and see who would advance to play them, now having to beat them twice in the championship game.

The team took a drive to Clovis to watch the fourteen-fifteen year old team play in their State tournament on the day off. John was friends with the coach and had coached several of the fifteen year olds on his team last year. The drive was longer than the game as they arrived in the third inning and the game was fast, Roadrunner winning that game as well.

The ride back to Roswell gave the boys time to talk about things with John. They had spent so much time together and really had never talked with him. Except for Tim. Todd was riding "shotgun" and started the conversation talking with his coach about their time together at the High School where Todd was the batboy John's senior year of school.

The team had all the potential in the world. A possible draft pick as the number one pitcher, the state's leading home run hitter and a center fielder that could run out of site in five seconds on flat ground. They were like so many groups to come through that area of Albuquerque, the world in their hands and an empty bag to show for it in the end.

"How'd you play?" "Did you hit home runs?" "What position?"

All the questions at once and with each one, before John could answer, Todd would do it for him. "He played first base!" "Long, long home runs!" "He was great. So was his team."

"Why didn't you win it all?" C.J. asked. The one question John didn't want to hear.

He thought about his answer for a minute. No leadership, too much leadership. Bad coaching. No teamwork. Not enough effort on his part. Not enough effort by anyone. There were so many answers and so many reasons. He started to rattle them off; explaining each one as he went then Ambrose asked a question.

"Aren't those all just excuses coach?"

"There are reasons and there are excuses." John started. Then he realized Ambrose was right. They were just excuses and he was teaching the boys there were no excuses. "You're right 'Brose. We just didn't play well enough as a team to win."

It felt good to come to grips with something he had wrestled with for years. Just say what happened and move on. If you have the chance, fix it and never make that same mistake again. He made sure he put that in the boy's heads as they talked more about John's team and this team, all the similarities and differences. Where this group could go and all the things they could accomplish. The drive went by almost too quickly for the coach, as he wanted to spend more time talking to the team.

He decided too much talk might spoil it. Besides, he was hungry and if he was hungry, the boys must have been starving. Another round at the cafeteria was just what they needed.

It was again almost five when they arrived to eat. Once again, the boys looked the part as the quietly strolled into the restaurant. The manager met the coaches at the front of the line.

"Your boys are back!" The man said with a smile. John cautiously shook his hand waiting for the manager to ask them to leave. Maybe the boys had done something he didn't know about. Maybe another team had done something to not allow this team to eat there. John waited to hear what the man had to say.

"They were so well behaved last time coach, I wanted to give you the twelve year old discount."

At first, the coach thought perhaps this manager was giving him a hint that they had acted immaturely the last time. Then he realized it was for real, a compliment for his team. He shook the manager's hand, thanking him for the gesture. Bryce noticed John's chest push out another two inches or so with pride.

During the meal, Kris' parents sat with Bryce and John. They talked baseball and business laughing most of the time as Chuck, Kris' father was quite possibly the funniest person the young men had ever met and without a doubt, the quickest witted.

Kris' mom put her hand on John's shoulder. Taking a deep breath she spoke. Again, John was waiting for bad news.

"When you first said the boys couldn't stay with us on this trip, myself and several of the other moms were about ready to have you castrated." There was laughter from Bryce and Chuck but John knew there was a bit of truth to it. "After having been here and seeing how much fun Kris is having as well as how much time we parents have to ourselves and with ourselves..." she winked at her husband,

"You were right." John smiled. That really meant a lot to him. Not only in being right but in gaining the respect of the parents. That's all he ever wanted to do was make people happy and not let them down. He always felt as if he were letting them down.

"That said..." She continued, "You may never be allowed to give them back." everybody laughed and finished their meals. John couldn't get enough of a night like this.

As the team walked out the door a small hand took John by his hand. It was cold as ice. He turned to find an elderly couple, the woman having taken his hand.

"Are these your boys?" The gentleman asked.

John hesitated first because he was again worried something had gone wrong then because he couldn't think of a witty way to say "yes." "Not by birth but they are mine." It was weak at best.

"They are the most well behaved bunch of young men I've seen in here in ten years and I've seen you twice now. You must do a great job with them."

"Thank you very much. They are great boys." It was all John could say. Not to the point of tears but overwhelmed nonetheless, the coach was almost speechless. For the first time in many, many years, John felt like he was doing something right. He remembered what it was to like himself and the things he was doing.

He let the boys and Bryce walk out, into the fading light of the day. This group meant everything to him. Not for the baseball but for the way it made him feel. Yeah, he was doing something right.

Chapter 16

The phrase "A love for the game" is thrown around all to often. Professionals play either for money or competition. Sure, they have fun playing but it is the competition both against an opponent and themselves they enjoy most. Fans watch it to see greatness, to relax or to quench the thirst for what they themselves couldn't accomplish. Really, the only ones who have that love are boys and the elderly. The frail, hunched embodiment of that love was John's former, now assistant coach Derry.

As the team walked across the parking lot from dinner, Derry and his wife were just arriving. Little League rules specified that only two coaches were permitted in the dugout during games. John had chosen Bryce to be in the dugout. Nonetheless, Derry had attended every game, along with his dedicated wife. Now, they had made the trip to Roswell to watch the boys play.

In his thirty plus years of coaching, Derry had his share of All Star teams, though none of them had ever advanced past the City tournament. He had lasted well past the time of his own sons' playing days simply out of a true "love for the game." Never, has any one person had a greater passion for a game or for the children that play that game than Derry.

From the day John had met this small man nearly ten years before, it was obvious why Derry coached. He loved the boys. Even now, at twenty three, John didn't understand how anyone who wasn't directly attached to a team, as in a son or a daughter or someone who had an agenda, like himself, trying to move up the coaching hierarchy, could spend so much time around the game or love every minute of that time. Still, Derry did it, most every day.

As a fourteen year old, John had a respect for Derry but it was mostly born out of a respect for all elders and certainly one who was his coach. Even after moving on to High School ball and College, John would see Derry at many of the games. His respect for the man grew with each year as he realized what a commitment this man was making to the boys he had known for only a short while. After his playing days were over, John would still see Derry at the High School games watching boys he didn't even know.

It was this dedication to the game and the players which had caused the twenty something coach to go to Derry's aide when he was forced out of coaching by the politics of parents who knew nothing about him or his years of service. In their eyes, they saw an old man whose time had passed him by. Thinking it was about winning and losing.

John knew that games are played to win, if not, we wouldn't keep score. However, these parents and League politicians thought they had better ideas for the boys than a man who was out there day in and day out for those boys. John knew that he was in a position to do something about it and did just that. It also didn't bother him that he was bucking the system just a little.

So, having his friend and a person he admired there by the field and watching him give his best to the boys, allowed for a great sense of pride in the young coach. He knew as well, that the boys had taken to Derry like he was their treasure to look after and learn from as well.

It was a good thing, Derry and the boys, as much of this journey seemed to be.

Chapter 17

As the evening sun fell behind the horizon of Southern New Mexico, midnight blue followed by a tapestry of black covered the sky. The morning would bring the State Championship, a title the boys could not stop talking about. From the time dinner had finished, Ambrose had been slapping the fellas on the back asking them if they were planning on being a State Champion or discussed how they would "dog pile." It was a way of easing the tension that would no doubt, if it already hadn't creep, into the boys heads as they were now on unmarked ground. None of them had ever been in a situation like this with a prize such as the State Championship.

While Bryce felt the same anxiety as the boys, John felt a complete calm. He was the picture of confidence. The Roswell team would have to not only beat his team twice after having already been beaten but would have to beat both Tim and Ambrose if necessary. John was so confident; his starting pitcher would be Kyle rather than either of the other two.

His reasoning was two-fold. First, he knew he could bring in Tim or Ambrose in a close game and finish off his opponent or give it up and save both the "big guns" for a final "do or die" game. Secondly, when he was thirteen, his coaches had pitched him in this same game, saving the two aces for just the same reasons John was doing now. There was no doubt in the coach's mind. This time tomorrow, the boys would be champions.

The game was scheduled for a ten A.M. start. With the prospect of having to pack, eat and get to the ballpark, which was still a thirty-minute, or so drive, John wanted the boys to bed early. As the nine o'clock hour approached, he pulled all the boys into his room to give his "pump 'em up" speech.

He talked about where they had been, meaning never having won before and where they were now, already champions but a step away from the next step. He talked of how the boys no longer made excuses for mistakes or failure but rather took challenges head on and overcame their obstacles. Most of all, John talked about how this team was the very definition of the word "team" in how they worked together on the field and looked after each other off it.

As he finished, Ambrose stood up, clapping his hands together. "I wish we could play right now, I'm so pumped up!" His enthusiasm was genuine as he truly enjoyed every aspect of the game of baseball. The rest of the boys' excitement could be read in their body language as well. In an effort to relieve themselves of some of the tension, they piled on top of Ambrose and the bed he was next to.

John gave the boys about ten minutes to get ready for bed. He knew they needed to wind down and many of them would have trouble sleeping anyway. After the ten-minute period, he turned the boys over to Bryce, asking him to keep the boys in bed and get them to sleep while he went to fill the vans with gas for the journey home.

He made his way down the stairs to the foyer, which held the swimming pool and hot tub; it was completely dark, as it was after their closing hours. He nearly tripped on the last step because of the dark. While walking across the swimming pool area, water reflecting what light there was in "waves" across the ceiling, John heard voices, coming softly from the hot tub area. He stopped to listen.

Sure enough, a couple, which couldn't be seen, was enjoying themselves in the hot tub. In most cases, this wouldn't have been anything more than a short smile for John but the young lady, whomever she was, couldn't seem to contain her passion. Louder and louder she became as John stood listening in the dark. As this was too much fun to enjoy by himself, he ran back up to the rooms to allow Bryce in on his find.

To John's delight, the couple was still there when the two coaches returned and the woman was still quite amorous in her breathing. For ten minutes the men sat on the steps, in the dark, covering their laughter as each made more than one joke at the couple's expense.

After one particularly quick-witted shot by John, there came laughter behind them. It wasn't the laugh of an adult. Without even looking, the coaches knew exactly who it was. Turning slowly around, to no surprise at all, three steps full of thirteen-year-old boys held their hands over their mouths in an attempt to contain their laughter.

Immediately, the coaches shooed the group upstairs to their rooms. There was no way of reprimanding the boys for their actions as they were even more guilty for not only doing the same but starting the whole thing anyway. Instead he just told the boys to get into their rooms with a reminder to wait until later in the night if they ever decided to have a "friend" in a public hot tub. With that, John did go to fill the vans and returned to four hotel rooms filled with boys dreaming of baseball.

Chapter 18

Kris slept, Tim played a video game and Todd talked nervously as the van rolled toward the dust-covered city. John fast-forwarded and rewound the hitting tape he had made for the boys batting practice. The sky held only a hint of light clouds against a pale blue; it would be a hot, hot day.

With cactus shooting by, even as the pulled into the city limits, John remembered looking out the window of vans he traveled in as a player. It was the time spent traveling, thinking about the game, teammates and the future he enjoyed most about baseball. Shoelaces were taken from their shoes, tied together and flown from van to van with messages on road trips with John's thirteen-year-old team. There were so many insignificant things they did which amounted to so many wonderful memories, the coach could only hope these boys were able to have the same.

No more than a mile from the ball park, the song "Good Vibrations," kind of the team's song, as it had the lyric's "in it to win it or get the *@#& out!" came on. The boys in John's van began singing it at full tilt rolling down the windows to let the other van know what they were listening to. As both vans pulled into side-by-side parking spaces, the boys jumped out, asking the coach to "crank it."

Here was a team preparing to play what should be the biggest game of their lives and the were standing on and around vans in a dirt parking lot dancing around, playing "air guitars" and banging their heads against the air. No pressure here.

As all this was happening, the Roswell team pulled into the parking lot beside them. To see the looks on those boy's faces as well at the look on the coach's was priceless. John nudged Bryce to look at their opponents. It was all the two friends could do not to laugh out loud. This had to put it in the Roswell player's minds there was no way this team would lose today.

It's a rare and perfect thing when a team comes together in a season, when no matter the situation, a team is unstoppable. This was one of those times. Not a hint of nerves, anxiety, or fear was in the boy's minds. Just the notion they would be playing a game today, together and the end result would be well, perfect, just as the day would be. It was as if everything else in the world had come to a stop or at the very least, was moving so slowly it couldn't be noticed. The only time that seemed to move was that on the field. The day, week, month, none of that mattered. Not even the slightest breeze dared to stir the perfection in this day. It was the boys' time and for one moment, it seemed as if they had the ability to not only recognize it but enjoy every second as well.

The Roswell coach must not have had the foresight the boys did, as he made sure to let John know this game would not have the same result as their first meeting.

"You used all your tricks last game coach." Referring to the a couple of back door pick off moves and odd base running moves the team had used in the last game. "You'll have to play us straight up this time."

John smiled and played the "no comment" card for the moment. He knew there was plenty left in the bag of tricks his team had worked on so often at practice. Upon returning to the dugout he told Bryce to remind him of anything he might use against this coach. "We need to send him a message early."

As if the Baseball Gods were watching and on the brash young coach's side, the Roswell team was throwing a left handed pitcher. Perfect for one of John's unused "tricks." Right away, in the first inning, with two outs, John had runners at first and third base. With the left-hander only able to see first base, the runner there was to take a false step, pretend to fall, drawing a throw from an anxious pitcher. At that moment, the runner at third would break for home, hopefully having the element of surprise and enough of a jump to beat the throw. Usually, John was willing to trade an out for a run but if all were perfect, everyone would be safe.

Sure as a blue-bellied lizard's tail will grow back, Ambrose "tripped" at first, Tim broke for home. The first baseman hesitated, not sure weather to throw home or tag Ambrose. He chose to throw home, late of course and Ambrose moved on to second. The Roadrunner fans cheered loudly. It had become fun for them as most of the fathers had learned to think like John and watch for his signals in certain situations, knowing what was coming, then seeing it executed was as much fun for them as it was for the boys.

Rattled, the pitcher lost command of his pitches, walking the next two batters. After a chiding from his coach, he delivered a fastball belt high to Steve. The ball rocketed to the right center gap, scoring all three base runners and the game was on. It wasn't going to be close. Kyle, though he had many balls hit hard, didn't give up a run. Tim came in to finish, looking as if he were throwing a hundred miles an hour. Following a pitcher like Kyle who relied upon location and deception, a power pitcher like Tim could be nearly untouchable. Everything the team did was perfect. If John called for a bunt, it was there, hit and run, steals, everything was perfect.

There was only one mistake, in fact and it really wasn't a "mistake." With the game in hand, the coaches wanted to make sure every boy got as much playing time as possible. Jon had entered the game at first base. A long cry from his performance in the City Championship, Jon had really been struggling to hit. The coaches knew that when Bret was pitching they would need Jon at first base so he needed as many innings as possible.

With two outs in the top of the seventh and final inning, the next one to be the final out, a pop up hit right over the first base bag was sure to be it. Jon put his glove up to block the sun, just as he was supposed to, then started to look as if he needed a compass to find his way. Forward then back, side-to-side and backward again finally tripping over the base and ending up on his rear end. The ball landed right between his legs, humorous site to everyone except his coach.

John wanted to be done with this game and save Tim as many pitches as possible. He snapped at Jon from across the field, though it really didn't matter. Tim threw the next three pitches by the following batter, ending the game and winning the State Championship eight to nothing.

The celebration was not as John had expected it to be. It was happy and fun but also "matter of fact." It seemed as if the boys expected this. It was what the coach had wanted to see when he first thought about winning championships with this team but he didn't want the boys to miss out on the feeling of accomplishment. The feeling that only comes when you stand side by side your closest friends and know that you worked toward this, as hard as you possibly could and this is your reward. He didn't want the boys to miss out on that.

John met the tournament director at home plate, along with the Roswell coach. While the director had very nice things to say, it was the other coach's words, which really meant something to John. "I've done this for about ten years now, and I've got to tell you," his words had a slight southern drawl to them, "this team will represent New Mexico better than any other I've seen. You've done a great job with them son." As a player, John had over heard people say he was a good ball player and as a coach he figured some might think it but to that point, no one had ever spoken to him like that. Not that he was looking for praise but at twenty-three, he was always the younger of the two coaches on the field and usually didn't get much respect for it. If he won, he was "cocky" or "lucky to have such a talented team" if he were to lose, it would certainly be because of his age. Taking the coach's hand, he thanked him feeling as high as he had felt in a long while.

After accepting the State Championship banner, the red and blue letters upon a white triangle flag, John turned to find the boys dumping water and Gatorade over one another's heads. Now they looked as if they were little boys playing at recess. This was more what he had hoped for. A confidence that said, "this was expected" but a joy of youth that can never be matched.

By now, the parents, all of which were there, some having driven down for the day if they weren't already staying with the team, had come onto the field for hugs, congratulations and pictures. Several handshakes into the crowd, John came to Derry who had a tear running down his soft, wrinkled cheek. Dressed in his red, two-button, collared shirt, blue jeans and the Roadrunner All-Star cap John had given him, Derry didn't say a word but hugged the six foot plus frame of his former player before gripping his hand with both his smaller ones in a quick handshake.

A horrible feeling swept over John all too fast. "Derry are you alright?" He asked with panic in his voice.

Derry's voice trembled as he fought back more tears. "Yes."

"John" he paused to gain some composure, "that was the most beautiful game I have ever seen played. It was perfect." He hugged John again.

There was more praise to be heard but if anyone had asked the coach to repeat what good tidings he had been given, he wouldn't have been able. He was lost in the day, doing his best to take it all in. The boys, his boys had accomplished something there. They had become something greater than even someone with John's expectations could have hoped for. Ambrose had his arm over Kris' shoulder while Todd kneeled between them for a picture. Kyle posed with his little sister for a picture, then with mom. The three amigos, Brad, Jason and Steve stood like a chain, arms over one another for their picture. John looked around, so much bigger than he had hoped for. His expectations had been to come together as a team. Instead, these boys had come together as a family.

Chapter 19

The alarm blared loudly, causing his body to literally jump out of sleep. He slid his feet over the edge of the bed, causing him to sit upright. John hated mornings. So many had passed with a struggle to find a reason to get out of bed. A fear that the only thing he could accomplish that day would be to disappoint someone new.

This morning, he lifted himself from the bed and into the shower without a second thought. No reason was needed except that today was a new day and he had responsibilities, a job, bills to pay and errands to run. There was no baseball this day and still, he was cautiously optimistic.

It had been nearly two years that he listened to the radio on the drive to start a day. Fearing that a good mood to start a day could only be ruined by the inevitable. Something he had done in the past would come back to bite him today or worse yet, the next bad decision would be made. Yet today, he not only turned the radio to a music station rather than talk, he sung along with it and tapped the steering wheel as he went.

He caught his reflection in the rear view mirror. There was no despise or contempt for the person he saw looking back at him.

Instead he accepted the man he saw and better yet allowed that the person he saw was not a bad person but rather someone who had made mistakes and no matter where he went, the memory of those mistakes and poor decisions would be going with him.

To have become part of the family of which he had now become was enough to change the way he thought of himself. When a man can look at himself and like who he is or at the very least, come to grips with the person he is, then and only then can a man allow others to like him as well. Somewhere along the line, he had given a group of young men the ability to work for and achieve things they had never been able to before. He was a good person. He did things for others as often as he could and never did anything out of malice. Though they say some of the worst things in history have come out of the best intentions, John realized everything he had done in life was done with the best intentions. By some chance of fate, he had been rewarded with this group of boys, finding their way into manhood and he had given them direction and lessons he wished he had learned when he was their age. As a group, they had been given a new friend in Ambrose and John had been given them.

They would probably never know it but simply by showing up, these boys had given a man more than he could ever give them.

Chapter 20

"You are the only team in New Mexico practicing today!" the coach shouted from the dugout toward the boys playing catch in the outfield. The Southwestern sun had barely risen over the Sandias that morning. A quiet weekday morning, traffic's rushing sound kept out by the surrounding trees and scattered buildings. A sprinkler ch-ch-chattered on the smaller field next to them while small sparrows darted up and down trying to steal a sip.

It was true, at least as far as the age group was concerned. Roadrunner was the only thirteen-year-old team still practicing. Two days of practice before leaving for Tucson, Arizona where the Divisional tournament was to be held. It would take two more steps, the Divisional and Regional tournaments before reaching the World Series, two very difficult steps.

The week would be hectic for the coach, as John not only had to prepare the team and pack himself; he also had his best friend's wedding to attend. Here, these friends came out to play every day, looking forward to whatever they had lying in front of them while their coach was taking part in bidding farewell to part of his past. No longer were he and Craig boys talking about their baseball memories but men who were moving on. John had played ball with his friend on the very field the boys practiced on now and the following night he would watch that same friend be married. Was it irony, rite of passage, who knew? None of it was lost on the young man. He now had an understanding of how, whether he wanted to or not, older just happens and it is part of a person's responsibility to do so. He also realized this was part of life to pass on to these young men all he could to help them get along without the struggles he had.

Practice that morning was completely John's responsibility. Bryce had to work and Derry had a "honey do" list of things to get done. Most days like this had the boys doing what was referred to as "hot shots" where John would hit ground balls as hard as he could at the boys. More often than not, a bad hop or two would hit the fielders in the chest, which had the coaches hollering for the boys to "rub dirt on it." No sign of weakness or whimpering allowed. Rubbing dirt on it was just as way for ball players to say they weren't hurt.

This morning was no different; Ambrose took one in the chest and Jon in the chin. Of course, Jon heard about it from his buddies, reminding him of how he tripped over the bag in the State Championship.

"At least the ball hit you this time!" Todd chirped.

"Lose that one in the sun too?" Steve hollered from the foul line.

It was that kind of looseness which seemed to infect the whole team. It seemed to be an endless summer. There were no spats between players and no pouting over playing time. Tim, who had a history of pulling away, even seemed to enjoy every day as much as the others. If a practice was two hours long, the boys did all they could to get every minute out of it and if they couldn't, they'd extend it by planning the day together. It was amazing.

As was the bride's dress at the wedding. Now into August, the church where the wedding took place was hidden away in the surrounding foothills of Albuquerque. A beautiful adobe building nestled amongst the Pinon trees of the area. Teal dresses and white tuxedos made a statement for the times. Being made of adobe, didn't allow for air conditioning, which is not a good thing in New Mexico in August. A heavy sweat came over John and the other groomsmen as they stood witness.

Looking at his friend's face, John saw true love, which he knew would never be forgotten. The feeling of happiness, which came over him, matched that of the days leading up to this. It had been so long since John had felt so many good days in a row. It was almost as if he could feel his world turning. As if something special was in the near future. Happiness was all around.

Through this joy, John was preoccupied with the thought of the next day's travel. A six in the morning beginning would get the boys on their way to facing a team from Denver, Colorado. After winning the State Championship, John had been given a packet with hotels and restaurants for Tucson as well as the brackets for the tournament. Colorado was first, with the winner to play the Nevada team, which had received a bye.

All the maps and recommendations were unnecessary though, as Ambrose's family had come from Tucson, where his father had been the head coach at a Junior College there. John had received permission to practice at that J.C.D.'s facility and what family was still in Tucson would have the team over for dinner as well as recreational time. Ambrose had been beside himself counting the days until they were able to leave. Finally, they were on their way.

A caravan of four cars, Ambrose's, Kris', Kyle's and Bryce's sped toward Arizona playing leapfrog most of the way. Saguaro cactus seemed to wave at them as the crossed the border between the two states, though few of the boys were awake to witness it. As teens tend to do and now that traveling was "old hat" to these boys, sleep was of the utmost importance.

Bryce had bee able to convince his job that this would be his last week of coaching, allowing him to drive the coaches down. If they were able to win this tournament, it would be Bryce's last. The two spent the seven-hour drive talking about how well each boy had played and remembering the years they had played together. It was the fastest seven hours either of them could remember.

Arriving in Tucson, the weather was a good seven degrees hotter than it had even in Albuquerque. There was no doubt as to why all the games would be played in the evening and at night. So practices would have to be early morning as well, otherwise the heat would take too much of a toll.

Three hours remained before the coaches meeting. There would once again be a barbeque but no parents this time. If the teams wanted, a AAA baseball game would allow the boys in for free. Upon hearing all this, the few parents which were there, decided to go off together, leaving the boys and the coaches to themselves.

The stares and chest thumping at the State tournament were nothing compared to what the boys witnessed in the dining hall of the swank Arizona hotel. Dressed in their collared shirts and pressed shorts, the team was greeted once again by silence but this time the boys responded with a confidence that announced they belonged there. Without hesitation, they walked to the buffet line, scanning over the room as they went; the boys went right to work. The buffet was no match for mouths like C.J. and Brad.

John and Bryce kept to themselves, noticing that all the coaches seemed to do the same. Lines of rectangular tables made up a military configuration for eating. The two friends took their seats toward what they determined to be the front of the room, nearest the food. Quietly, they took the whole scene in. There was no one walking around trying to feel one another out. No, everyone here was confident in the fact that they could win with whatever it was they brought with them. There could not have been a more stereotypical gathering of sports crazy, testosterone filled men anywhere in the world. The establishment of dominance could have been cut with a knife, much like a tension filled room. John was as much a part of that as any, thought Bryce really was there as a spectator. His mentality was much more a secondary role and he was quite comfortable in it.

The boys took a quick like-hate relationship with the team from Utah. While several of the boys from the Utah team, tall blonde and most likely of the Mormon faith, offered to befriend the boys from New Mexico, there were a few who took to making comments to Jon and C.J. which could have been left unsaid. C.J. must have been savvier than his coaches knew as he somehow quick wittedly snapped back with a comment about their possible religious beliefs. Not that C.J. had a malicious bone in his body but he couldn't help taking a shot in self-defense. Had his coaches heard it, they would have no doubt made sure it never happened again. With that small portion of quarrel, were the two teams to meet up in tournament play, it would be a good match up. However, it wouldn't happen until the third game if both teams were to win their first two.

While they sat, enjoying the food, barbequed brisket and beans on high-end Chinet paper plates, John surmised that the Nevada and Utah teams would be the ones to beat. Just looking at the Nevada team, as big as they were, it was easy to see they would be a strong team. They also reeked of money, probably coming from a suburb of Vegas just off the strip. Money usually translated into expectations athletically and the like. Expectations that would be enhanced by any mean necessary. It didn't mean they would be unbeatable but surely they were better than average as they would have access to facilities, equipment and obviously, the weather in Nevada would allow them to play year round.

The Utah team just carried themselves in a way that spoke of confidence. Two players stood head and shoulders above the others but it was more in the way they walked together, much like the boys from New Mexico, which reminded John of his own team, a team that worked well together because they were friends off the field. Though he looked and looked, the coach could find no sign of the Arizona team.

Plates covered in barbeque sauce and wadded up napkins, half finished plastic cups of soda were signs that the dinner was winding down. The Colorado team began running through the dining hall and through the hotel, another sure sign of the end of dinner. It also made John smile as they were the boy's opponents the following day and this sign of a lack of discipline was a good sign that they wouldn't be much competition. Still, he was taking no chances; Tim would be the starting pitcher, hopefully allowing the team to move on to the next game.

With no way to get the boys to the baseball game which had been arranged by the tournament and no parents to get the boys back to the hotel the team would have to stay and occupy themselves while John and Bryce attended the coach's meeting. The foyer of the hotel was amazing, with huge vaulted ceilings, well designed Renaissance style statues and arches with tapestries draped meticulously throughout. John sat the boys down and explained his expectations of them. No running, obscenities or boys being boys. "Basically, don't be the Colorado team." The coach finished with. He had no worries, as the boys had always behaved but he wanted to reiterate his rules just the same.

It took all of about three seconds for the boys to settle in on four couches, which surrounded a huge wooden table in the middle of the foyer and a beautiful, hand woven carpet, which must have been twenty feet by twenty feet. Jon called it a magic carpet as he sunk down into the soft leather of one couch. Ambrose was halfway through his first joke as the coaches walked away.

In a medium sized meeting room just down the hall from the entrance of the hotel, five manila envelopes laid on the dark wood laminate of four circular tables. As ten coaches from the five participating teams found their seats, a large man, looking as if he were a transplant to Arizona from somewhere down in the bayou began laying out the guidelines of the tournament.

The salt and pepper haired, walrus mustached man, whose hat really didn't fit over his large head, spoke loudly with a Cajun accent, though John really couldn't hear him. The words really became nothing more than background noise as he looked around, people watching. While there weren't many to watch, John still took great pleasure in attempting to size up his competition.

Two dark haired, heavily Hispanic gentlemen sat at one table by themselves. As he hadn't seen them at dinner, John surmised they were the Arizona coaches. They whispered loudly in Spanish to one another as the director spoke. Growing up in Albuquerque, John was able to make out several quotes, mostly directions to the field and how far it was from their hotel.

The Utah coaches were older, probably forty something. Neither had a cap on and they dressed as if they felt, as John did, look classy, you'll be classy. The taller of the two didn't take his eyes from the director but the other looked quite bored.

Little was distinguishing about the Colorado coaches. The manager, or at least it seemed, as he was the one who thumbed through the packet from the envelope first and received it back from the other man after he had looked at it, was a shorter man, mid-thirties maybe. It was difficult to tell whether he was Hispanic or Caucasian as his darkened features gave light to both. The assistant was older than the first man, by about ten years. He was no doubt, Caucasian and seemed more interested in the speech than his partner.

The two men seated across from the New Mexico coaches were a sight to see. Both men seemed to be in there forties but physically looked much older due to the wrinkles caused from the desert sun of Nevada. Their skin was bronze but weathered from that same sun. Both had on blue ball caps with green and white letters. Their hair was cut "mullet" style, colored light from the sun as well but giving way to the silver highlights of age. One of the men was doing the same thing his younger counterpart was, surveying and assuming. He seemed to be the manager but had no interest whatsoever in the meeting which took place. After looking over the room, his gazed fixed on Bryce. It probably would have been John, where he stared if not for the fact John was already looking his way.

As if he were in charge of the meeting, the Nevada coach stood up right in the middle of the director's speech, no regard for politeness, speaking loudly.

"I find it unacceptable that we are all here and the New Mexico coaches aren't. I thought we were all told this meeting was mandatory." With that, he returned to his seat looking as if he had just finished Martin Luther King's "I have a Dream" speech.

"What are you talking about?" John retorted, almost angrily. "We're right here."

The mullet haired man looked at John a moment chose his words and replied, "Aren't you both a little young to have a team here? Younger brothers on the team, maybe?" Not a sound of apology in his voice.

Too many times in his life had John wanted to be quick witted and wasn't or worse off, he would reply and later wish he had said something better.

"I guess we'll see." That was all he said, leaning back in his chair. No hand gestures or ego checked response. Just exactly what he wanted to say.

The director continued as if nothing at all had been said. Bryce leaned over to his friend, writing in pen on the back of the manila envelope, *that couldn't have been more perfect.* John felt the same.

As the two walked back to the foyer from the meeting room, John was beside himself with emotion. How dare that man question him as a coach or his age! Age has nothing to do with the ability to coach! The young man's inner dialogue was going crazy. Had there been another second go by before they reached the boys, he might have blown up but now they were within earshot of the team.

"So what you're saying is, Papa Smurf is basically God to the Smurf population?" Kyle H. asked.

"No, no." Ambrose replied. "I'm asking if there is only one female, Smurfette, and only one leader, Papa Smurf and there's a whole population of Smurfs, how'd they all get there?" Some of the boys laughed but Ambrose, Kyle H. and Matt truly seemed caught up in the conversation.

"I don't think it was pro-creation." Matt piped in. "I think Papa Smurf created all the other Smurfs, including the girl."

Ambrose smiled triumphantly as to what he was about to say. "If he is creating all these creatures and he creates a girl, you know he didn't do it for all the others, he did it for himself."

"AHHHOOOHHH!" All the boys moaned and laughed in the same breath.

The two coaches stood just out of the conversation, next to a huge, palm tree looking bush, listening intently. This was the most amazing conversation either had ever heard. The boys leaned in over one another's shoulders, piling elbows on the varnished wood of the large coffee table. Here, these groups of adolescent boys, just beginning to look at girls, let alone think about them were having a completely intelligent, adult-style conversation about cartoon characters. It was exactly the transitional elements teen boys go through on their way to manhood. So many books and arguments John had read or participated in as a student were now revealed before his very eyes. The whole concept of God, evolution versus creation and natural instincts was being played out right here. It was completely real, serious and yet so funny, he couldn't contain his laughter and for the moment, forgotten was the slight against him.

They stood listening a while longer, the scent of prime rib lingering in the air from the nearby hotel restaurant, until the subject became boring and several of the boys noticed the coaches waiting. Bouncing over, the boys looked ready to go on to the next thing. John looked at his watch. A quarter to nine. By the time the returned to the hotel it would be time for bed. It would be an early morning if they were going to beat the desert heat.

Into the vans they piled. Off to the hotel they drove. John turned down the music in the van in order to hear more of the boys' conversations. It didn't matter what they talked about, it was the bonding and sharing that was taking place that mattered. Against the backdrop of a city full of sparkling lights, standing bright below a clear sky of sparkling stars, the van rushed quietly across the darkened canvas. An oasis of color hidden in the darkness of a desert. All cities are beautiful at night, colorless buildings, standing side by side become rows of reds, greens and oranges this city was as well, tonight though, it seemed all the more.

Chapter 21

Inch by inch, minute by minute, the tiny crack of sunlight, which snuck between the dark blinds of the room, crept up the bed. Bending to fit the terrain it made it's way to the very edge of the covers, over the man's chin and finally tickled the John's nose. Todd, who slept between the two twin beds, was hidden from the light, as were Tim and Kris who's bed couldn't be reached by the invading light. Their side of the room remained in darkness.

Rolling over to turn off the alarm before it woke the boys, the coach threw his legs off the bed and did his best to avoid the sleeping boy on the floor. It was a far cry from his normal morning; looking for any reason he could to rise, today he looked forward to the day and any challenge it might bring. In fact, it had been a number of days since he had felt that terrible feeling of wanting to sleep the day away, knowing only something more disappointing than the day before could happen and then not wanting to sleep at night because falling asleep meant the next thing that would happen would be the next day. No morning went by however, not knowing that the fact he didn't have to make up a reason was a good thing and to appreciate every day it happened. A jump in the shower had him awake as a few drops of water from his wet hair and a shake had the three boys from his room stirring.

A blinding flash of light greeted him as he opened his door, the sun rising behind a row of Palms came through the huge leaves as no breeze at all left them hanging just so. Several birds chirped in unison as they welcomed the sun as well. Two steps out the door reminded John why the games wouldn't be played until evening and they needed to get a practice in early, ninety-seven degrees and only seven thirty in the morning, August in Tucson. One by one, the three doors to the rooms containing the other players and coach opened. Not a drooping eye in the bunch.

After a short practice of ground balls, bullpens and batting practice, the team returned to the hotel and walked next door to a Denny's. The boys had been all over the coaches to take them there to eat. After getting the bill, John remembered why he had hesitated to do so. With only one hundred dollars per player meal money for the week, they could only afford to eat there once or twice. The time they spent there though was priceless.

C.J. had four chocolate milkshakes, Brad had two full meals while Ambrose took a bite from everybody else's meal and made sure he received and hash browns which weren't going to be eaten. It was one laugh after another smiles and giggles. Chocolate milkshakes for breakfast, which most of the boys had, didn't bother the coach much, as he was a chocoholic but for C.J. to have four, later the coach had wished he had said something.

In heat like that in Tucson and with limited funds and transportation the coaches were left with the dilemma of finding something to keep the boys active or at least interested and not sleeping all day. *A body at rest stays at rest while a body in motion stays in motion.* Thinking long and hard, they decided fifteen minutes in the pool after a hard and early morning wouldn't be bad then they might try to see a movie. Unfortunately, the nearest movie theater was too far to walk and nothing age appropriate was available. To solve this problem, the coaches piled everyone in one room and chose a pay per-view movie to watch.

While Mike Meyer's made fun of teen age life in suburbia, Illinois, in "Wayne's World," some of the boys laughed, others played their video games and several, including the coaches, nodded in and out of sleep. The room was extremely cold, windows drawn shut allowing only the glow of the television to light the room. Plied legs over arms, three and four boys napped on one twin sized bed. Ambrose lay forward chin in his hands, watching the movie. Brad snoozed, laying back, legs over 'Brose's back. Kyle and Kris lay, almost spooning with their legs over Brad's also sleeping. Jon sat up, against the wall sleeping next to C.J. who's hat was over his face, falling off when his body, completely limp from relaxation, toppled over from sitting to lying on his side.

Dozing only a few minutes, John looked over the room with a sense of calm and self worth. Here were his boys, so closely knit as to lay over one another with no worries or bothers, nothing but love for one another, a closeness, which seemed never to be matched or broken.

A relaxed silence came over the room as the movie had ended and a blue screen now lit the room. Two or three minutes passed. Not one body in the room moved as they all had fallen asleep. One by one they began to move, most of them looking first to the clock.

Three-forty. The game was at six. With an hour of warm up at the field, twenty minutes to travel and time to dress, the coaches got the boys up and moving in an attempt to get the bodies in motion once again. Upon opening the door to the room, it was obvious a summer shower had passed through, dampening the ground and cooling the air. Cooling it only to about ninety-five degrees from the high of one hundred five, which had been reached around noon. The boys waked on the short Bermuda grass in front of their patio areas, squishing their toes in the cool moist ground as they got their energy up.

Without a word from either coach, the boys faces were already turning from relaxed, vacation hang out with buddies looks to their game faces. Ambrose was already giving pep talks and slapping backs. Just as in the State Tournament, there was no sign of tension. The boys were loose and excited.

If you are nervous, you're not ready. It's not ok to be nervous. It is ok to be anxious. Anxious means you are excited to play. John could never remember which coach he had learned that from or if it was even a coach. Maybe it was a quote from a player. Whoever it was, the saying had stayed with him and he had passed it on to these boys more than once. Now, more than a month after getting this group together for the first time, he could see in the boys' faces and their manner, they believed that too.

Chapter 22

Red jerseys with yellow, white and orange piping on the edge of the sleeves were paired with white pants with red pinstripes, red belt and stirrups. Being obsessive compulsive about uniforms, John hated the yellow and orange in these tops but liked the overall look of these uniforms better than the "clown" combination. Tim had chosen this night's uniform because it felt more comfortable to him. Not every night but once in a while, John would let the starting pitcher choose the uniforms.

It was quiet on the vans but without tension as they rolled toward their destination. As quiet as a van can be driving down an interstate with windows down allowing the wind to blow through at seventy miles an hour. The music strained to be heard over the roar though the dial was twisted as far as possible.

The soft, gray clouds, which had dumped the cooling shower on the hotel earlier, now hovered over the horizon ahead of the team. The diagonal lines, darker than the clouds themselves, gave notice that it was raining steadily in the near distance.

Almost as if it were a game of chase, the front window of John's lead van would hold three then four and five drops of water as they would reach the edge of the storm, then dry again as the storm would pull farther ahead. Drops, no drops, for about five miles this went on until a steady beat of rain fell upon the road. Not enough to delay a game but enough to relax a person's mind.

They arrived at the High School, just outside of Tucson after their Colorado counterparts. Fourteen baby blue and dark blue jerseys ran out from the third base dugout into left field for batting practice, which was fine with John as it left open the batting cage itself making it easier for his team to hit and not chase balls.

A small crew of three men and a woman worked to smooth the dirt of the infield as well as dry out the damp spots around home plate where the rain had left two small puddles. The field was in good shape, large for a High School field, four hundred feet to center field, three forty down the lines. A good size area, completely surrounding the field had obviously been cleared of debris and brush, reminding the coaches of something they were supposed to tell their team.

"By the way," John brought the team in close to hear his announcement, "there is a possibility of tarantulas, scorpions and even rattlesnakes coming on to the field so be aware."

The boys looked around, not certain of whether the coach was serious or not. Kyle, who was playing left field eyes, became large. "What do we do if we see one?"

John could tell there was a real worry in his player's eyes. "Throw up your hands, as you would for a ball under the fence and I'm sure they'll call the ball dead." Reassuringly he added, "You'll be fine, I doubt you'll see anything, that's why this area has been cleared and burnt away." He didn't want it to be anything more than a note in the boy's heads so he motioned them to get started with batting practice and not to talk anymore about it. Of course, expecting teen boys to let a subject like snakes and spiders go is asking too much. Ambrose could be heard explaining a time when he saw a six-foot rattler one time when he lived there as he walked out to the cage with Matt and Chad, who else to make a small worry bigger. John knew they'd get over it as soon as the game started which he hoped would come soon.

The "Star Spangled Banner" was barely decipherable over the sound system employed by the High School ball team. John stood tall near the first base end of the first base line as his team was at attention for the playing of the song. Gazing off toward the horizon, which now was clear, save a small group of clouds, the young man noticed it was a different blue than the sky of New Mexico. Not that it was really possible but wherever he had traveled during his short life, the sky never seemed quite as blue as it did in New Mexico, not just in Albuquerque but anywhere through the land of enchantment.

"Play Ball!" brought his mind right back to baseball. As he had done time and time again he brought the boys together, told them to relax, play hard, play well and sent them off with what had become a tradition. "In it to win it!" they hollered together and the starting nine players sprinted on to the field as fast as they could ready to play ball.

Tim made short work of the Colorado boys in the first inning, striking out two players on eight pitches and getting the third to pop up to Todd at second. He bounded off the field as if he actually was enjoying his time out on the field. It was the first time John had ever seen this in his player, as his demeanor on the field was usually stoic. The twenty-three-year old took it as a good sign as he strolled over to the third base coaching box.

Before any player on his team was unfortunate enough to make the first out, John's team had scored five runs and before making the third out of the inning, Roadrunner had scored nine. A whole new sense of confidence came over the team. No longer was there a question of whether or not they would win but rather, what would be the final score and how long would Tim pitch. There really was no sense in pitching him too far so he could throw again with energy two days later. Most teams had pitchers throw every other day, as that was what the rules allowed but John didn't want to hurt any boy's arm so they only threw every fourth day if possible.

The coaches decided to allow him to throw five innings, enough to ensure the victory, get some good work, then allow Kyle and Jon to each throw an inning. The tournament couldn't have started any better for the boys from Albuquerque. A nineteen to one win, a starting pitcher who saved his arm and a second round meeting with the team from Nevada, best of all, no scorpion, tarantula or rattlesnake sightings.

Chapter 23

Money earned is sweet money won is sweeter. The same is true for victory. To earn a win, grinding it out, working for every run is great. To win a game when you spend little, work little but play well, is very sweet.

Pats on the back and firm, quick handshakes kept John's attention for the two innings of the nightcap game between the host Arizona team and Utah. The boys tried to watch the game while eating complementary hot dogs and chips but at thirteen, distractions come easily.

Every game has a moment or even moments when the direction it is going, changes. Series of games can even change on one play, decision or mistake. A weak ground ball between the legs of an aging first baseman turned a World Series. A heroic at bat and one perfect swing allowed an underdog to dominate a hundred win team in another.

In the bottom half of the third inning, while John and Bryce stood watching the very impressive and extremely large Arizona team, Utah had them on the ropes with two runs in and the bases loaded.

After a strikeout took the out total to two, a double down the right field line threatened to clear the bases. As the runner from first crossed home plate, the large, Hispanic coach from the Arizona team walked halfway to the baseline, shouting in Spanish to his pitcher. John elbowed Bryce jutting his chin out as if to tell his assistant to watch what was happening. He had seen it but wanted see how it played out.

The pitcher took the ball, to the mound, set, then stepped off and appealed to the home plate umpire that the first runner, the one from third when the at bat took place, had missed home plate when he had come home to score. John had been watching and noticed the umpire had not even been looking in the direction of home plate when the runner scored. Instead, he had been making sure the ball was fair and not gone into a dead ball area down the baseline.

Still, he pointed into the Utah dugout then signaled the runner was out, negating all three runs, changing not only the inning but also possibly the game and even the entire tournament.

Of course, it was bedlam for about twenty minutes while everything was straightened out. In the end, the call stood and Arizona came to bat. It wasn't only the runs the Utah team lost it was momentum. For one brief moment, Arizona, which really carried itself with a chip on it's shoulder and a confidence which stated they couldn't be beaten, looked shaky, as if they might fall and Utah was looking to knock them over. Instead, the game was tied and Arizona had a moment to regain their composure. A moment which turned into seven runs and a win, putting them into the winner's bracket final against the winner of the New Mexico/Nevada game.

The draw couldn't have been worse for the boys. While they got an easy win against the Colorado team, they were then set up to have to beat Nevada and Arizona on back to back nights, then after a day off, beat one of them again. The Nevada team had already had a night off with no pitching being spent, while Arizona now had a night off then would play the winner of a tough game where both teams would have spent precious pitching and if they won, would have another night off before playing again, home state advantage.

A second day of early morning practice, movies in a darkened room and a cool afternoon shower had the boys back on the field. "Clown suits" were the uniform of choice or necessity, as they needed to wash the others. Nevada wore white pants, piped with royal blue and Kelly green. Blue jerseys with "Green Valley" scripted in white trimmed by green looked sharp and new. No doubt they were well funded and by the look of their round of infield, well coached.

John admitted that to Bryce, which struck the red head a bit odd. He had never known his friend to admit that about another team of which had put a burr under his saddle as the Nevada coach had at the coaches meeting. He wasn't sure whether it was an admittance of defeat or a hint of worry or nothing at all. Honestly, it made Bryce nervous.

Apparently it made the boys nervous as well. During their own round of infield, John hit six fly balls, two of which were dropped, then airmailed over the infielder's heads. Three ground balls, none of which were fielded cleanly and again, thrown over the heads of there cut offs.

Only two ground balls were hit to the infield before John reached the breaking point. After Kris bobbled, bobbled again, then threw wildly to home plate, the angered and now embarrassed coach flipped his bat and pulled his team off the field, the biggest game of their lives, no real warm up.

In practice, it was common for John to throw his fungo, pull the boys in and "go off" on them. It was already to the point where the boys weren't even fazed by it. Often times they would wait until the coach was out of site and mimic him. They understood his theatrics. He wanted them to expect the most out of themselves and each other. The body language, bat throwing and raised voice were just show. They knew that. They also knew he would never swear at them. It was as much a product of not being his style as it was something he felt would make him sound less intelligent. He never swore at them.

If a time ever were to come, when he might curse at them, this would be the time. Bryce sat in the corner, his head down waiting to hear the tirade. No yelling, no knocking over of bats, no book throwing. Instead, he sat down, hands folded on his lap, right leg crossed over his left. His head leaned back until it rested against the wall of the dugout, his hat lowering over his brow as he did. A deep sigh as he closed his eyes just a moment then he looked across the field. He almost looked at peace rather than upset.

Todd ambled over, bat in his hand, sitting down next to his coach. John cocked his head to look at number seven; a question waited to be asked but never was. Todd smiled, and then looked out onto the field. "Coach, the boys and I just decided," an eyebrow rose over the coach's right eye as he waited for the rest, "that was the best bat flip you've ever had." Both eyebrows wrinkled inquisitively but John said nothing. "Didn't you see it?" Todd continued, "It landed against the wall just like you put it after good rounds." He patted his coach on the knee as he stood up. "This will be a good game coach, I promise."

A smile slowly widened on the twenty-three-year old's face. Not enough to show teeth but a smile nonetheless. Not because Todd had said they would play a good game but more at the fact his tiny second baseman read him so well and acted so mature. It was a microcosm of this team. Up and down his head bobbed as he nodded in approval. He wasn't upset anymore, no not now, the only thing he felt was proud.

There was toughness in the way Nevada went about their game. Often times, white-collar teams have softness but not this team. They seemed to follow the mannerisms of their three best players. Bigger, stronger and better than most players they carried themselves like they were just that. The rest of the team did so as well. They didn't however, and John had noticed it at the barbeque that first night, carry themselves like a family.

The game had started off both great and poorly. As Kyle had come on strong hitting the ball during State, the coaches had moved him to the lead off spot and moved Todd to ninth as a double lead off type of order. Kyle singled to start, followed by a short gapper by Kris. Great start but while the coach waved Kyle to third, he hesitated allowing himself to be thrown out in a close play at third. No runs to start the game.

While Ambrose battled, holding the Nevada team to no runs during the first four innings, John noticed the arms on the first baseman, who was left handed and the catcher who threw down to second during warm ups on his knees. Really, that was just a way of showing off but showing off a great arm isn't a bad thing. The pitcher Nevada employed was no slouch, throwing hard and mixing his pitches well but was no doubt, their third best.

"They're taking us lightly Bryce." John said as he rose to coach third base to start the fourth inning. "Their looking past us and it's going to cost them."

The sun had already set but soft streaks of orange still hung in the sky as the game entered it's second half. The air cooled but was by no means comfortable yet. The coach looked across the field toward the distant horizon. He could coach games like this at venues like this for the rest of his life. Could there be anything better? No way. Then again, it wouldn't always be this team, these players. For a moment he was sad. Maybe he wouldn't want to coach any other team, any other boys. These were his boys and this was their team, theirs together. Think about it another time.

Just as he pulled himself back into the moment, Steve drew a walk. A past ball and a ground out to second put the first run of the game in scoring position. Thinking the game would probably be low scoring, John touched his arm, chest then the bill up his cap. He followed that with four touches and a second touch of his cap. Squeeze play.

Kyle acknowledged, followed by Steve as John put his head down, swiping at the dirt with his shoe as if nothing at all might be going on. A run here could put the game away, maybe. A mistake here could swing what then was no momentum to Nevada's side.

Steve took his lead, short and wide, as not to give anything away. Kyle, who had moved his position to the front of the batter's box waited for the pitch as if he were swinging away. As the pitcher started his motion, he gave a quick glance toward Steve at third base; Steve held his ground just as he was supposed to. As the pitcher's stride foot landed as the ball was delivered to the plate, Steve broke for home, running as hard as he could. At the same time, Kyle pivoted his body to and pushed his hands in front of him. The lights of the field lit the top half of the ball in a bright, luminescent glow as it rotated quickly toward home plate. The pitch was a strike, just on the inner half. Kyle, as he had practiced with the team so many times, made sure to get the ball down before running himself to first base. Steve crossed home plate, making sure to touch it, without having to slide. The pitcher fielded the ball, throwing Kyle out at first but first blood had been drawn, one nothing New Mexico.

A few players met Steve as he came into the dugout but the majority of the team met Kyle as he came back in. Everyone wants to be a hero but these boys knew that being a hero meant doing your job and helping the team. Kyle had made an out because he had sacrificed himself for the team. That has heroic.

The game remained one-nothing going into the fifth inning. Ambrose battled with each pitch, giving everything he had to keep the powerful Nevada hitters off balance. The boy's body language gave away the fact he was tiring. John strode to the mound after a triple had tied the game and left a runner standing at third.

"Want to hear a dirty joke? John asked as he neared the mound. Ambrose nodded, taking a deep breath. "Two white horses fell in the mud." He smiled as he reached his pitcher.

"Coach, that's bad." Ambrose replied gaining some wind. "I'll give you a book of jokes when we get back to the hotel." He looked over his shoulder to third base. "I'm gonna get out of this inning but you may have to use Kyle next inning, OK?"

"I can live with that. Just get out of this inning." John said turning back to the dugout.

A pop up back to himself got Ambrose the first out. Two strikes on the next batter had the young man in position to get the second until that batter pivoted on the next pitch just as Kyle had two innings before. One upping the younger coach, Nevada's headman called for and received a two-strike squeeze. Two to one, Nevada.

As the boys came in from the field, John met them outside the dugout. He wanted to make sure they understood how well they had played and to recognize how hard his pitcher had worked. Still, they trailed and he wanted them to see they had more work to do.

A one, two, three inning left only one more at bat for the boys to score. On top of that dilemma, they would have to hold Nevada scoreless for six more outs. That task would belong to the two boys responsible for the team's first score, Kyle first and Steve if necessary.

Kyle did all he could, facing the sixth and seventh batters, getting them both on hard hit line drives to Todd at second base. Close calls on balls and strikes plus a hung curve ball forced John to call on Steve to try and get Nevada's lead off hitter out as Kyle walked the eighth batter and gave up a double to the ninth. Three straight slow balls produced a pop up to Kris, bringing to close the sixth inning. Three more outs to score at least one run and keep the game going or two runs to take the lead once again, either task a daunting one.

The right fielder had been brought in to pitch the final inning, once again prompting John to talk to himself. "They're making a mistake." over and over again in his head.

Nothing worth having ever comes easy, a quote from his mother. She would always say that when John or his brother would complain as children about how hard they had to work. Moments like these always reminded him of that. In this case, Bret was due up first, hitting in the sixth spot, followed by Brad and Steve. At this point, even with all of Ambrose's encouragement and the coach's efforts to fix mechanics, Bret hadn't hit a ball hard since arriving in Tucson. Pop up to first, out number one. Brad, who had always been hot and cold, struck out swinging at a curve ball, which bounced in front of the plate. Out number two. John knelt in the coach's box, motioning for Bryce to have Kyle H. hit for Steve who had done nothing but walk six or seven times in his last ten at bats. At least he would get everyone but Chad in the game and if Kyle were to get on, Chad would run for him and everyone would have played.

It always seemed to the young coach that if his team were ahead by twenty runs, it was never enough yet a one run lead against him could seem insurmountable. Still, he never hung his head. This game always produced funny hops.

Two pitches, two strikes and not even a check swing. It looked to the coach as if Kyle wanted nothing to do with the pitcher. Ball one. Ball two. A foul ball on a weak swing followed by another, this one barely rolling foul down the first baseline. Ball three. The crowd raised its collective voice as ten or so relatives of Ambrose worked to gain some energy. You never can tell. Foul ball. Finally, as one more pitch sailed toward home plate, this time with the catcher diving to his right just to catch it, Kyle earned a walk.

Before he could reach first base, John motioned to Bryce to have Chad run for Kyle H. Two things were in the team's favor here. First, everyone got in the game, making not only John's promise to his mom still complete but also put the fastest runner on the team at first base. Everyone in the stands knew John would think about trying to steal second base but would he do more than think against a catcher who really changed the game with his arm? Really, was there any doubt?

One the first pitch, with Todd standing in at home plate, Chad broke toward second. Just as John had hoped, Nevada had so much confidence in their catcher; they didn't try to pitch out or rush the ball to the plate but relied only on the ability of the catcher. On a close play, closer than John would have liked, Chad slid safely into second. The dugout cheered wildly. Suddenly the game was turning. Todd called timeout.

As the tiny second baseman jogged down to his coach, the world seemed to take pause. Right then, right there, nothing else in the world seemed to matter. In fact, nothing else seemed to even exist, simply a glowing patch of green, spotlighted in a sea of pitch black, like a picture on a coffee table, a moment frozen for all time.

"I just wanted to let you know, I'm gonna get a hit, so make sure you send Chad." Todd whispered loudly to his coach. It was so matter of fact John couldn't respond at first.

"Make sure you go two and get in scoring position if the throw goes home." John responded as matter of factly as he could sound, a pat on the butt for Todd as he returned to home plate.

The boys had been drilled on how to run the bases, particularly with two outs. Chad knew to run hard for home as soon as the ball was hit. He would have a jump, if Todd could come through. The coach looked around the outfield. Center and left fields both played shallow, looking at Todd's size. The right fielder played deeper as Roadrunner had hit several balls that way earlier in the game. In fact, the boy now pitching had thrown Ambrose out at first from right field. The boy in right field now had a great arm as he had moved from first out there when the pitching change had been made.

Todd dug in, as he loved to do, digging out a rut with his back foot then taking three short, half-swings. His statement had been brash but he looked now as if he would back up every word of it.

The pitcher looked in, taking the sign from the catcher. A tall boy, he came set looking twice at Chad and second base. The kick and the pitch, a fastball it looked like maybe away but a strike anyway. Short to it, long through it. A way John had of reminding the boys what type of swing to take. Todd struck the ball, a solid, maybe too solid single to right.

Chad didn't hesitate a second. He broke on contact, whizzing by his coach at third base who was waving him home all the way. Up clean with it, the right fielder hopped and launched the ball toward the plate. Everything went slow motion, except Chad. The smallest player on the New Mexico team motored toward the huge catcher, sliding as he and the ball arrived at the same time.

Most balls thrown to the plate by thirteen-year-olds have at least a small arc to them as arm strength is still developing. Not here, the ball looked as if it were on a frozen rope from right field to home plate. Still, Todd read that the first baseman wasn't going to cut the throw off and headed toward second in case Chad could beat the throw.

Beat it, maybe not but the ball was just off line enough to force the catcher to have to block it to keep it from going to the backstop. Safe! Two to Two and still, Roadrunner was at bat.

After everything settled, the New Mexico team going crazy as were fans from everywhere in the stands, Utah, Arizona and Colorado teams now watched as well, the Nevada coach called a time out to change pitchers again. He motioned for the right fielder to come in.

No doubt, they had watched the game between New Mexico and Colorado, noting that Kris, who stood on deck was hitting left-handed. The right fielder was left-handed. In baseball, coaches always look for match ups. Over time, it has been established that left handed hitters don't hit left handed pitchers as well as they do right handed pitchers. Nevada was going for a match up which favored them.

After getting loose, the new Nevada pitcher walked Kyle intentionally to cause a force out situation as well as set the match up of lefty versus lefty. What no one in royal blue and Kelly green knew was that Kris was a switch hitter. It was only due to John's asking that Kris had only hit left handed to that point in the tournament.

While the lefty had been getting loose, John had seen Kris' dad come to the fence and talk to Kris. John knew what they were thinking. Though he hadn't hit right handed for several weeks, this would be the time to do it. Kris had jogged over to his coach while the new pitcher loosened. Before he could even speak, John interrupted.

"Can you?"

Kris smiled, "Yes I can."

"OK, get off early." Meaning, look to swing early in the count. That was the extent of the conversation. It was so easy. Like siblings know what the other is thinking before they say or do it, this team was on the same wavelength.

Now, what seemed to be a foregone conclusion fifteen minutes earlier now turned into the greatest game any of these boys had ever been part of, including their coach.

As Kyle reached first, Kris stepped in from the right side of the plate. Shuffling questions and near panic could be heard in the third base dugout as he did. John looked in and smiled. They had no idea Kris could do that and now they had even less and idea of which side he was better at. They may have just put him in the drivers seat. John just smiled and clapped his hands. He knew it was a huge risk to have Kris do this. No right-handed swings in nearly a month? The odds just weren't in Kris' favor but what about the game to that point had gone according to odds?

"Get a jump!" The coach hollered out to Todd. He knew Todd would need every advantage to beat a throw to the plate. The outfield was shallow as Kris wasn't much bigger than Todd. Kyle too, had to get a jump to avoid being forced at second.

Watching the lefty's warm ups, John knew he threw hard, harder than they had seen so far in the tournament. Kris would have to be quick. Real quick. The umpire pulled his mask down and signaled for the pitch.

Not even looking at second, the left-hander balanced and let it rip to home plate. Kris wasted no time, hacking at the first pitch. "Ping!" The ball rocketed over the shortstop's outstretched glove into left center field. Todd raced for third, knowing he was heading home. Kyle would no doubt reach second safely.

The center fielder must have not switched his positioning when Kris went right handed. He was playing a bit shaded to left, as he would have if Kris were hitting from the left side and were going to be swinging late. He picked up the ball cleanly on about three hops. Todd was just past third when the ball came out of the center fielder's glove starting upward in his arm arc and coming out quickly.

John could see the ball was going to reach the catcher before Todd. Unknowingly, his fists clenched as if it were he, heading to the plate. Stepping toward the foul line, he looked over Todd's shoulder to see what was happening.

The ball bounced once, then a second short bounce, just in front of the catcher. It was the second hop that allowed Todd an extra split second to reach the plate. He gave a small jump into the air, hoping to get a little more behind his slide and perhaps knock the ball away.

Ball hit glove. Cleat hit glove. Ball bounces out harmlessly and Todd is called safe.

Absolute pandemonium. Fans, players, everyone watching who wasn't a parent of a Nevada player and it looked like perhaps some of them, were cheering with all they had. Games like this in tournaments like this by thirteen-year-old boys just weren't supposed to happen. Stripes of red piled one on top of another, overlapping like swatches of fabric laid out on a cutting table, as the Ambrose and C.J. worked to get themselves on top of the pile that was ten friends enjoying to the utmost, the moment they were in. It was absolutely beautiful.

Too quickly it all ended, as Tim chased a curve ball in the dirt for out number three. He took off his helmet and spun it toward the dugout as he headed for center field. Before it could stop spinning, the other players had begun their sprints to whichever position they were playing while the others gathered any equipment lying on the ground.

As John walked back from his coaching box, Bryce met him in front of the dugout, motioning his head toward first base. No one was there. During the rally, John had hollered for Bret to start throwing on the side, as he would pitch the seventh inning. Usually that meant Jon would play first base. After his circus act at State, however, no one was sure if he would ever see time at that spot again. Arching his neck and exhaling, the coach raised an eyebrow and sent the awkward young man over to first base. It was, after all, where he always practiced.

Bret would have to face the heart of the Nevada line up. Number one was just that, number one jersey and the lead off hitter. To that point in the game he hadn't been much of a factor and it would suit John just fine if he didn't start now.

After taking strike one, the batter lined a ball sharply to right field exactly where Chad was standing. If it had been only a step to either side, Chad would have been chasing it for days it had been hit so hard. Not tonight. Out number one.

Batter number two was a pinch hitter, as the starting player had gone zero for three to that point in the game. Replacing the starter was a thick, stocky, red headed player who proceeded to hit a ball even harder than the batter before him but with the same result, a line drive right at Chad. Two down.

The number three hitter had already proven he could hit, lining a double and a sharp single in previous at bats. He was now the pitcher of record and just as he pitched, he batted from the left side. This worked to the New Mexican team's favor with the lefty-lefty match up, if Bret could keep the ball in, no harm done. First pitch, out over the plate, the batter doubled to the left center gap. Suddenly it seemed that ol' Moe, momentum that is, might be changing teams.

The Nevada team came to life just as the visitors had in their half of the inning. The tying run on second with the best hitter on the team coming to bat. Both John and Bryce gained two or three years of age in about thirty seconds. To slow the momentum, the young coach called a timeout, talking first to the umpire about the number of visits to the mound he had left, then a short trip to the mound, where he said nothing but only looked at Bret, crossing his eyes, hoping to relax his left-hander. John returned to the dugout thinking to himself all the things that had gone right, hoping for one more. The cold, cement bench felt hard as he crossed his legs looking out onto the field once again.

Brad called for the pitch to be low and away, hoping to get the batter to chase a pitch or not be able to get the barrel of the bat to the ball. Instead, Bret's pitch was in, with movement running farther in to the batter's hands. A left handed hitter usually likes the ball down, as he can drop his hands and drive the ball, so hand high can be a tough pitch to handle or it can be a ball he "turn on," allowing his hips to open and again, drive the ball. Fortunately, the ball got in on his hands as the batter tried to turn, causing a harmless pop up in the foul territory behind first base.

The entire New Mexico bench, consisting of four players and the two coaches, rushed to the front of the dugout to see if the ball would be playable. Hot white, glowing brightly against the now blackened sky, the ball seemed to hover, almost holding still up in the night, red laces turning slowly as it finally returned to Earth. All arms and legs, Jon had turned his back to the infield and now ran looking like a newborn giraffe trying to gallop for the first time. If the moment hadn't seemed so huge, it would have dropped his friends to the ground, laughing and holding their stomachs. Todd and Chad raced toward the ball's landing zone as well; though it was obvious they couldn't get there. Jon on the other hand, had every chance to make the play.

The ball dropped out of sight behind Jon's running figure. In an awkward, last ditch effort; he shot his glove out in front of him, hoping for a miracle. As if someone were listening, his "enchilada" as he affectionately called his glove, opened enough to snatch the ball from the air somewhere just above knee high.

This play, as big a play as the team had witnessed through the tournament, couldn't have been a bigger surprise. Only a week ago, the gangly first baseman had tripped over the first base bag and here was making a highlight reel catch. Three outs, game over and the biggest win not only in these boys' lives but also probably in Roadrunner Little League. Teams before had advanced this far in the tournament but to play a team of this caliber, match them and beat them was a magnificent feat. On top of all that, they had earned it.

Continuing his path toward the ball, Todd ran right into Jon, hugging him as they fell to the ground. Chad was next to arrive, followed by the rest of the team. John would have liked his team to act as if they had been there before but decided to let them enjoy the moment and each other. As a team they had arrived at this moment, they deserved to celebrate it.

The boys composed themselves, forming into a line for the traditional team handshake. As the two lines passed each other, the coaches met shaking hands as well. The Nevada coach stopped John as they met, pulling closer with his handshake.

"I was wrong when I questioned your age at the meeting the other night."

"You have a very good team and they are well coached." The salt and pepper haired man seemed sincere in his words. "Good luck tomorrow and we'll see you in the championship." He smiled as he finished.

Thanking the man, John was stunned. He would never have expected that. He wanted to feel proud but wasn't sure anymore what was pride and what was arrogance. Which one was he? That question would continue to bother him for some time to come but now, it was time to enjoy his "family" his team and all they had accomplished.

Chapter 24

Mariachi music played on a medium sized, portable AM/FM, cassette player, which stood on the edge of a counter on the back porch. Ambrose's father and uncle sat with the two coaches, eating green chili stew and warm tortillas.

The boys sat in the living room of Ambrose's cousin's house. A large screen television played a videotape of the 1988 Olympic baseball team of which Ambrose had been the batboy and his father a catcher's coach. It was a highlight video, set to inspirational music. 'Brose would watch it before games and had began a tradition of several of the boys doing so with him. Now, arms around each other, leaning side by side against the couch, the boys gathered as the team they were, their closeness showing as, in one way or another, they all were touching, legs or arms or shoulders.

Out of the corner of his eye, John caught site of the boys. He only half listened to a story, which the uncle was telling, choosing rather to look in at his team. He wished he had been that close to his friends growing up and imagined most other people would feel the same. What this group had was special, a once in a lifetime type of bond. No guarantee that they would remain friends, even beyond that summer but now, in this perfect moment, they were like brothers.

Turning his head slightly, without even realizing, he drifted off into a memory. The memory of himself and three friends, collapsed on a living room floor, exhausted from hours of "pick up" basketball. So tired they ached, even though they were only in their teens. Looking up at the ceiling, the four friends tried to decide who would have to spend the energy to call and order pizza. John smiled at the thought.

Seeing the boys sprawled across the floor as they were reminded him of that time. Good times. Something struck the young coach, maybe this was the reason he struggled so hard to enjoy his life. The fear that all the bonds of youth, all the great times, shared with friends would never come again. There was no innocence to be found or worse yet, no innocence to be lost, just the same thing every day. A swell of depression came up from inside, the feeling he had fought off so many mornings.

Why suddenly, did he feel so bad? Was it the realization of why he had these feelings of depression? Maybe it was the thought he would never have those times to share again. He felt sick to his stomach, excusing himself, walking inside, through a screen door, down a hall and into a bathroom.

A pool of clear, bubbling water welled up in his cupped hands. John splashed the water on his face in an attempt to cool his rising temperature. Water, dripping down his tanned face, John looked at himself in the mirror. What exactly was he living through right that very moment? Wasn't this one of those memories he would have forever, being put away, in the back of his mind to use or call upon whenever he needed? Yes! That's exactly what was going on.

His stomach immediately felt better, the dark cloud that had covered his head was swept away and at that very moment, he knew from right then, for at least the foreseeable future, he wouldn't have to fight off that feeling again. The moments he so deeply treasured, the memories he feared so badly to never live through again, would always be there. All he had to do was continue to live each day, not looking for them but knowing they would reveal themselves. His boys would make sure of that.

For so long, he had been lost within himself and just like that, this group of boys come along, changing his whole outlook on life after they themselves had their outlook changed by the arrival of Ambrose.

Chapter 25

Tangerine orange, cotton candy pink, the colors just began to color the sky and the clouds hanging just over the horizon. John had always believed New Mexico was home to the most beautiful sunsets, until now. Standing along the first baseline, hand holding his cap over his heart as the National Anthem played meekly over the loudspeaker, the coach stared into Arizona's late afternoon sky.

Huge billowing "thunder boomers," clouds that piled one on top of another reaching high into the atmosphere, looking down as if there really were "Baseball Gods" standing overhead in a city made of clouds. It was almost as if you could see the silver lining of the clouds as the sun warmed their edges. Puffs of white mixed in among the gray quickly being over run by the pastel colors of a Southwestern sunset. The desert ground seemed to hold not only the heat of the day but the color as well. No doubt, this was the most amazing sunset John had ever been witness to.

The game had been delayed a half hour or so due to the afternoon showers, allowing the day to cool a bit more, making for a more than pleasant evening. By this time, only the two teams on the field, Arizona and New Mexico and the team from Nevada remained in the tournament. Earlier that day, Nevada had beaten Utah, sending them home with the Colorado team that had been eliminated the evening before.

A calm, relaxed team took the field, John had won the coin toss and decided to take the field first. There was no pressure. Every imaginable goal had been accomplished though John still felt like this team could advance further. He had put expectations and accountability on the boys and they had risen to the challenge. Two championships and what the coach had felt were two perfectly played games. Whatever happened from here on out, the season had been a success.

Growing up in New Mexico, both John and Bryce had learned that Hispanic boys tended to grow earlier than Caucasian boys did, allowing them to often be not only bigger but better athletes as pre-teens. Holding true to that theory, the Arizona team looked gigantic as the first three hitters stood waiting for the umpires to start the game. Two of the three boys had mustaches, nearly full grown! The small group of fans that sat in the Arizona bleachers cheered and spoke loudly, all in Spanish. It was an intimidating site, not only for the boys but the twenty-three-year old coaches as well.

The visitors started swinging early, with a single, double and a hard hit line out beginning the game. Bret, the starter for John looked rattled but managed to get out of the inning with minimal damage. More than once, Ambrose walked to the mound from third base, acting as an on the field coach, attempting to calm his friend down, bottom of one, two nothing Arizona.

The intimidation continued as the home team batted, as Tim was hit by a pitch and Bret was knocked down, nearly being hit by a pitch as well. Still, the New Mexico team wouldn't be pushed around, battling for a run in the first and two more by the end of the fifth. Unfortunately, their opponents had scored eight times of the combination of Bret and Steve.

Now, runners stood at second and third with the best hitter on the Arizona team up to bat. Already he had doubled and tripled. John had no desire to throw to him again. A feeling of despair started to brew through the dugout and John could feel it on the field as well. From nowhere, a light went off in his head.

Standing non-chalantly, John took two steps forward and hollered out to the field, "Hey!" Their attention gained, John raised his right hand over his head and made a couple of small circles. As if it were no big deal, he returned to his seat adrenaline now racing through his veins. *A duck on a pond.* While on the surface, everything looked calm; under the water things were churning a mile a minute.

The play was designed to fool the opponent into thinking the ball had been thrown away, drawing the runner off of third, thinking he could score. With everybody chasing an imaginary ball, the chaos would allow the pitcher, who still had the ball, to tag the runner out. As a teen, John had seen the play run in the College World Series by the University of Miami. It had worked for them but no team of his had ever tried it. While there was no risk, as no one could score if the play didn't work, there was the feeling of foolishness to deal with.

Steve came to the set position, beginning his motion to the plate. As his leg lifted, Ambrose broke toward third as if a pick off were coming. The runner saw it coming and moved back to the bag. Suddenly, Ambrose fell to the ground, reaching behind him as if the ball had been thrown away. After hitting the ground, he scrambled to his feet, turning his back to the infield and ran toward the fence. Kyle, who was in left field and Kris at short, also ran hard toward the fence chasing something that wasn't there.

Yelling in Spanish while looking down the line, the coach waved his arm toward home urging his runner to go. Hesitating for just a second, it was obvious the runner couldn't locate the ball and was uncertain what to do. Following the coach's instruction, the runner turned and ran for home.

Not more than five steps down the line, Steve was now waiting, having kept the ball and broken toward the line. He tagged the runner with the ball in his glove, and then showed the umpire what he had done. Three outs.

The contingency of New Mexico fans went crazy, as did the players both on the field and off. It was fun and a team executed play, swinging the momentum of the game and lifting the impending feeling of dread, which had been looming nearby. As the team came in from the field, John met them half way.

"You have played all summer as hard as you could, never quitting but right now I can tell you're just about done." His voice began to pitch. "Don't you dare!" John's fists clenched and his face reddened.

"I came here to win a game! Who's coming with me?"

He turned quickly from the huddle, walking away without having the boys bring it in. From behind him, he could hear Ambrose call the team together. "Why are we here?"

"In it to win it!" The boys shouted in unison as the energy level jumped again.

The first three batters, Kris, Tim and Ambrose, reached base safely to start the inning bringing Bret to the plate. So far in the game he was nothing out of two with two weak pop ups. Better than the two previous All Star summers, the boy still had not swung the bat as well as everyone would have expected.

John thought about calling a time out to relax his player but though better of it. Instead he clapped his hands, nodded and hoped for a hit. Bret stepped in and swung through a fastball for strike one.

Before the next pitch, Bret stepped out of the box, raised his head to the sky with his eyes closed and sighed deeply in frustration. Here was a huge situation and the batter didn't have a clue.

"Believe in yourself and us!" a voice shouted from behind Bret. Hitting from the left side, he turned his head to where the voice had come from.

It was Ambrose, down at first base. He clapped his batting glove covered hands together, looking down at his teammate. "You can do this." He said to himself but Bret could read his lips.

The next pitch looked to be the same as the first, a fastball a little low but over the heart of the plate. Just as he had, before the tournament began, Bret put a short, quick swing to the ball and sent it screaming into the night sky. Straight away center field the ball went, turning the center fielder's back to the infield as he was already on his way to chase it.

The three runners read the flight of the ball and saw the center fielder had no chance of making a catch, so they were off to the races. Kris stayed on third base, waiting to tag up if by some miracle the ball was caught. When the ball finally bounced, one hopped to the fence four hundred and five feet away, Kris started for home, Tim about two steps behind. It looked like a relay race as Ambrose chased after Tim, rounding third as well. All three scored easily and Bret ended up where Kris had started, third base.

A smile of joy and relief covered Bret's face as he stood beaming.

The boys had come out of the dugout to greet their teammates, shouting down at Bret as well. This was the moment he had tried so hard to reach. His eyes welled up, causing him to take of his glasses to wipe his eyes. John choked up for a minute as well.

It took two of the three outs left in their half of the inning to get Bret home but finally, Jason singled to right, scoring the seventh run. With that, the boys ran back out to battle the Arizona hitters down only a run.

Steve and Kyle did all they could, throwing every pitch to every location. It seemed there were no weak hitters in the line up. One more run came across making the score nine to seven with one more at bat for John's team.

As he walked to his coach's box, John couldn't help but wonder what might have been if the Utah runner had touched home plate or if the umpires in that game had called the runner safe. As well as they were playing, he was certain his boys would win this tournament if they could catch a break. That would have been the biggest break imaginable.

No sense worrying about what might have been. As he had discovered within himself the night prior, worry about the moment and find those memories that you want to have.

Top of the line up, Kyle, Kris and Tim would have to face the Arizona "ace" which had been called in to pitch. No doubt they had seen Arizona's two best. As the starting pitcher went to play short and the shortstop had now come in to pitch, a sign of respect shown by the Arizona coaches.

After the first two swings, John had wished the pitching change had not been made. Both Kyle and Kris rocketed balls toward the left-center gap only to have the now shortstop leap and make snow cone catches. Tim followed with a single but Ambrose's bid for a single up the middle was met with another outstanding play by the shortstop, diving to his left, jumping up and throwing on to first for the final out.

The loudest sound of quiet John had ever heard came over the field. Suffering their first defeat, the New Mexico boys weren't sure how to handle it. Exhausted by the effort as well as the reality of the whole thing had silenced them. The fans that had been so supportive were quiet, waiting to applause the effort when the time was right and the Arizona team could feel it wouldn't be right to celebrate until after leaving the field, as they had been fortunate the game was only seven innings long. One more and they would have given in to the will of their opponents and they knew it.

The cheers they so richly deserved as they left the dugout greeted the team. Nearly ten o'clock, the boys said nothing as they piled into the cars to get back to the hotel. While there was disappointment, there was more satisfaction, from the coaches and the boys. No one would hang his head over this loss. It happened, it hurt but it was a loss they could live with. Tomorrow was quickly on its way and to have a second chance at Arizona, the boys would have to win again tomorrow. For tonight, even in defeat, together they had accomplished nearly everything.

Chapter 26

Tim's lips formed a tiny "O" shape as he blew the fourteen candles out on his birthday cake. The Cottonwood trees surrounding the porch were littered with yellow leaves trying to hide among the green ones. It was September now; still warm enough in Albuquerque to have a birthday party outdoors. The boys had spent the better part of the afternoon playing Home Run Derby on the twelve-year-old field. Two hundred foot fences were nearly too small then, now the balls sailed majestically over the chain link like Major Leaguer's did during batting practice. Tim was having his party at the Little League fields, allowing him to play the sport he loved more than any.

A month had passed since the Nevada team had eliminated their team. It really wasn't much of a game. The boys hadn't quit, not a chance of that, no it was something more. The sense of accomplishment everyone had felt after the prior night's game seemed to signal enough. Even winning that game wouldn't have matter much. They had come to that point as a team; baseball had brought them as far as it could; now they were ready to move on to the next step, together.

Middle School was winding down. They were now in the eighth grade, the end of a wonderful time in their lives. Not that there wouldn't be more, it was simply the passage to High School, a year to celebrate the end of their innocence and prepare to once again be young.

The boys realized, for all their success as athletes, academically and with the girls beginning to look longer and more often, they would once again be the little fish in a big pond, freshman. Kids begin to chose their own directions in High School, some play sports; others focus on getting to college. Girls become more of a focus and friends become less. Would this happen to this group? Not one of them could answer honestly "No" if asked had they thought about that possibility. For now, they ruled the school and it was football season. That's what mattered.

Sitting under the shade offered by the slatted porch just off the concession stand, John sat with Tim, Ambrose, Kris and Kyle. The rest of the boys had taken to throwing a football around on the biggest field. While all the boys loved baseball, they also enjoyed playing whichever sport was in season. Tim in fact, was playing organized football for the first time that fall. Still, his heart belonged to the Pastime. The other three boys felt the same. Together, the five of them rehashed the tournament, all its glory and in the end, it's sorrow. Arizona had gone on to win, beating Nevada in just one more game. Advancing to the regional part of the tournament and even to the World Series where they played in the championship game against a team from Puerto Rico, eventually losing three to two.

In a way, it was a moral victory for the boys from Albuquerque, knowing had they played again or even an inning longer in that game, the outcome would have been different. The boys talked of how they would have done things differently and what it would be like to do it again. They had two chances at it; their fourteen and fifteen year old seasons still to come.

Though they talked with such conviction and stars in their eyes, they all realized it really was a one shot opportunity. Only a handful might make the All Star team as fourteen year olds as the team was mixed with fifteen year olds as well. Really, that one shot opportunity would be a reach too as Brad might move on to just football and any number of boys, including Tim and Ambrose had a good chance of playing for the High School summer team. If so, they might have to choose which team to play for knowing full well they would play for the High School.

The conversation carried on for hours, well into the evening. Blankets covered bare legs and jackets were pulled on. Off and on, other boys would join in; some of the boys left but Ambrose, Tim and Kris remained until nearly midnight, talking with their coach.

All the while, John watched Tim as he interacted with his friends. He was polite and fun, laughing most of the time they were there. He was enjoying himself and allowing people to see him doing so. That wasn't like the thirteen-year-old John had spent so much time with over the past months.

Tim was the best athlete, best baseball player in the group. Even with the arrival of Ambrose, Tim remained the best. Several adults, including his coach had wondered aloud if there were now too many Stallions in the barn for Tim's liking. A slight reservation to begin with had turned quickly to acceptance. Now it looked a bit like admiration.

Superstars, in professional sports can often have personalities that turn people off. They don't say the right things or talk to the media often enough. Aloof, high maintenance or arrogant are often words associated with great athletes. In this town, at this age, Tim was just like that. Maybe it was something simple, an uneasy feeling about getting attention. Perhaps it was the inability to say what he felt, always turning it around and whatever he meant to say coming out wrong. More likely, he really was just a jerk. John saw something else. A very intelligent young man, blessed with everything a boy could want who liked to be alone. It frustrated most, including his parents but made perfect sense to John. He liked to be alone as well, mostly for fear of disappointing others but alone nonetheless. Tim seemed to like being alone almost as an escape from having to be the best at everything he did. Ambrose allowed Tim to sometimes just be part of the "gang." He liked that and now, for the first time since John had met him, Tim was being a fun loving, likeable kid. Ambrose allowed him to do that, just by being his friend.

Over the next two months, seven of the boys had birthday parties. All the players and coaches from the team were invited and most of them showed up. Occasionally, a game or prior engagement kept one or two people away but for the most part, everyone attended. By the end of the year, only Kyle H. and Chad were not to be found hanging around. Just the first part in an inevitable change every group of friends goes through. "Hello's" would still be exchanged, as would stories of the summer past it was simply a fact of life, people grow apart. Baseball was just around the corner.

Chapter 27

Through the winter months, afternoons were spent on a number of things. Kris, Tim and Ambrose spent many of them either playing catch, lifting weights in Kris' garage or doing both. Todd was often invited by the fellas to join them but couldn't find a ride or was looking after his younger sister. The recent months had become difficult for the normally positive, happy-go-lucky, toe head. Todd's father had been promoted within his job, forcing him to commute north to Santa Fe, an hour drive everyday. There were only a handful of minutes each week the two were able to spend time together. His mother, feeling guilty, had begun either coddling the teenager or letting him get away with most anything he wanted. Still, Todd remained focused on baseball, tossing a ball to himself or swinging a bat for hours at a time.

Brad, Steve, Jason and Matt played basketball most everyday. Brad had potential to play in High School though football would probably be his sport of choice. The others played mainly to keep busy and have more time around one another. Ambrose played on the team as well, though he was playing only to be with his friends.

When Tim wasn't working out, he too played basketball, on

another team in a different league. His athleticism allowed him to play in a competitive league with players from another school. He had ended up here as he had signed up late but it really improved his level of play. Unfortunately, it was also giving him a different outlook on life. Jon played on the team as well. Not because of his athleticism but because they had needed a player and he and Tim were growing closer. Jon certainly wasn't bad; he just wasn't quite at Tim and the other boy's level.

C.J. was finding a passion for football. In the months following Tucson, C.J. had grown two inches and gained nearly ten pounds. What hadn't changed was his speed. He still could run faster than any of his friends and with his increased size, now made for a nice sized running back. He too had begun to work out, though his time was spent with older boys already on the High School football team.

Kyle's father was one of the most successful High School wrestling coaches in the nation and certainly the history of New Mexico. He didn't know a great deal about baseball but he understood the need for discipline and repetition. In a perfect act of parenthood, he let Kyle come to him; rather than tell his son it was time to practice. Kyle was beginning to find his love was baseball. More and more often, he would ask his father to take him to the High School field to throw, hit or take ground balls. Now, if he would only grow six inches.

Six hours of school everyday gave the boys even more time to spend together. At any given moment, three or more of them could be found together, walking to class, eating lunch or traveling to and from the events they shared. All nine of the boys made the honor roll, both semesters of that eighth grade year. No small task, considering all the items on each boy's list each day.

Ambrose's list included a few more items. For years, his family had taken part in their church's soup kitchen on Thanksgiving Day as well as taking blankets and coats to the less fortunate people in the downtown areas of both Tucson and Albuquerque. The family introduced several of the boys to selfless acts such as these. As they drove from place to place, if one of the boys was with them, it was Ambrose who took the time to explain why he thought it was important to do things like this.

"Without doing anything but being a kid, I have been given all the gifts anyone could ask for." He had made this speech so many times it almost had a rhythm to it. "How hard is it for me to take some time from my life to give back?"

Anyone who might have heard Ambrose say this without any background on the young man would think he either was exaggerating or had been told what to say and it had become second nature to repeat it. Those who knew him, knew he meant every word he said and it wasn't something he had been told to say. He believed that giving back or going out of his way for someone else was as important as the time he put in believing in his faith or honing his craft as a ball player.

One Friday afternoon, Ambrose came across a classmate, head collapsed on an open math book, in the library of the school. The classmate was not a baseball player, football, basketball or athlete of any kind, just a boy Ambrose knew from class. The two boys sat at the round, maple table trying to grasp the concept of the Pythagoras' theorem. Ambrose had little trouble with math while most of the eighth grade population struggled mightily. While talking, it was discovered that the two lived only blocks from one another, so Ambrose offered to come over that evening to continue the tutoring.

No great offer, except for the fact it was Valentine's Day and a school dance, which Ambrose had already saved numerous dances for young ladies. Gatherings like school dances were also times for the fellas to get together with no time line, no practices or classes to interrupt their time together. To miss it or at least miss part of it was a big deal and here Ambrose offered his time without a second thought. The young man went on to get an "A" on the next test.

While the boys participated in all the pieces of life they could find time to hold, John was waking up each morning and getting on with his day without the need to find a reason. It was his life and he was looking forward to living it. Really, he was minding his time until the baseball season arrived. Those dark days of wanting the day to end and never wanting the night to were things of the past. He kept in touch, making his way out to watch basketball games or to throw with the fellas on days warm enough to allow it. He was amazed at how they had matured in such a short time. In talking with any one of them, there were no longer complaints of how life might be treating them. No excuses about teachers or parents or coaches who were out to get them. Less than two years had gone by when everything was someone else's fault, now they were responsible for their own actions. They held themselves and each other accountable for mistakes that might happen. In talking with C.J. one afternoon, the young man explained how he had received a "D" on a school paper. At first, when he saw the disappointment on his coach's face, he stammered about not being able to get a ride home from working out causing him to not have enough time to get it done. Before he finished his second sentence he paused, "No, that's not right. I just didn't get it done, sorry coach, it won't happen again." looking his coach right in the eye.

Not long ago, that admission would not have happened. Shoot, John might not have been able to say it himself. That was the difference between him and these boys and the flaw he wanted to correct in himself. These boys were becoming not only men, but also good, caring citizens as well. It was one of the reasons he felt he would never, could never let these boys down.

Chapter 28

Two huge snow falls, totaling seven inches between them, several flurries and numerous blue sky, icy cold days was the extent of the Albuquerque winter. March ides had arrived and with them the fourteen year old baseball season. It had been a long time coming for all those involved.

As the boys were now moving from thirteen to the fourteen-fifteen year old division, all the boys would have to go through the draft again. Just as the year before, John was allowed two "options" as he had no children to put on his team. Tim and Bret had been his options the year prior but this summer John wanted to make sure Todd was part of his team with all the young man was going through at home. Ambrose and Bret would be fine playing with someone else, just as Kris, Kyle and Brad would be.

Really, the summer was uneventful, except for the usual summer bonding, bike rides to Dion's pizza, afternoons laying around the swimming pool in Brad's backyard, hoping to see his unbelievable sister in her bikini and of course, baseball games.

Tim had his usual summer, looking like the best player in the league though he was only fourteen. It wasn't a surprise however, he had always looked that good. Brad, Kris and Kyle played well too. Todd was having his best summer ever until a broken arm put him on the shelf for several weeks. It was Ambrose who stood out, surprising even John, who thought of Ambrose as Tim's equal. 'Brose had grown a few inches, adding bulk and strength to his already solid ability to play baseball. The year before he had been a good hitter, having the ability to hit the ball the other way, now he added power. On the mound his velocity had jumped nearly five miles an hour, making him the second hardest thrower in the league next to Tim.

Those two spent the summer in a friendly competition of who could top whom. Tim might throw a shut out, Ambrose would throw a two hit shut out. Ambrose would go three for four with a home run; Tim would have a four for four day with two home runs. Never once did they argue or cease to talk to one another. They didn't even jokingly talk "trash" to each other. It was hugs when the game started and arms around each other when the game was over. All the boys were that way, games would have ended hours before and still some part or the entire group would be sitting together in the bleachers or under the porch talking girls and baseball.

Once again, John's team was leading the league, though his mind was on the All Star season. He had once again asked Derry to coach with him and now had a former player from his first Little League team helping him coach. Justin had been the smallest player with as many doubters as he didn't have pounds. Still, John believed in him, using him not only to play second base but pitch as well. Eventually, Justin had become a big part of the High School State Champions earlier that spring. Knowing he wouldn't be playing baseball in the future, he had begun coaching with John, as his younger brother was the catcher. Quickly, the relationship between John and Justin went from coach-player to good friends.

It was John's focus on the upcoming All Star tournament that cost his team the League Championship. New Mexico showers had postponed several games, which John wasn't willing to make up, wanting instead to get on with the tournament. The League decided the Spurs would forfeit those games, putting them in second place to finish the season.

Depression had taken its toll on John for a number of years. Now it seemed that arrogance or the belief that the world owed him something was taking depression's place. Which was worse? After accepting his second place trophy, John kneeled at the edge of the dugout. He realized his focus on nine boys had forced him to sacrifice the ten on this team that wouldn't be making the All Star team. It wasn't fair to them and he knew it. Quickly, he shook that thought from his mind. The boys he would be working with for the rest of the summer had given him something in his life to believe in and look forward to. A sacrifice like this was worth it.

No, it wasn't. Perhaps, if all the boys John cared so much about were playing with him the rest of that summer it would have been. Maybe. Instead, he had given away the possibility of their memories for only five of them.

When the team was announced, with all the same pomp and circumstance as the year before, only Tim, Ambrose, Brett, Kris and Brad were selected. The first three were "no brainers" each had a very good summer and were equally deserving. The last two, Kris and Brad were surprises. Brad especially. He was a good ball player and had played well during the summer but the ugly head of popularity seemed to be raising its head, as it always seemed to do during this event. Kris' selection was a surprise as well, though it had looked for a while as if the race for the final spot on the team was coming down to Kris, Kyle and Todd. Not that the coach, once again, John minded. He loved these boys and had the utmost confidence in them as players. In his heart he had wanted, even voting for Todd, as he truly had earned it. In the end the time out of the game with the broken arm seemed to have cost him.

As the ceremony ended, John walked off the field into the crowd of parents and friends congratulating those whose names had been called. A few steps into the crowd, he came upon Kyle. The boy's handsome face was almost mournful, his beautiful dark eyes welling up with tears. John put his arm over the young man's shoulder, steering him out of the crowd.

"When I was eleven I didn't expect to make the team." Kyle started, "At twelve and thirteen it was kind of a surprise but a I sort of expected it." he paused a moment as he choked up and needed to swallow. "This year I worked so hard and really feel as if I deserved to make this team!" Kyle started to breakdown but composed himself quickly.

John's eyes welled up too, almost feeling his player's pain. Once again it was time for a speech he had given the year before.

"Don't ever allow this to happen again, work so hard and become so good that no one can ever leave you off the team." The taller man looked right into the boy's eyes so Kyle knew how much John meant what he said.

Kyle looked back at him as the expression on his face changed from sorrow to determination.

"It won't ever happen again." With that, Kyle walked away to meet his parents, turning back after ten steps or so, "Thanks coach!"

John watched him until he met up with his mom where she put both arms around him in a loving embrace. The coach really felt something when Kyle had said it wouldn't happen again. "I believe you Kyle, I believe you."

Todd was waiting for John at the coach's pick up truck. He needed a ride home. Expecting to have to give the talk one more time, John asked his second base man what he was thinking.

"I'm OK," Todd replied, but John knew Todd would rather keep things inside than let people know he was hurting. "I know my broken arm kept me from making the team. I had a great summer."

"Really?" John almost believed him.

"Yeah, really." Todd smiled. "Next year is the one that matters anyway."

Truer words had never been spoken. The majority of the All Star team was made up of fifteen-year-olds and despite John and Justin's best efforts to play the five fourteen-year-olds to save the tournament, the older boys wouldn't play hard. Maybe they resented the coach's affection for the younger players, maybe they cared more about being teenagers than they did about baseball. Whatever the reason, the team was beaten in the City Championship game by it's rival, Altamont Little League. Tim took the loss, three to one, the only bright spots were Tim's pitching and the fact Roadrunner had only six hits, two by Tim, one each for Brad and Bret, the only run batted in came from Ambrose's bat, a bittersweet ending to the tournament. Though they were done playing, his boys had played well. Everyone could now look forward to High School and one final summer of Little League baseball.

Chapter 29

Layers of light and dark gray covered the sky completely, from the tip of the Sandias to the petroglyphs of the West Mesa as John drove to work. He thought about his first day of High School, walking to school on a day almost identical to the overcast day he looked up into this morning. Overcome with anxiety, his steps were short, taking as much time as possible, yet he was so excited to finally be there he wanted to get there as quickly as possible. Little had he known that these conflicted feeling would be commonplace for his four years of school. Always excited to take the next step but unsure of what would happen when he did, the bittersweet complexities of adolescence.

Tim, met with Todd and the two walked to school, few words were spoken and those that were, mostly were awkward and pointless. Basically they were mutterings to break an uneasy silence. Ambrose and Kris were dropped off listening to music but also speaking very little. Kris did however, stay awake the entire ride. Kyle rode with his mom who was a counselor at the school, there was no talking at all in that car but when is there ever when a mom drives her son to school. All the feelings John had felt ten years earlier as he made his way to school were running through his players this morning, one more connection between the coach and his players.

The step to High School is one of only a handful of moments when a person can grow up in a single day. A young man walks into a hallway and sees many of his dreams come true right before his eyes. Girls. Young ladies. Women. He is at a point in his life when, whether he outwardly admits it or not, he thinks about girls. Here, there are more than he can count. There are of course, those girls he has known for years but even those girls are different, having either grown up themselves during the summer or now see a way to attract the boys they know or even the older ones. More importantly, there are now older girls, juniors and seniors that, to many boys, seem to be big screen fantasies come to life.

If this weren't enough, there are the older boys which already have the attention of those young ladies because of not only their mature physical features but more importantly because of their mental maturity. Sitting in class, next to the upper class men or just walking down the hall, a curious young man can hear the difference in what is spoken and not spoken to gain affection. In most cases, certainly the case of these incoming freshmen the end of that first day of school meant the end of their boyhood simplicities.

Eldorado High School, home of the golden, fighting or truckin' eagles, depending on what sport you played. All the fellas from Brad and Steve to Tim and Kyle, had grown up knowing they would someday be here waiting, anticipating and now, here they were, soaking in the moment. Ambrose, who had not grown up here had gotten the bug from hearing the other fellas talking about being here also walked into school that first day, nodding to himself that he belonged here. The next four years would be his and he would live them to the fullest.

Chapter 30

Ambrose stood looking into the midnight blue sky, hands jammed into his pockets in an attempt to keep warm. He shivered as the cool morning air nipped at his cheeks and nose. From the corner of his eye, he could see Brad's breath in a wispy looking cloud as its warmth met head on with that morning air. Todd and Kris' hot chocolate caused steam to rise into the air as well. The four stood close together to create body heat.

A loud sound, somewhat like a blast of air exploded in the air around them, followed by another then another. Bursts of light filled huge canopies like lamps being lit, one by one, huge lamps, glowing against the early morning sky as the lifted gently off the ground.

The boys were taking in the first morning of the International Balloon Fiesta, held annually in Albuquerque. Hundreds of colorful and odd shaped balloons would come to participate in a number of events, showcasing skill and beauty in balloon aviation. Thousands of people milled around the dirt lot which housed the lift offs, watching as these beautiful, quiet shapes lifted themselves into the Southwestern sky.

The morning sky, pale blue washing over it's darker night companion proved to be a magnificent backdrop for the balloons to sail into. While the boys had been here many times before, this morning was Ambrose's first time. The simplicity and the beauty amazed him, staring upward as the shapes became smaller and smaller. He had seen the balloons from the ground now two years in a row, which is a sight in itself, as hundreds of dots rise into the sky, filling the usually clear skies with many blemishes. From his house it seemed that balloons were still life paintings that moved almost too slowly to pay any attention to. Now, seeing it from up close, he realized how quickly they really did move. Occasionally, a balloon would make its way into the neighborhood, grabbing people's attention by blasting its fire, keeping the craft afloat. Children would gather to watch, as its descent was soft, ending in a touch down of wicker basket to desert ground. Ambrose had seen all that before but this was different, wonderfully different. It was a first for him and he was able to take in the moment, enjoying it with his friends. As the cool air around him warmed, Ambrose stood with his three friends looking up into the New Mexico sky, taking in the moment.

The fall held so many moments, so many firsts. Football games on Friday nights. The Homecoming dance. Real final exams.

For years, the boys had attended the Friday night games with wide-eyed excitement. Now they were there as students. It was a totally different feel, the colors brighter, and the sounds greater. Sitting in the east stands for an early season game, the band would be warming up as a cool blanket settled in over the stadium. Players went through drills, Texas orange, white and gold trimmed on their uniforms as the reds and oranges of the sky mixed with the black and blue of the night sky. Brad would sit with the fellas but for minutes at a time he would become lost, imagining it were he out there preparing to play. He loved baseball but it was becoming apparent, football was his passion. Soon enough, he would be out there on Friday nights.

The early school year awkwardness was gone by mid-September and all the boys mixed socially with friends of all classes. Several of the boys, Tim and Brad mainly, had already gained the attention of older girls whom they sat with during the games. This social acceptance allowed the boys to attend their first Homecoming dance, though it was Ambrose who stole the show as a junior, a young lady who had the attention of all the boys in school actually asked Ambrose to the dance rather than the traditional, boy asks girl.

It was physical, for the most part when the girls noticed Brad or Tim or Todd but Ambrose had more phone calls from more females than any boy in the history of High School near as anyone could tell because he was so real, real in a sense that he could talk to anyone about anything and be sincere. He had maturity, selflessness, and something else. No one, not even his parents could put a finger on what quality he possessed which brought people to him, they just did. He was special and everyone knew it. A person couldn't even be jealous of Ambrose if a girl preferred 'Brose to himself or if Ambrose received more attention at a gathering. He just made it easy for everyone to like him.

To a man, every one of the fellas could say the first three months of their High School experience was more than they ever could have dreamed. *Having the world by the tail,* couldn't even cover how exciting and satisfied the boys were. If there was a complaint to be made and one would have to look for one, it would be in respect to Tim, who was beginning to distance himself from the other boys, not because of jealousy or a feeling of "better" but simply because of his personality. He had decided his future lay in the realm of professional athletics and he preferred to put his extra time and energy into working out. Any time he had beyond that went to his girlfriend, which the fellas had not yet quite gained an interest in exclusivity, so there was a small rift between the boys' ideas.

Rumor had it that Tim had not only a chance to play at least at the JV level in baseball but basketball as well. At Eldorado High School, players of freshman status just didn't play JV and didn't even think about Varsity. Sure, it had happened before, just not very often. Just that thought of making that level made Tim believe he was good enough to go on to college and even the pros. He decided early on, his effort would be to go as far as he could.

Often times, athletes of Tim and Ambrose's caliber become distant or difficult to deal with. While Ambrose would never be like that, Tim was taking his first steps toward becoming that type of player. The fellas didn't know it and really, neither did Tim. Without knowing, he was falling into the trap of high exposure sports. It was the time of the

"Fab Five" in college basketball, a group of rebellious young players at the University of Michigan who went out of their way to dress, act and play on the edges of the rules. He was enamored with college hoops, which also now had tattooed players and oft troubled teens making it big. Chest thumping, self-promoting athletes were everywhere on television and Tim was taken in by all of them. Not only did he know there was a possibility to get there, he wanted to be just like them. Not just play like them but act like them. He thought that was the way to be if he wanted to get noticed. The fellas as well as John, began to see less and less of Tim, though no one really thought too much of it as his personality lent itself to times like this. Still, it had little affect on the great times the boys were having with each other and all the new friends they were meeting.

John had gone to work at another High School, allowing him to coach both football and late in the year, baseball. In fact, the second game of the freshman football season pitted coach versus players, as most of the fellas played football. The outcome was ugly as John, for all his ability as a baseball coach didn't translate to football, compounded with a lack of talent allowed the game to get out of hand in favor of the fellas. Forty something to nothing was the final, though John wasn't upset. He loved seeing his boys in his Alma matter's colors, looking like the great young men he knew they were.

That fun moment was one of the few, as John was again having trouble maintaining a positive outlook on life. He claimed he was a realist, rather than a pessimist, as he viewed each day as something bad waiting to happen and anything good would be a bonus. He wouldn't even listen to the radio, thinking that a song might put him in a good mood thus leading to a bad day happening.

His friends and family urged him to go to a doctor, get medicine, to do something to try and regain the easy going, fun nature he was known to have growing up. He would refuse, justifying his moods by saying he used to be naive and now saw the world for all the bad things it had created. He could snap out of it if he wanted to. He chose to be in a bad mood. He chose to keep to himself and be quiet. When the time came, he would change his emotions. There was a problem though, when would that be and could he really do it? Inside, he doubted it.

Really, it was as much John's mood swings which had Tim wondering about his life and contributed to his mood change. Here was this friend, a mentor and teacher who saw the world in a negative way. Why should he be any different? Maybe John was right, the world didn't reward the good person, the hard worker. Instead, maybe he should make his future happen by doing things the way he saw it on television. Unfortunately, the coach never saw his affect on his favorite player.

John was lonely and hated himself for all the bad decisions he had made in the recent years. He never wanted to go to college. He should have waited. He went, so he should have worked harder, instead he was lazy. He wanted to play ball at Nebraska, he stayed to go to school with his best friend. He dropped out of school thinking he could pursue baseball anyway. He didn't make it. He should have gone back to school, he hadn't. No matter what he did it seemed to be the wrong decision. Following his heart had led him here and now, he knew another mistake was waiting for him. Why did he always follow his heart instead of his head?

All of this seemed to go away when he was coaching the boys during the summer. Maybe it was being around Ambrose that caused him to make good decisions. Perhaps it was knowing he was a role model to the boys and he never wanted to lose that which kept him from making these life-changing choices. Whatever it was, he needed the fellas, more than they would ever know, in fact, they would never know. He couldn't ever tell them for fear that the pressure of knowing how much he relied on them might affect them negatively. That, he would never do to them.

Not a day went by in which he didn't wish he could force himself to live by the same rules he asked the boys to live by. No excuses take responsibility and give everyday the best effort you can, thereby allowing you to look anyone, including yourself in the eye. Many days, John combed his hair looking away from the mirror. On days that he drove by the school, John would think of the boys. Hopefully, they would never know the person he was underneath.

Chapter 31

By the time basketball tryouts rolled around, the bug to play baseball had taken a good bite out of Ambrose. He wanted to get the winter over with and get on to playing ball. Many of the boys, save Tim and Brad, who both looked forward to basketball, wanted the same. To quench their thirst and take up some of the time, Ambrose and Kyle tried out for basketball along with Tim and Brad. While both Tim and Brad made the JV all the other boys, Ambrose, Kyle, Todd and Steve made the freshman team. It was a compliment to their athleticism and work ethic though the mainly did it to kill some time and keep in shape for the upcoming baseball season.

A cold, Tuesday afternoon, gray skies laying on top of a frigid thirty mile an hour wind had the bones and muscles of even fourteen and fifteen year old bodies feeling the chill. Ambrose and the boys talked about their dread, knowing they would have to walk outside as they bent over between wind sprints. Halfway through a following sprint, Ambrose felt a sharp pain in his right hip. He continued the run, finishing up, though his pain became nearly unbearable. None of the other boys even noticed as Ambrose had established long before that, he never complained nor took time off when his teammates were working hard.

It wasn't until the locker room, as the boys dressed, that anybody said anything. Noticing Ambrose gingerly putting his leg into a pair of pants, Kyle asked if he felt OK to which Ambrose shook his head but still said nothing. His limp, as the boys walked to the parking lot to wait for their rides home drew more questions and looks but 'Brose just blew it off as a cramp. Enough said.

Three days later, Ambrose took himself out of practice, as he could no longer stand the pain in his hip. For the young man to do this, the boys on the team realized something had to be seriously wrong. Their goading, along with a concerned mother, forced Ambrose to concede to see a doctor.

No athlete wants to see a doctor. For one, a doctor will undoubtedly say they have to sit out a game. Athletes hate to miss games. Second, a doctor might find something wrong which means more games missed. Athletes hate to miss games. Finally, if an athlete misses games, there is always the risk that teammates might lose faith in that athlete because they are missing the hard work the rest of the players are putting in. Ambrose never wanted to be seen in that perspective, though no one ever would think that anyway.

As often happens when people visit the doctor, the wait to actually be seen took longer than the actual check up. A few pokes and prods, combined with some movement of the legs and a few questions about stretching and activity led to a diagnosis of "pulled muscle." a relief of sorts to Ambrose, until a remedy of a week of " no activity" was suggested. Bothered, Ambrose remained quiet on the ride home. His mother, always a thoughtful speaker, gave Ambrose positive things to think about rather than pouting. She spoke softly but definitively. Ambrose listened and quickly came to grips with the idea of missing a week. After all, it could have been worse.

Two games were played while Ambrose took his time on the injured list. Not that he would have been the difference, but the team lost one and won one of the games. A weekend practice would be the last missed before he was allowed to return. He chased balls at practice as to keep busy and put himself as close to working hard with his friends as he could get. As he jogged slowly after a ball, his hip continued to ache, causing him to press his thumb into it in hopes that the pressure might take some of the pain away. It didn't

"Dad, I know you have taught me never to complain," Ambrose

spoke softly as his father drove him home from practice, "but my hip still hurts. In fact, it hurts worse than ever." At a stoplight, his father looked at Ambrose, noticing tears welling up in his son's eyes.

Not thinking twice, Ambrose's father took out a cell phone and made a call. He called a colleague at the University for which he coached. Two hours later, Ambrose lay on an examination table, shaking slightly as he was both nervous and cold, dressed only in the paper-thin gown patients are given at a hospital.

This time, a series of more serious and in depth examinations took place. X-rays and a MRI were part of those examinations. Between tests, the doctors wrote many items down and whispered things to the nurses who helped out. The longer these tests went on and the more they whispered, the sicker Ambrose felt. Anyone who has to visit specialists like these would have a pit in their stomach. Imagine being only fourteen and having all this going on. Even the strongest of personalities, such as Ambrose could even get through. By the end, Ambrose was a wreck.

Finally finished, the men and women helping Ambrose through the examination told him to dress. Already, as he pulled his shirt over his head, Ambrose could feel the soreness from all the pushing and stretching, creep into his body. His mind was some distance away, thinking of many things at once, his friends, baseball, basketball, a particular Arizona afternoon years earlier and at the same time he thought about nothing. Without knowing, it took Ambrose nearly twenty minutes to dress, as he slowly put his wardrobe back on. It was almost as if he were taking his time in an attempt to avoid his next appointment, though that had nothing to do with it. Something was on his mind he just didn't know it.

Both Ambrose's parents were sitting in the office where the nurse directed him after dressing. The doctor sat at a large, dark, cherry desk, polished to a wonderful shine, his hands folded in front of his chin as he paused from whatever conversation he had been having with the mom and dad. Pictures of athletes, both Alma matter to the university and others adorned the walls of what really was quite a cheery, relaxed setting. The empty feeling in the fourteen year old's stomach calmed for a moment as he looked at his parent's faces. They seemed to be fine. Maybe everything was all right.

The doctor smiled, "Ambrose, have a seat."

Chapter 32

Everyday a person wakes up; there is an underlying fear that something horrible might happen. A car accident, a grandparent passing away, a Columbine type tragedy. No one ever speaks about it, really never thinking about it anymore than just a passing thought in hopes that if it is out of sight it is out of mind and hopefully won't happen. What does a person or a family do when reality hits? Teenagers, more than anybody, feel they are invincible, as they haven't lived long enough, in most cases, to understand their own or anybody else's mortality. It isn't arrogance but a naivety. An innocence that hopefully isn't lost too soon. Occasionally, it is.

The pain in Ambrose's hip was coming from a baseball-sized tumor, which had developed. Through all the tests the tumor was determined to be malignant. Ambrose had Cancer.

The ride home was quiet but relaxed. Before Ambrose had a chance to panic both the doctor and his parents explained to him the statistics of those who survived this type of illness. They talked about the types of treatment which were available and what they would entail. The doctor was very adept in his explanation of what would happen to Ambrose's body and his ability to continue in sports. That explanation was what Ambrose needed to hear. Not so much for himself as from the moment the word "Cancer" had been spoken, he could think only of his friends. What would they do? How would they react? Would it be his fault if they didn't reach their dreams in the upcoming summer?

Not a single thought of himself came to Ambrose's mind. Only of friends and family. There was no "Why me?" or "It's not fair." he didn't even have a fear of dying which would seem to be the first thing to go through most people's mind. Not this young man. As his family's car pulled into the drive, Ambrose already had a list of whom he needed to call and how he would break the news to them.

One by one, the young man called the fellas, Kris, Todd, Tim and so on. There was no worry or despair as he described the battery of tests he undertook and all he had to do in his near future. In each instance, his news was greeted by silence. Who ever know what to say to news like that, particularly fourteen-year-old boys? Each time the phone line went silent, Ambrose would do something to bring the conversation back, a joke or some other reassuring comment.

By the end of the night, the digital red on the clock reading eleven fifteen, Ambrose was too wired to sleep. All the energy he was forced to give to his friends in breaking the news had actually energized him. It seemed to him that he could almost feel his body working to fight off the sickness invading his body. He could beat this. Darn right he could, not only could he beat it, that night Ambrose decided he would beat it. With every fiber of his body he would beat this. He couldn't wait for the next day to arrive.

It was only due to the extreme nature of the treatments the doctor's and his family chose to fight the Cancer did Ambrose leave the basketball team. Never in a million years would he have quit. In fact, he didn't quit so much as remove himself from the playing part of the team. When time allowed, along with physical ability, Ambrose made practices and games to keep score, cheer or anything else he could do to be around his friends. To a man, they noticed when he was there and when he wasn't; never taking for granted their friend's efforts. With each day, some sort of change was taking place with Ambrose's body and none of it looked as if it were good for him.

Chemotherapy, radiation treatments and so many injections people lost count, within only a few weeks, the one time, hundred and fifty pound physically fit and gifted young man now looked more like a waif thin shadow of himself. The treatments had taken its toll on Ambrose physically, leaving him now a hundred and fifteen pounds, maybe.

Everyday, people of all ages, races and backgrounds look in the mirror, preparing them for a new day. In most cases, no matter how much money, how strong, handsome or beautiful that person is, the find some flaw to complain about. A pimple, a mole or simply a bad hair day, something could be better and teenagers, everything with the under twenty group is an emotional roller coaster to begin with, causing tears, outbursts and ruining days completely. Here was a young man whose body was withering away in front of him, not a single hair on his body to comb and yet he never once complained, pouted or even pounded a fist in anger. Instead, Ambrose looked himself square in the eye saying to himself, "One more day, I'm here and it's going to be a good day." and off to school he would go.

Instead of worrying about his own plight, Ambrose went out of his way to worry about those around him instead. When C.J.'s grades began to decline, as did his attendance, it was Ambrose who pulled him aside to get things straightened out.

"I'm confused, nothing makes sense," C.J. complained. "You are like the greatest person I know and look what you have to deal with, why should I have good things if you can't?"

It was a theme Ambrose would hear in one form or another over the first few months of his sickness. Friends all around him seemed to feel as if his being sick gave them an excuse to fail or at least not give their best effort. In some cases, like C.J.'s there really was a feeling of self-destruction as a way to try and equate themselves to Ambrose. He would have none of it.

A warm, blue sky, Sunday afternoon had all the fellas sitting in Ambrose's living room watching an "elite eight" college basketball game. The sun shone through a pair of sliding glass doors, leading to the back porch, causing a sunlight shadow to cast itself into the room. Potato chips, carrot sticks and dips to go along with them sat on two coffee tables. Empty soda cans and half finished glasses stood on the tables as well. It was just as it had been; two summers before when they had gathered in Tucson after their memorable win. No one even thought about Ambrose's sickness.

At halftime, Ambrose turned off the television and gained his friend's attention. As he spoke, his voice started quietly and steady but as he went on, his voice rose and his body animated.

"Some of you and other friends at school have begun to slip as far as grades or attendance or in the decisions you make. You feel as if you can't have fun, enjoy life and succeed if I can't." His eyes welled up off and on and occasionally he stopped for fear of breaking down. "Some people even have a hard time looking me in the face because they are worried about how I look, as if I needed hair." At that moment, he pushed the sides of his bald head up toward the top of his head. In doing so, the extra skin on his head gathered, squished on his head like a bowl of spaghetti. The boys laughed, though it was an uneasy laugh at best. "I will not let you use me or my illness as an excuse for failure! I am fine, I have been and I will be. Yes, I am sick but I am already getting better and I guarantee I will beat this. I need your help. Allow me to focus on the things I need to instead of worrying about you guys." Many of the heads in the room dropped, knowing he was referring to them. "For two years now, we have done nothing but think about and talk about the summer we are going toward right now." Pointing at himself, his hand going up and down, he continued. "This doesn't change anything. I will be fine by the time we play this summer and we are going to win that World Series we have talked about for so long! Every one of us in this room is an exceptional person, who can and will achieve great things. I am not about to let you fail because of me. Do you understand?"

Ambrose went on a while longer, as heads went from bowed to looking him straight in the eye. A short "rap" session followed before the boys got back to the game. One of the items the boys discussed and arranged was a study hall, twice a week to get homework done and one other night a week for athletes to get together to not only talk about sports and this time in their lives but also discuss religion, all of this from a fourteen-year-old boy. All on his own and all out of the goodness of his own heart. When the game was turned back on, the roar from the boys was as if they were at the game itself. Energy came over them, as if it were a pep talk before the big game. A new sense of worth filled each one, including Tim, though it couldn't be seen on the outside.

When 'Brose got to school the next day, he was greeted at his locker by Todd who looked different to say the least. Shortly, Kris and Brad came by as well, looking different than themselves but similar to Todd. All three had shaven their heads and their eyebrows in support of their friend. As the day went by and Ambrose went from class to class, more of his friends, not only the fellas closest to him but also through out the school had done the same. By the end of the week, a new trend had swept over Eldorado High School, one of shiny heads and naked faces.

What had started as a small group of friends looking to show support for all Ambrose had done for and meant to them had spread to all his friends and as is prone to do in the "fad" conscience world of High School, become a popular thing to do. In a school with a population of nearly two thousand students, over four hundred of them now looked like Ambrose. Never had there been a more beautiful sight.

Chapter 33

Anyone who has ever lived in Albuquerque knows how the February winds can cut through a person's body, chilling them to their very bones. While the sky is a magnificent blue and not a cloud in sight, the cold wind runs from the Rio Grande face first into the Sandia Mountains with nothing to break it. Maybe it's because most days it is warm but on those cold windy days, it seems to be below zero.

That cold is felt by everybody, big and little alike but for Ambrose, now carrying just over a hundred pounds on his once "buck fifty" frame, the cold seemed to be hiding in his bones. No hair to aid in holding in any warmth he could get didn't help. Still, Ambrose met each day with a smile.

The early spring was the busiest and hardest time for Ambrose. His treatments had reached full strength and were wiping him out each time he took part. Baseball, both High School and Little League had begun, though he was still to weak to practice or play. The best he could do was attending practice when he felt up to it, which as he had proven so many times already was most everyday. Cold sores on the roof of his mouth from the radiation, nausea from the chemo, the shakes from everything else, Ambrose still managed to make most practices for both teams just to be there. His grades had improved, though mostly A's to begin with is difficult to improve upon. In what seemed to be an odd twist, there seemed to be an epidemic of a lack of excuses going around.

By the end of April, Ambrose had only played a handful of innings for the JV team and none for the Little League. This, of course bothered no one, as everyone now saw what was really important in life. To Ambrose though, it was important to be out there playing. He felt it was the only way to show his friends that he really was winning this fight and to back up all his talk about no excuses. Also, he knew there was a rule about the number of games he participated in for the Little League to be eligible for the All Star tournament.

The Varsity baseball team at the High School was on a tear, winning all but two of their games in route to what they hoped would be back-to-back State Championships. At practice, whether it was Varsity of JV which Tim, Kris and Ambrose were all a part of, there was a blue collar, "bring your lunch and go to work" mentality. Part of it was due to the tradition of baseball at Eldorado High School but also in part to Ambrose. His hard work and positive attitude had given birth to a work ethic, which could not only be seen but almost touched on the field. The older boys, many of whom had never played a single inning with the young man, seemed to pick it up a step whenever he was around. The entire program seemed to go to another level as the last leg of the season wound down.

After winning the District Championship, the coach sat his Varsity players down to talk about which players, if any, would be coming up from the JV for pitching depth he planned on Tim. For hitting and defense, Kris. Each time, the team held up a hand in agreement of disagreement.

Before mentioning the last name he had in mind, the coach paused and went into a short talk about life, he finished by mentioning Ambrose and the fact he probably would be unable to help them physically due to his illness. Before he could continue, fourteen arms shot into the air. Without even hearing what the coach had to say, every member of the team voted him on. If the coach had not mentioned it, they would have. There was no way in the world Ambrose wouldn't be with them as they played for the State Championship.

Some would say it was a gesture of good faith or a mercy selection. Not in this case. The boys on the team knew, not only did Ambrose bring them to a new place on the field; he did the same for them in life. He was a leader and an inspiration. They wanted that in the dugout with them. What they also knew, though it had never been seen or proven, the players knew that even with his illness, if he had no energy in him whatsoever, Ambrose would drag himself onto the field to play. His love for the game was that great but also, his love for his teammates. They wanted him with them and win, lose or draw, they wanted to be with him.

The three youngsters sat next to one another, watching the first game of the State Tournament. They had played in huge games against great competition but to see the magnitude of the State Tournament, held on the field where the Los Angeles Dodgers' AAA baseball team played was almost overwhelming. Tim, who had followed the AAA Dukes all his life thought about all the different players whose baseball card he kept had played on that very field. Kris watched, imagining it was he out there playing for the title. Ambrose stared out onto the expanse of emerald green and red clay through tear filled eyes. It was unimaginable beauty, the game, the field, the colors and the day itself. He wouldn't have to play an inning and he would be satisfied. He loved the game. He loved where he was at that moment.

Eldorado had a battle on their hands in that first game. An upstart team from Las Cruces and yearly rival was giving them all they wanted. By then end of the sixth, they had been able to chase Eldorado's All-State starting pitcher, trailing by only one. In making his pitching changes, along with moves throughout the game, Eldorado's coach was left with a move he never imagined in all the scenarios he had gone over before this game. To have the best defense possible, in relation to the changes and options he had left, it was necessary to use a freshman third baseman, which had maybe a total of twenty innings under his High School belt. Ambrose was going in at third base.

As he took his warm up ground balls from the first baseman, Ambrose could feel his heart racing. His hands shook as he fielded and threw wildly to first base on the first warm up. The senior shortstop walked over, putting his arm around he freshman to reassure him. Two more throws and Ambrose calmed a little.

It was the single most exciting moment in his life to be out there playing in a game like this. He looked around, taking everything in. Hundreds of people, in the stands, clapping, standing one by one in a rousing ovation. Ambrose was confused. He looked to the pitcher, who stood off the mound rubbing the ball looking back at him. He looked at the dugout. All his teammates stood at the edge of the field clapping as well. As if someone had suddenly turned on the volume to a television, the roar of the crowd finally could be heard by the young man. It was a standing ovation for him.

For nearly two minutes, the crowd cheered, causing what seemed to be a monumentally huge moment in the game to be almost trivial. This moment was about a young man battling for himself in the most selfless of ways. This moment was for him.

Ambrose could feel his throat tighten as his body wanted to bawl. He knew he couldn't, so he swallowed hard, grabbing a handful of dirt to rub together between his hands. His eyes were filled with tears so much that he couldn't see more than a blur or brown as he knelt to pick up the dirt. Smoothing the dirt in front of him with his cleat, Ambrose then tipped the bill of his cap. Finally, the cheering softened and that other thing continued.

Out number one was a long fly ball to center field, which was no problem for Ambrose's teammate there. Out number two came after three balls were rocket past Ambrose, just foul each time, quickening his heart rate again but helping to acclimate him to the speed of the game.

As the ball went "around the horn," ending up in Ambrose's glove, he flipped it to the pitcher with a smile. The senior looked back at him. "Make this play for me?"

Ambrose smiled even bigger as his heart jumped, "You got it." back pedaling to his position at third.

Ambrose put his glove out in front of him, walking gingerly on his toes as he got into a ready position, following the pitch to the plate. Just as the ball entered the hitting zone, 'Brose squared his body to the plate. A fastball, running in on the batter's hands jammed him, causing a pop fly into foul territory...near third base. Ambrose ran ten steps or so, shielding his eyes from the noon sun, getting his body under the ball. Just as he had for the past thirteen years of his life and as if he had been doing it everyday that spring, Ambrose caught the ball for out number three.

It was only a first round game, with two more to go but the excitement which ensued, players running onto the field, fans standing in unison, cheering at the top of their lungs made it seem as if it were the greatest play of all time. Ambrose stood tall as he was mobbed by his teammates, his hat falling off from the pounding, allowing his head to be rubbed by more than one of the fellas. Later that day he would feel the affects of this friendly mauling but for that moment, it was the greatest feeling in the world.

During the next two games, both of which Eldorado went on to win, securing their back-to-back run, Ambrose didn't play. He cheered and talked, running onto the field in the celebratory dog pile. He soaked in the moment, posing for pictures with family and friends loving his fortune. A reporter from the local newspaper pulled Ambrose aside hoping to get a story about the young man and his tribulation. Through all the questions, mostly about him, many about the Championship, Ambrose talked only about his friends and all they had accomplished. Never once did he use the word "I." Words like "we" and "team" were always in his sentences. Finally, as the reporter got the message, asking what he looked forward to most, Ambrose did talk about himself, and then excused himself to hug his mother.

"I look forward to the best summer ever, playing ball with my friends."

Chapter 34

As the weather warmed, inching closer to summer, so had John's emotions. Though the spring months were spent coaching players who weren't the ones he looked forward to most, it was still coaching which always helped increase his self worth. Early on, Todd had been playing for the freshman baseball team and Tim the JV and later the Varsity. That meant limited practice time with the Little League team. Not that those two needed it. Every ball player knows the need practice, which they were getting with the High School, the just didn't need time with the team.

As they did most years it seemed, the league had changed team names, as they had received a large donation from a former player there and Albuquerque legend now employed by the Los Angeles Rams of professional football. The Dodgers, complete with spring training replica jerseys now adorned the shoulders of John's team. New players wore the name as well. Most notably a boy named Justin whose family had moved from the Valley in an attempt to improve their son's academic outlook on life.

It was Justin who had pitched such a great game against Roadrunner when the boys were thirteen, taking them to the last inning before losing. John knew this and had also known of the upcoming move. A phone call had let Justin and his family know that John would do all he could to get Justin on his team also improving the possibility of Justin making the All star team which would help their pitching depth immeasurably. It probably wasn't above board to do that sort of thing but John's sole motive in life was to give his boys and Ambrose the best possible chance at reaching their dream, even if it meant soiling his integrity to do it. The boys were worth it.

Little League rules state that a player must participate in half the games actually played in order to be eligible to take part in the All-star tournament. This brought into question Ambrose's ability to play. By the time school let out and the summer began which was the tail end of May, left only twelve games left for Ambrose to get his ten in as the season was twenty games total.

So the remainder of the regular season went, though any of the boys participating or parents watching could tell there was something missing. The joy of the game didn't seem to be there. The normal sense of competition, both friendly and not so friendly no longer resonated through the complex. It was baseball but there seemed no joy in Mudville.

While everything was as it should have been in the younger age groups as well as the softball, the fourteens and fifteens just didn't click. It was always tough at that age as so many of the best players were splitting their time between High School and Little League but now those same boys were playing without their best friend, without their compass. John, who could always raise the ire of opposing coaches, now went about his business as if it were just that, a job. No comments, no trickery to make his all too well known statements. He too felt the sadness of missing his friend. The entire family was struggling to make it through.

Finally, the first week of June, Ambrose felt strong enough to get back out to playing ball. An angel must have looked down upon them, weeping perhaps, as two weeks of on again off again rain caused four rain outs, games of which Ambrose would have missed but now could play in, allowing him to be eligible for the All star tournament. No one would have even thought twice about someone looking down if not for rain delay during a game between the team John coached and the one Ambrose played for.

With Ambrose standing on third base, a cloudburst caused the teams to leave the field. Ambrose ran into the dugout with John, Tim and Todd. With the rain beating down on the cement roof, water dripping down like a wall in front of them, all four stood on the bench to keep their feet from getting wet. Ambrose brought up the taxi driver from two summers earlier.

"Coach, do you remember that cab driver, Angel?" Ambrose half yelled to be heard over the rain.

"Sure, he was looking out for us that day." John responded, wondering where this might be going.

"You think maybe another angel is looking out for us now, with all this rain, making it easier for me to get all the games in I can?" His brown eyes were wide open as he spoke, allowing his coach to see all the hope the young man had inside.

"You know Ambrose," John started, and then paused, as he needed to regain his composure just a bit. "If you hadn't said anything, I don't believe I'd have thought about it but I do think that maybe someone is looking out for you or us or…yeah, I think maybe there is." He smiled, looking out beyond the rain, to the sun, which was now fighting through the clouds. When the game continued, there was more energy, more enthusiasm, more…something.

That energy continued through the remainder of the season. People talked again, competitive banter returned between the coaches, John in particular. It was fun again; the dark cloud of doom, which had hung over for that short time were gone for good allowing the summer to finally heat up.

Chapter 35

It is in some men's nature to not allow them any amount of success. For whatever reason, they find a way to be self destructive in one way or another. John was a very good student through his school years, mostly due to his mother's urging and insistence that achieve a level of academics he was capable of. As a player, he had insisted upon that same level of achievement from himself and his team mates, then as a coach, anyone who watched him run a practice could see he demanded the same.

Kicking of dirt, hollering at the top of his lungs, occasionally throwing a bat or ball, all were theatrics he used to get the most out of his team. By this, their fifteen year old season, the boys who had been around John had become accustomed to those theatrics and often times would make friendly wagers as to what he might do that day. Todd, being a comic at times, would often mock his coach, when John wasn't around of course, doing quite a good imitation. They knew all he did was for them and not once did he mean it in a negative or belittling way.

However, for all he demanded of his players, John had that self-destructive nature. He had more than struggled to fulfill his academic requirement in college, leaving eventually to take his chances playing ball. After his playing days had finished, he refused to return to college to get a degree for whatever reason, even he didn't know himself. Even his personal life was a problem, never allowing him to care for someone he should then jumping into things with ladies he shouldn't. All he did, all he had in his life seemed to go bad and he knew it was his fault through whatever decisions he made. It never failed.

Now, with all he viewed at stake, John found time every day to look himself in the eye and tell himself not to self-destruct. Already he had made mistakes in life but not to let those mistakes affect the boys. He began his journey to work for the boys by making a promise to himself to take care of every detail. *It's the little things in life that matter* and now he meant to live up to that.

Just before the Fourth of July, the All-star team was selected. John again was fortunate to be selected by the players as coach, who in turn expected Justin and Derry to help again. Matt, Kyle H. and Chad didn't make the team, while the new boy, Justin, Chris and a single fourteen year old, Sean did make the team.

John's first order of business was to alter the traditional uniform of the league. For years, Roadrunner Little League had been seen in pinstripes of some sort for each level of their All-star teams. The young coach had liked this but now felt these older boys should stand out from everyone else. He had discovered that many of the previous year's uniforms had come up "missing" so new ones would have to be ordered. He took it upon himself, going down to an acquaintance of his who made uniforms and ordered a new set for the fifteen-year-old team. He also liked the way his team had been able to wear two different uniforms when they were thirteen so thought it would be nice if they could do so again. Again on his own, John found a sponsor who would pay for a second set of jerseys, tee shirts really, which the boys could wear as well. Finally, he redesigned the logo which had adorned the caps of the players for years, altering what had always been two, plain text letter "R" side by side between two stars to what was now two capital letter "R" in a script font. When all was said and done, the boys would have a set of white uniforms, Roadrunner in script across the front, a red jersey with the same two "R" on the left breast as on the new, solid red caps.

When the team arrived for pictures, along with all the other age groups, the new look was the talk of everyone. The other teams couldn't stop talking of how "cool" they looked and if they might get to wear them when they reached that age. The parents not only spoke of how nice they looked but how the cocky young coach was showing off again. Then, quietly but with obvious animation, the members of the league's board spoke of how John had gone out on his own and they weren't happy about it.

None of it mattered to John, as his entire focus was the team. He wanted them to have everything, to look great and feel great plainly, for the sole purpose of enjoying the final summer of their youth. It was all he wanted, all he had been able to think about for the past three years. Any consequences, he would face without worrying.

As the tournament grew closer, the intensity of practices seemed to pick up. Two years earlier, John had done most of the practices by himself, using Derry as best he could as Bryce was working. This year, Justin was around for everything, allowing John to pay more attention to detail in everything he did.

Ambrose's strength seemed to be returning little by little as well, giving new life to practice. The velocity of his pitches, coupled with balls jumping off his bat as they had before would bring cheers and comments from the fellas, which seemed to raise the level of enjoyment and intensity each time it happened. Everything seemed to be regaining a sense of normalcy, which felt good to the entire team and it's coaches. They could almost feel as if all this was right and just and maybe it was simply a bump in the road, which they needed, to remind them of all the good things they had. Baseball was bringing this "family" together again, this time even closer than they had been before.

One Tuesday afternoon, two days before their first tournament game, as an afternoon shower did it's best to cool the desert ground John received a phone call. He had been working for the High School still, which allowed him to have summers off meaning many of his days were spent playing golf with his assistant coach Justin. It was almost lucky that he was home to take the call.

On the other end of the line was a woman from a sports magazine, quite popular in the sporting nation, who had heard about a young man who was battling cancer but still found time to play ball and do all he could for his friends and school mates. She explained how amazing this story was because of the selfless nature the young man exhibited. She also spoke of how quickly and how often this story was coming up within the sporting community. No doubt much of it was due to the fact Ambrose's father was an NCAA baseball coach. In finishing, the woman asked if the magazine would be allowed to send someone to a practice in an effort to interview Ambrose. She also mentioned, in passing or maybe to grab the coach's attention that perhaps a nationally recognized sports program might be calling as well.

The young coach, who had learned quickly the rights and wrongs of interviews and "coach speak," gave his blessing if Ambrose was willing to do so. Of course, he had no idea why a fifteen-year-old boy would not want to have his fifteen minutes of fame but still didn't want to give a complete "yes" until he had spoken with his player.

After hanging up the phone, John paused to think of how excited he would be if it were he, at fifteen, who was being interviewed. He felt good for Ambrose. Then, as he picked up the receiver to call his player, he remembered something that had happened in Tucson three summers before.

A local newspaper had come to the first game of the Regional tournament that year, looking to do an article on Ambrose, his father and their return to Tucson. Ambrose had done the interview though reluctantly as he didn't want to be seen as anything but one more member of his team. In no way did he want to be seen as bigger than his teammates. Would he feel the same now? Maybe he would want to speak more about his struggle to fight Cancer. The coach made the call.

As he listened, Ambrose's heart raced, he was so excited, his team would be mentioned in a magazine he had been reading for years. Maybe a picture of the team, Kris or Kyle's name mentioned as well. He almost couldn't wait for John to finish talking.

"They want to come look at our team!" Ambrose's voice almost cracked as he spoke.

"I don't think so, Ambrose." the coach's voice softening so to let his player know to relax his excitement. "They want to talk to you. This article would be about you."

There was a silence on the other end of the phone as the reality sunk in. When he spoke again, Ambrose was quieter and matter of fact.

"If it's only about me, then no, I don't want to do it. If it's about the team then yes."

The coach responded, not really knowing what to say. "OK, I'll let them know, then I'll let you know. See you at practice."

Hanging up the phone, John stared blankly at the wall. What he had just heard, witnessed really, was one of the most incredible things he had ever known. A fifteen-year-old boy turning down a chance for a little bit of publicity, a small taste of fame in essence, for the respect of his friends. His team meant more to him than personal gain. Once again, a boy was teaching this man what parts of life were really important and how a truly "good" person should act.

By the time the two saw one another at practice, John had called the woman back, explaining to her what Ambrose had said and what he wanted. She was almost as amazed as the coach. Out of respect for the young man who was making such an impact, she agreed not to send anyone but left it open if he ever changed his mind. As the coach explained that to him, Ambrose smiled, "That's what you've preached to us, isn't it coach? Team first?"

John nodded and turned away to prepare for practice. He felt so small and yet so big. Ambrose was leading him to becoming a better person and still made him feel as if he were teaching Ambrose.

As the sun set against a sky completely empty of clouds, the boys left the field only one full day away from the beginning of all they had been waiting for. One more run at their dreams. One more run, together.

Chapter 36

Earlier in the day, Justin and John had played a casual round of golf. Not only could they kill time, the sunshine and stillness of the warm July day could ease any tensions. Tensions that only existed outside of their baseball world as the team they would match up against later that day had about as much chance of winning as the coaches did of hitting a hole in one before their round was over. Two years earlier, Roadrunner had beaten this same opponent forty-four to four, without any effort to run the score up. In fact, John had backed off in the second inning.

It was the perfect opponent for their first game. Confidence wouldn't be an issue but both coaches were curious as well as concerned to see how the boys would react, this being their first game together again. It also gave John a chance to pitch Ambrose, who was just gaining his strength back after all his medical procedures. Hopefully, an outing against an inferior team would give both Ambrose and the team more confidence in the young ball player's comeback. If he struggled, the team would be able to recover and overcome any adversity. The situation couldn't have been set up any better if John had done so personally. All they really had to be concerned with was how to take care of two hours between golf and baseball.

Three shadows, reaching like long fingers began to crawl over the backside of the third base dugout as game time approached. As it had two summers before, one of the tournament sites was Roadrunner Little League. John looked west, across the central area of the complex and over the smallest field toward the horizon. Everything seemed so calm, so quiet as it always did at five thirty in the evening. The world seemed to slow down; all the hustle and bustle that was life, slowed as if all that mattered then was family and time to reflect. The coach looked up, as the huge Cottonwood tree, which had stood in that same spot even when John was the same age, gave shade to both the home and visitor bleachers. Standing where it did would give more shade and even cool the visitor's side to the point that the end of the game might need pullovers.

Looking over it all, John felt like there was more activity than usual, even for the first game of a tournament, as cars pulled into the dirt parking area to the South of the complex. Fifteen minutes to game time and already the home side bleachers, newly painted red, already neared capacity. All the fields, four in total were still filled with teams practicing when usually, at that time of year, they were empty. Three lines, standing four to five people deep crowded in front of the concession stand as well. There were more people around than usual. The noise began to rise.

Somehow, word of mouth had spread that Ambrose would be pitching that evening. By the time the National Anthem finished, there must have been five or six hundred people, standing room only, as more and more arrived each minute. There was a loud murmur rushing through the crowd as the boys ran back to the dugout, John walked next to Justin commenting on the enormous crowd.

"Are you kidding me?" He asked with an almost laughing tone. Justin simply shook his head and smiled. Both men knew it was a moment to take in rather than ruin with words. Ambrose deserved this, even if he would have preferred it not to happen. A short speech and a quick team cheer had the team sprinting to their positions; Ambrose took a second to let them go before he started his walk. He exhaled, long and slow then out he trotted.

The ovation was amazing. Not quite as loud as the one he had received during the State High School, as there was a building for the sound to echo off of there. A chill ran up and down John's body, causing him to well up inside. Fortunately, the boys had given him a gift, a pair of sunglasses that he wore, covering his eyes. All these people, not only from the league and the close community but from all over the city, stood cheering together for the fifteen year old boy, standing on the mound in front of them, who's first pitch sailed to the backstop, nerves, tears in his eyes, keeping him from seeing where he was throwing, who knew. It didn't matter. The same chill his coach had felt moments before now ran all over Ambrose.

Finishing his warm up pitches, Ambrose took the ball from Kris after the throw down to second. He paused, taking in the moment. Looking around at first base where Bret stood tall, then to Todd, Kris and Kyle. Tim, Jason and Steve looked back at their friend from the outfield, dressed in their white pants and red tops. This was his place, Ambrose's sanctuary. Nothing was wrong with him there, no sickness, no disease, and no worries at all.

Remembering a line from a favorite book, a line he had always wanted to utter, Ambrose toed the rubber, peering in at Brad. "Do your worst." He said to himself, referring to life and all it might throw his way. He had no fear. Time to play baseball.

John removed Ambrose from the mound in the fourth inning. There was no need to have him continue as the game was well in hand and the pitcher seemed to be tiring. At the time of his removal, when John allowed Sean, the fourteen year old to finish, the team led twenty six to one and it wasn't that close.

After walking the first batter he faced, Ambrose proceeded to strike out the side and five of the next nine batters. In fact, the only ball put in play by the other team was a bunt to sacrifice one of the runners that Ambrose had walked. To go along with his stellar pitching performance, the kid went three for three hitting with two singles and a double. His first at bat was a single, which again drew a standing ovation from the crowd.

A line of people, stretched around the field like a human picket fence cheered the young man. Justin pointed out to Bret and Kyle, who sat next to him, a father holding a toddler, maybe two years old, who clapped her hands just like everyone else. As Ambrose walked off the field, exhausted from his effort, his eyes welled again. Not from hurt or fatigue or even the overwhelming thought of what he had just accomplished. Rather, it was because of his love for the game and his team, which not only could be felt now but seen as well. He reached the dugout, those teammates not in the game at the time greeting him at the steps, engulfed Ambrose in a small group hug. A more memorable moment could not be thought of by anyone present that evening. Not that it mattered, final score, forty four to four.

Three more games had the fellas once again in the championship. Now, with the confidence Ambrose was near to his old self, the boys made short work of their opponents. John knew Ambrose was nowhere near one hundred percent but didn't want to let the boys know any different. He saw Ambrose gasp for air between bases. He watched while Ambrose rubbed his hands up and down on his knees trying to make whatever pain he was feeling go away. No, Ambrose wasn't his old self but his willingness to overcome and not allow anyone to see how much he hurt made his coach reach a new level of admiration for his young player. John would never betray Ambrose's heartfelt masquerade.

Ambrose was forced to miss that third game, slowing the team's momentum just a bit. Not because he didn't feel well but rather because he had an appointment with the doctor's for another treatment, which couldn't be rescheduled. The treatment took so much out of the young man; he simply wasn't able to play. Without much enthusiasm, the team won the game, putting them into the championship, a game that Ambrose would not miss for the world.

Again, in front of a huge crowd, Roadrunner battled to win that championship game. A tough minded North Valley team started a pitcher who showed as much courage as his opponent, taking the field with a deformed arm, which he had been born with. Just as had been the case two summers before, Roadrunner trailed late in the game, needing heroics to finish it off.

After jumping out to a one nothing lead in the first, The fellas seemed to back off, as if the game was in hand and it was only a matter of time before North Valley fell apart. Not the case, their hard fighting opponents took the lead in the fourth when they turned three singles into two runs.

The team seemed to lack the killer instinct they had shown in earlier games. John thought maybe it was the fact Ambrose had missed the last game and the boys had bigger things to deal with than a baseball game. John's intuition proved to be right when Ambrose pulled the team in to give a pep talk before they hit in the fifth inning. Neither coach heard what 'Brose had to say but it must have worked. The team's response made both coaches think it was a case of the boy's minds being elsewhere.

Todd led off that inning with a rocket of a line drive right at the left fielder for out number one. It was the first hard hit ball in four innings for the team. Kris followed with a hard single up the middle, which rattled the pitcher who walked Tim on four straight pitches. Ambrose, who was clearly tired from the treatment two days earlier, grounded weakly to short for the second time in the game. Fortunately, the ball was hit so slowly, both Kris and Tim advanced to third and second safely. Bret strode to the plate. It seemed that Bret had reverted back to his old self, struggling to hit during the All-star tournament. What John thought he had fixed in Tucson now was broken, again.

The North Valley coached called for time, wanting to talk with his pitcher, the breather game John time to ask Justin if he should pinch-hit for the left-hander. Both Steve and the new boy, Justin were available for hitting. The younger coach didn't hesitate at all in answering "No" causing John to pause. He really had felt it was time to hit for Bret and that his assistant would agree. Justin's answer threw him. Hands on his hips, the twenty something coach stared off into the now eye level, huge, orange sun.

By the time he came to any sort of conclusion, the time out was over and Bret stepped in to hit. Ball one, ball two, right away, Bret had things in his favor. Maybe it would be all right. The next two pitches, both right down the middle, luke warm fastballs, Bret looked as if he'd never swung a bat before, taking one and missing badly on the other. As he was prone to do, John turned and walked away from the batter, letting him fend for himself. John then knelt, grabbed a handful of dirt and waited.

Kris led from third and Tim from second. Any ball hit, John would be scoring Tim who ran well so the game would change, if only Bret could do his part. Sure enough, just as baseball always seems to do, when you've got it all figured, something else happens. Bret smoked the next pitch to the right-center gap, scoring both runs and changing the lead. Ambrose waited until the rest of the team went to greet the two who scored then walked out next to his coach at third. He high fived John then motioned to Bret who was already looking at him. A thumb up was the signal, to which Bret tipped his helmet. The game was now in hand.

It's not often a game can be in hand with only a one run lead but after Ambrose's speech, which no one ever found out what exactly was said, there was no way the team would let him down. Sure enough, Kris finished the game striking out four of the last six and not allowing a runner to reach base.

When the celebrating ended, this year with much less excitement, the team headed to the nearby old fashioned burger shop. There was a sense of "matter of factness" about the team or maybe it was more a sense of "this is wonderful but we have found that there are bigger things in life than this" whatever it was, it was good but not overdone. It was a good thing, for the team, for the coach, for Ambrose. After all, this is what he had been looking forward to for so long.

Usually, at least in the three previous years in which his teams had won, John draped himself in the championship banner. Flags of large size, adorned with red, white and blue lettering, recognizing the champions at each level of play. While sitting at dinner, enjoying an old fashioned burger, John took the flag off his own shoulders and draped it over 'Brose's. "You deserve this kid." The coach said, winking as he spoke.

"Thanks coach," Ambrose replied, his voice hoarse from yelling and all he had been through during the week, "you know I love you, don't you."

His eyes welled up and his throat tightened as he tried to respond. "I do, Ambrose, we all do."

Chapter 37

When the boys were thirteen, John had implemented a rule, when anyone was hit by a pitched ball or a ball took a bad hop, striking them anywhere, all the boys were allowed to do was grab a handful of dirt, rub it on the spot and move on as if nothing had happened. *Never let your opponent know you are hurt.* It was something he had learned early on as well. Now, with the boys being fifteen, John had not even thought about that rule because the boys wouldn't let anyone know they were hurt anyway. It wouldn't be cool or they might be embarrassed.

On the last day of practice, before the team was to leave for the State tournament, John sat in the dugout with both Derry and Justin, watching their team warm up, discussing possible match ups and pitching rotation. Of course Derry, bless his heart, had all kinds of wild theories to pass on, all of which John pretended to take out of respect and love for his friend but really had no intention of using. Justin knew he didn't know as much about the game as John so he only offered minimally, realizing he had given his input for the month when he insisted Bret hit in the championship game. After a short while, the boys were loose and headed into the infield for ground balls. Derry took the outfielders while John and Justin took the infield. John would hit to the left side, third base and shortstop, while Justin hit to the right side. After ten or so ground balls, while Kyle and Ambrose switched off after every other one, John saw Ambrose standing behind Kyle, grabbing handfuls off dirt and pouring them over his head and body.

"Looks like Ambrose has another joke to tell." John mentioned to Justin between swings, motioning with his head for Justin to look. Peering down at third, Justin saw the same thing, Ambrose grabbing handfuls of dirt and dousing himself with them. Not wanting to get sucked into one of 'Brose's comic ploys, both coaches let it go, waiting to see what the practical joker would do next.

After fifteen minutes or so, as the players scrambled to pick up all the balls they had just fielded, no punch line was evident so John walked over to his third baseman that was gathering balls down the line. When he got there, a dust covered player looked up at him.

What John had intended to ask had something to do with cats and sand boxes but when he and Ambrose's eyes met, he forgot everything. Ambrose had mud caked on his face, under his eyes and nose from where the dirt had mixed with his tears, sweat and mucus under his nose. It was obvious Ambrose had been and still was crying. Softly, to himself so none of his teammates would know.

A feeling of panic raced through the coach's body, "Ambrose! What's wrong?" He said it loud enough and with enough in his voice that Ambrose knew right away his concern but not so loud as to attract the other players.

"Coach," Ambrose said, half coughing, half gagging as he had so much crap in his mouth, "you have always said, if it hurts, not to complain but just rub dirt on it and go on with your business." John looked dumbfounded as he strained to remember Ambrose being hit with a ball. "Well, it hurts right now, it hurts real bad." For a brief second, Ambrose began to break down but just as quickly; he regained his composure, shaking himself to clean up a bit.

Not knowing what to say, John stood, his mouth agape, hand on his player's shoulder. "Ambrose, I meant on the field, what you have going on, I mean…anytime you need to, anytime you have to…" He felt stupid and shameless.

"I don't want the fellas to know, ever!" The boy's lips were trembling both with anger for his situation and pain in his body. "They need to see me be strong so they will be strong when they have to face something in their life and I am on the field!"

Both young men smiled and sort of laughed at Ambrose's statement. No matter how dark his situation and now obviously no matter how bad he felt, Ambrose could make someone smile, all the while thinking of anyone but himself. It made John, once again; shake his head in disbelief and amazement. After several minutes, John finally, with the threat of Ambrose losing playing time, convinced Ambrose to take a break, get his medicine and relax in the shade of the dugout. Before too long, the entire team sat or lay in the cool of the brick dugout. The desert sun beat down all around them but they felt nothing. Known for working the boys as hard as they could go, even John could feel it was one of those times, a moment to enjoy. Justin used his father's key to the concession stand where each boy filled a cup with ice and another with ice and whatever soft drink they enjoyed most. Returning to the dugout, the boys sprawled out, in some cases lying on top of one another listening to chirping of the katydid bugs in the nearby trees. Baseball could wait until tomorrow.

Every time Ambrose spoke so selflessly or showed such maturity, John came just a little closer to the realization that it wasn't the boys he wanted to change it was himself. Yes, he wanted to have an impact on the boys and help them to realize that in life, there are no excuses. There are reasons but not excuses. It had bothered him so greatly when he would hear a parent or player make an excuse for poor effort or a lack there of. Bothered him to a point of anger. Now, as he watched this young man battle and make no excuses, never once asking "why me?" the coach realized it was his own self he was angry with, disappointed in and fed up with. All those mornings he woke to a dark cloud overhead; they were his own fault, his own doing. He couldn't allow this to continue. As he led the caravan of cars along Interstate twenty-five toward Hatch, New Mexico, he realized it was time to grow up, to move on, past the dream of playing the game and accept the responsibilities of life. A boy had taught him that. The boy sleeping in the seat behind him as they rolled into the Southern part of the state.

"Thanks Ambrose." John said almost to himself, his eyes moving from the road to the rear view mirror and back.

"What's that?" his young assistant coach asked, waking in the co-pilot's seat.

"Just thinking about the next couple of days. Go back to sleep, we still have an hour or so. I'll wake you when we get to the State Tournament."

Chapter 38

With the exception of Albuquerque, Las Cruces and the area around Alamogordo and Carlsbad, where the caverns and white sands are, towns in New Mexico have almost nothing to do. Deming was no different. Of course, there were the "world famous" duck races they held annually but those weren't until September. As the caravan pulled into the brand new hotel, really it looked like a motel as everything was a single story high and cars pulled up in front of the rooms, the boys noticed the one thing that could be their savior, a pool centered in the middle of the complex.

Piling out of the cars, moans from stretching and the realization that it would be a long week of video games and cable television could be heard. John and Justin took care of registering, putting the boys in two groups of three and two groups of four. As he had in the past, John wanted to make sure the boys knew they were there to play baseball, not go on vacation. He would be in charge of one group of seven, Justin the other. The boys changed and jumped into the pool. It was a hundred plus day temperature wise and they didn't play until two tomorrow so the coaches gave them a half an hour.

Evening came, along with a short sprinkle of rain. The evening did very little to cool the day but the rain did the job quite nicely. The boys and coaches piled into two vans then headed over to the pre-tournament picnic as it was called this year. Three long tables, covered with burgers, hot dogs, buns and all the things that went with them, stood under a large canopy. Teams that were already there sat on the bleachers, in dugouts or stood around in between.

Word had traveled around the state of Ambrose's health. Instantly, he was a celebrity, teams and parents approaching him or the coaches to ask if he would be bothered is the asked him about himself. Of course the young man loved to talk and never hesitated when his sickness was brought up. He smiled and laughed, making light of an otherwise dark situation. It was amazing to see. It was as if a teenaged Pied Piper had come to town, playing his flute quite loudly.

The party lasted only a short while, as teams needed to get settled and rested before the start of the tournament. It seemed, because of their meeting this evening, there would be little rivalry between any of the teams this year. Athletes always look to find competition and rivalries tend to heighten competition but with as many players and coaches who talked with Ambrose that evening, it was understood that the games would be played, hard as they ought to be but that would be all. All the hand shaking and back patting foreshadowed a "gentleman's" competition. Perhaps.

By three o'clock the following day, Roadrunner was comfortable in knowing they would advance to the second round of the tournament. Again, Ambrose pitched the first game, dominantly, allowing no runs through six innings before giving way to the fourteen year old. While the town of Deming gave no reason for excitement, the tournament did offer something new. The field it was played on was also the High School field, meaning for the first time in their Little League lives, they were playing on a regulation-sized field. They had played, during their own High School season on one but not during the summer. Also, the infield was Astroturf just like some of the big league fields they saw on television. That small detail made what otherwise might have been a boring tournament, suddenly have a little life.

Finishing off their opponents, the team drove a short while, as that's all there was to the city, looking for somewhere better than fast food to eat. With no luck, they stopped for burgers before returning to the hotel. While they sat, finishing their meals, it was agreed that they would go somewhere better the following night as they were all tired of burgers. They laughed and joked, relaxed to say the least before they piled in the vans to get back to the hotel. While they were still eating, John had noticed Ambrose chewing very delicately when he chewed at all. When he threw away his trash on the way out, John noticed that more than half his food was left. The coach said nothing, knowing Ambrose would let him know if anything were wrong.

The team sat, feet dangling in the pool, under the stars that night. It was a comfortably warm night and again, they didn't play until seven o'clock the next night. The coaches let the boys swim if they wanted but the boys themselves decided not to swim but rather to relax. Brad and Steve had run across the street to a convenience store, when they returned, they each had a glass bottle of some drink never before heard of, "Doc Holiday's Sarsaparilla." One would have thought these two boys had discovered something from another planet when everyone tried a sip. It was the biggest thing since "suicide" drinks, where a person put a little of every soft drink into their cup. Really, it was a "Dr. Pepper" knock off but you couldn't tell the boys that. Two or three at a time, the fellas ran across the street to get one for themselves. Sure that the caffeine would have them up for hours, John put the boys in their rooms and told them to relax, hoping the sight of beds would over come.

By nine the next morning, several more trips across the street had been made, each room having an abundance of the empty bottles standing on night stands and dressers. The boys had discovered that these glass bottles could be refunded at the convenience store for fifteen cents. Of course, most bottles have refunds but this being the nineties, most drinks came in plastic bottles. It was more than fascinating as the boys collected from one another and even looked in nearby trashcans for more. They wouldn't have to pay full price for the drink they now enjoyed so greatly. The parents who were there as well as the coaches just shook their heads and chalked it up to boys being boys.

Shortly after noon, in the room next to John's, the one he was in charge of with four boys, Ambrose, Kyle, Kris and Jon, a shout rang out. It was loud enough to startle and concern the coach who shot out his door to see what was going on. The door to the room was open, as the boys were always coming and going, allowing John to see Ambrose and Kris holding Kyle down with one arm each and of all things, tickling him with their free hands. Kyle's face was bright red from the struggle and the continuous laughing he and the other boys were doing. Upon seeing his coach Kyle caught his breath and begged for help.

"Coach, coach, you've gotta help me!" Laughing again as he finished his plea.

"What is going on?" The coach asked, leaning against the doorway, crossing his arms and smiling, as the sight was too much not to smile at, "Ambrose?"

"I have never heard Kyle swear coach, you know, a curse word?" He grunted in trying to hold Kyle down. "I really want to, just to make sure he can do it." He turned his face back to Kyle "Even I have said a bad word or two."

Of all the things these boys had done, this one was as funny as any of them. Here, the nicest, most religious and selfless of the fellas was holding down another to make his say a bad word. The coach guessed things could have been worse and also realized how close the boys were, knowing it was all in fun, so he looked at Kyle, "Better come up with one fast." turning and leaving the room. From behind him, he heard Kyle yell a word, definitely one on the "mom wouldn't approve list" though not one of the better words, thereby ending the holdout and allowing the room to return to normal. As he walked back into his own room, John could hear all three boys break out in hysterical laughter, one of them even falling off the bed to the floor. It seemed to the coach the boys had found a cure for the boredom of Deming.

A pleasant but too long to be appreciated by ballplayers, rain shower delayed the start of the game that night. There is something different and exciting about playing at night. The ball seems brighter, though only the top half of the ball is illuminated. Velocity seems higher balls appear to travel farther. It is as close to playing the game with his heroes as a boy can get. From that point of view, the delay didn't bother the fellas but having to wait longer after such an exciting day was almost too much to bear.

Whether it was the lights or the delay or just being together, the game took on a life of its own. It was arguably the most fun the team had since the tournament started, everyone but Tim. He seemed to have a chip on his shoulder but it was apparent the boys were trying to look past it. With the game close, in the sixth inning, there still was no sign of tension in the New Mexico dugout. Bases loaded, two out and up by only one run, six to five, Bret stepped in. Ever since the double in the City Championship, the lefty had been on a roll. Now, the team needed another shot in the arm.

Bret worked the count full then fouled off a tough pitch, the ball sailed high into the night sky but not out of play. Plenty of room allowed the opposing catcher to settle under it. It seemed to be so simple a play that John began to walk back toward the dugout, watching the catcher as he took his first steps. One moment, the catcher looked comfortable, the next, his feet moved, his body wavered, it would not be so easy a play and sure enough, the ball hit on the edge of the catcher's mitt, bouncing off to the ground giving new life to Bret's at bat.

One thing John had always preached, as a coach was to *never* give an opponent a second chance by failing to make a routine play. Murphy's law stated that if you did, the next batter would hit a double. On the next pitch, Bret didn't hit a double but instead launched a ball so far into the right field night that no one ever saw the ball bounce. Gasps and ahhhs came from the crowd, an impressive swing to say the least. It was that series of events which sealed the game for Roadrunner. The other team could feel itself having a chance until that ball was dropped and the next hit somewhere across the border. What had been fun and relaxed in the Roadrunner dugout remained relaxed but now had a "killer instinct" about it.

On cue, Tim mowed down the next three batters on ten pitches, showing a brief second of joy as he skipped over the foul line on his way back to the dugout. No one said anything, not even pats on the back, as none of the fellas knew how to approach their teammate. It wasn't until four batters into their half of the seventh that they found a way to embrace their friend. Again with two outs, this time only two runners on base, Tim drew a count of three balls and no strikes. Usually, a coach has his player take the next pitch, hoping for a walk or at the very least, to make the pitcher throw more pitches. Not this coach. He knew Tim was itching to show off his ability, not so much as to show up Bret but to equal his teammate. Looking down at his coach, Tim expected the take sign but instead saw John put both hands on the bill of his cap and push them off toward the batter. It was the sign to swing away. A quick smile shot across Tim's lips, followed by a look of determination. As the next pitch neared the hitting zone, John could feel his own body tense, anticipating something big. Bret swung the bat left-handed, Tim swung from the right side. Since they were eleven years old, it was these two who always hit the home runs, a sort of game of one on one. With a smooth swing, Tim drove a rocket into left field. Bret's ball was lifted but had a bit of a line drive trajectory; Tim's ball was higher, more majestic and almost as far. Behind left field there was a short width of grass, a sidewalk, a street, another sidewalk and the backside of the football stadium. Tim's ball hit the backside of the football stadium.

As he rounded third, it was all he could do not to smile, slapping his coach's hand as he went by. He finally did crack when his teammates at home plate, slapping his head and backside as they returned to the dugout, mobbed him. A voice from behind him caught John's attention. It was the Deming coach.

"Coach, I've been here for eight years now, watching my teams and all the teams we've played. Never have I seen balls hit like those two your team just hit and they're only what, sophomores?"

John smiled, "Going to be sophomores."

A "proud papa" feeling came over John. While he couldn't take credit for ability like that, he sure could be proud of them. For three years now he had been with Tim and Bret, more than any of the other boys. It felt good to see them succeed.

Tim didn't throw his best game and still dominated their opponents. It was more his attitude than his ability that kept the game close. The players around him didn't want to play for him as his attitude was all about him, not them. It was a difficult situation for everyone. The moment near the end of the game helped to break whatever ice had built up. Hopefully, it would continue from there.

Returning to the hotel, everybody else wanted to slide into the pool as they had the night before. Tim chose to call his family and his girlfriend, who he talked with for nearly two hours. When he finally finished, he slumped into a chair, shaking almost uncontrollably. He cried, gently from all the overwhelming feelings he was overcome by. He wasn't selfish, he wasn't angry. He was confused and scared only he couldn't tell anyone, not even John. For years, he had felt like everyone relied on him to carry the team. Ambrose's presence took all that pressure away and now it was back. Beyond that, he felt like he was losing a friend, someone who made him push himself to be better, as a player and person. What if Ambrose didn't beat this? What would he do then?

Not wanting anyone to see him like this, he jumped into the shower, taking his time so that all his emotion could be put away. He would try again tomorrow to be a better guy, to open himself up. He would try anyway.

Only two games stood between Roadrunner and a return to the Regional Tournament where they had battled two years before only to come up short. One of those games would fall later in the day, again at seven o'clock. John wanted to get the boys something better to eat than the usual fast food so he had scouted the town looking for a suitable restaurant. On the far end of town, a total of six miles, he found a Mexican food establishment that he thought would be better than the usual. Returning to the hotel, he gathered the boys to explain the plan. They would dress in their collared shirts and shorts around four, head off to eat, returning to the hotel to change around five thirty, pitting them at the field by six or just after.

As the boys went off to change, some grumbling could be heard, as many of the boys didn't care where they ate they just preferred to make it quick in order to get ready for the upcoming game. While the coaches changed, a knock on the door had Ambrose standing on the other side.

"What's up kid?" John asked, pulling his shirt over his head.

"Can I talk to you a second?" Ambrose asked, almost sheepishly, a far cry from his usual manner.

Shutting the door behind, John sat his player down with only himself and Justin in the room with Ambrose. A sense of fear began to creep up from inside.

"I know you want to take us somewhere nice to eat." Ambrose began, "I would like that myself coach, but can we just go for fast food tonight?" Then quickly added, "Just tonight?"

John looked at him with a questioning look. Before he could speak, Ambrose continued.

" I have cold sores all over the inside of my mouth, making it really painful to eat." John recalled dinner the night before. "I don't want the fellas to know I'm hurting or get any special treatment, but if we go for fast food, I can mix a protein shake here but put it in a fast food cup, making it look like I'm eating just like they are. Can we do it just tonight?"

John looked at Justin who, for the first time since John had known him, had the look of a boy. It was clearly John's decision, not that it was a difficult one.

"Of course we can, tell the team."

A smile so wide John could count every tooth in his mouth crossed Ambrose's face. He jumped up and darted out of the room, small cheers rose from the rooms down the way. It seemed that more than a few players wanted to eat fast that night.

As he predicted, not a single question nor inquisitive look rose from his team mates as Ambrose drank his meal as the other boys ate theirs. Just one of the guys, Ambrose made sure to make eye contact with his coach during the meal. They said nothing but they understood one another perfectly. The boys needed to be unaware for their own good. Ambrose needed this for normalcy and to have a night where he wasn't fighting but simply living. The coach needed it to learn and to grow.

The fast food must not have sat too heavy as the team rolled again, defeating the host team from Deming, coached by the resident High School coach. The match-up reminded John not only did he have probably the most talented group of players on one team, ever to come through Albuquerque but that he was a pretty fair coach. While he may have begun his coaching career as a cocky young man, what he had witnessed that summer had helped to mold him into a confident but humble person. It was a pleasant reminder that he was good at what he did. He would always need to be reminded not to be cocky and that he was good. Everyone does. One more game and they would once again be State Champions. One time is hard enough; to duplicate the feat is a chore unto itself. No motivational speech, no movie where the underdog wins out in the end, just a good night's sleep and a game to play tomorrow.

The young coach was famous for wanting to wear the nicest uniforms, preferably all white in championship games. It was a statement, he felt, for the good guys always wore white. Having watched the weather the night before, he knew the temperature was supposed to reach into the hundreds. With the game starting at eleven in the morning, an odd time to say the least, John didn't want his players worrying about how hot it was on the field. The mental side of the game always equals the physical side, reminding him of a line from one of his favorite movies, *"If a player thinks he's playing well because he's wearing women's underwear, then he is!"* Normally, John wouldn't even give a second thought to what the boys wore, he had played in the same New Mexico heat before people became concerned with how hot the players might get. He had never felt the heat; he was always lost in the game, not in what he had on. However, he had played games on an Astroturf surface before. The material absorbed the heat of the sun and held on to it, raising the surface temperature fifteen to twenty degrees more than the temperature outside. For these reasons, the boys wore their red tee-shirt jerseys. It didn't matter what they wore. The next two and a half hours were only a formality.

Bret absolutely controlled the championship game from beginning to end, allowing only seven hits through his seven innings of work. With two outs and a lead of eleven runs, John became bored with the game and wanted to end it right then. Tiring, Bret had given up two hits and a walk, leading to a run and runners on second and third. John stood up, called out to his fielders, circling his finger over his head. As they had in Tucson, the team was preparing to run the "Miami" play, hoping to end the game. Some could argue it was unnecessary and even unsportsmanlike but just like his players; John was tired of Deming and wanted to go home.

Bret came set; taking a deep breath, then stepped off, pretending to throw to third. Ambrose half slid, half fell as if there really were a ball to catch, everybody went running. Like a fish chasing a worm, the runner at third bought the story hook, line and sinker, putting his head down and jogging for home. The look on his face was priceless when he looked up to find Bret in the middle of the baseline with the ball in his hand. Out number three, two-time State Champs.

There was jumping and high fives, but the celebration was minimal. Partly due to the team's expectations, they knew they should have won, partly due to the long week in such an "exciting" place but it was becoming obvious that all the boys had been through in the last six months was beginning to take it's toll, mentally draining all of them. Still, no one said anything about it, nothing to take away from their accomplishment or their time together.

The team gathered for a photo, holding the banner in front of them. Brad and Ambrose knelt at the end of the front line, arms around each other. Kris, Steve and Bret held up fingers showing they were number one. Kyle and Todd each held an end of the Championship banner, Kyle showing off his all-American smile, Todd a smirk of confidence and joy. Tim stood next to assistant coach Justin, a real smile of real happiness on his face, while John stood on the other side of the group, one arm on C.J. the other on Bret. He smiled but it seemed almost as if he wanted to step away and let the boys have their moment together.

Yuccas and Tumbleweeds gave the coach something to look at as he drove the van Northbound on interstate twenty-five. Tim and Bret lay sprawled out across the two back seats, sleeping the sleep of teenagers. John always did his best thinking when he drove but this time, there was little to think about. Maybe there was plenty to think about but he just didn't feel like thinking. Instead, he remembered, playing back the highlights of the weekend in his mind. A backhand play by Kris, his throw bouncing off the turf just like the coach had taught him, the long home runs by the boys sleeping behind him, Ambrose's face as he asked to have fast food. These were images he would keep forever. The coach smiled, taking his foot off the gas pedal just a bit, so what if the trip home lasted a while longer, it could only be one more pleasant memory.

Chapter 39

Endless rows of bright, blinking lights, surrounded by the almost deafening sound of bells and whistles caught the attention of everyone as they entered the terminal in Las Vegas. Fourteen pairs of eyes were as big as baseballs, straining to take everything in. Heads jerked from front to back as hands patted backs gaining the attention of others to point at something new. For most of the boys, it was their first trip to Vegas and everything the coach had told them about was right there in front of them.

John gathered the entire group, all the players, his assistant and three parents, both of Tim's and the fourteen year old's mom had made the trip. Making sure everyone understood where they were headed and what to do if somehow a player got lost, John looked over his group of young men. All of them looked quite nice in pressed shirts, ties and well, as teens tend to wear, tennis shoes. John had always felt that people feel differently about themselves when they dress up. Whether it is for church or a family gathering, there is a rise in confidence and self-esteem when people look at themselves in the mirror to see how the nice outfit looks. John wanted them to have confidence and show their class. Only Todd looked "off" as he had made an attempt to show some style. He had a pressed shirt, a tie and even suspenders, along with shorts. To his credit, they were nice shorts, actually part of the outfit; unfortunately it gave Todd a leprechaun look. In an attempt to make him feel better, Brad told his friend that it reminded him of a picture his mom had of himself when he was two. One of many quick jabs Todd had taken throughout the day.

One of the coach's instructions, upon parental requests, was to make sure no one took any of the many flyers that would be offered to them as they walked through the airport or later on if they walked on "the strip." After explaining himself, turning to head to the luggage pick up, John turned to his assistant, "I guarantee it will be Justin." chuckling out loud as his assistant agreed.

The tournament was being held in Ely, Nevada, a town about four hours outside of Las Vegas. The team had decided it would be easiest to fly into Vegas and drive the final leg of the journey rather than attempt to drive the entire way. The biggest reason for the decision was lack of drivers and vehicles. Only a handful of parents would be able to make the trip at all and most of those wouldn't even make it until the end of the week, leaving John, Justin, one mom and Tim's parents as the only chaperones.

As the team waited for three rental vans, John looked around the terminal, smiling. Only months earlier, he and two friends had taken a weekend and come to the city that never sleeps. It had been his first trip to Vegas and he was as unknowing of how to gamble as he was of the city itself. Immediately, he had been enamored with the sights and sounds, unfortunately he had only fifty dollars for the weekend. Not fifty to gamble with, fifty dollars to pay his third of the hotel room, for food and to gamble with. Not exactly a promising venture.

Lady luck can smile on even the saddest dog, however. After watching his friend work a craps table for an hour or so, John was able to figure only one thing, the field. Playing the "field" meant betting that the numbers two, three, four, nine, ten, eleven or twelve would come up. In his amateur mind, John saw this as a pretty easy bet. That's why Vegas is as big and bright as it is, suckers like that. In a case of extreme beginner's luck though, John went to bed that first night with eight hundred dollars in his pocket and finished the weekend with over sixteen hundred. At one point he had even been as high as two thousand but made more than one stupid wager, bringing him down just a bit. His system was simple, whenever he got overly nervous, bet five dollars, as he gained more, he bet more, that simple. It was highly unlikely that anyone was as naive and yet won so much.

As young and arrogant as he was, John realized a person doesn't beat Vegas twice and certainly someone as green as him. He had no intention of gambling this time around, save a few quarter slots. The slots of course, had already garnered the attention of the boys, who asked John to pull a few for them as they fed him their spare change. John obliged for a few minutes while they waited. Only Jason was a winner this time, having two of his quarters turned into two dollars. It was fun but John didn't want the boys to get the wrong idea about gambling and definitely not get the gambling bug. He was always looking to make a good impression and teach good life lessons, even if he didn't always live up to them himself.

Two hours later, after a short drive to the hotel, a change of clothes and one more lecture on the consequences of poor decisions while out, the team was walking "the strip." John had wanted to see some of the street shows again and thought the boys would enjoy them as well. Starting at the Mirage and its volcanic eruptions, the group made it's way toward Treasure Island and the pirate ship. Not more than two blocks into their walk, John, from the corner of his eye, saw a hand reach out from the center of the group, taking a pamphlet on girls. "Justin!" was all John said, using his firmest tone and the pamphlet was thrown to the ground. The coaches looked at each other and smiled. There are things a coach comes to know about his players and who they are as a person. Justin was not a bad kid but John had never doubted it would be him who stepped on "the line." After the pirate show and several more blocks of walking, the team ate Fatburgers before heading to the hotel for the evening.

As they returned to their hotel, Ambrose and Kris caught up with their coach as he led the group back inside. Ambrose had heard many tales of "all you can eat" shrimp buffets. Everyone on the team knew of Ambrose's passion for seafood, so it came as no surprise to the coach when the two boys asked if they could eat at one on the way back through after the tournament. It reminded John of something he and his friends would have asked when he was their age. "Of course." He responded, knowing there would be plenty of time and there obviously was no harm in a shrimp buffet. A quick night's sleep and they would be off to the great metropolis of Ely, Nevada.

Chapter 40

Most towns have a movie theater. Most towns have several stoplights. Anyone who has ever traveled, driving around the country in a station wagon or mini-van knows that fast food can be found most any place and McDonald's exist everywhere. Everywhere except Ely, Nevada. A sign, just down from the hotel stated that a McDonald's would be built sometime later that year but for now, nothing. Ely, population four hundred or so, had only one stop light, hanging on two wires across the main street in town, a gas station, one sit down restaurant known as the Kountry Kitchen and a pop up trailer which, during the day, would serve slices of pizza. There was a movie theater, which had one movie and two showings a week, seven o'clock on Tuesdays and five o'clock on Saturdays.

On the bright side, there was a nice softball complex on the North end of town, three fields and a concession area all of which John wondered about as there couldn't be enough people in the town athletic enough, young enough or interested enough to field the six teams necessary to require three fields and finally, the railroad museum. A museum dedicated to the history of the railroad, which went through the center of town, two dollars admission, only open on weekends, total tour time, fifteen minutes. Come to Ely, Nevada and spend a year one week.

Fortunately, the town, not a city but town, was set in a beautiful area, surrounded by mountains. It was hot, but not miserable hot during the day and actually cool at night. The field the tournament would be held on was part of the middle school's property, as there was no High School in town, set up looking West, a wonderful sight as the sun would set, just over a rise of hills. Pine trees mixed with Cottonwoods surrounded the area. No doubt the crowds would be big as there was nothing else in town to do except go watch the baseball games. It was Monday, a dinner at the field was planned but the tournament wouldn't start until Tuesday. The flight home wasn't until six in the morning the following Monday. What kind of week would it be?

John had the boys wear their white uniforms to the dinner, as all teams were asked to dress for a formal introduction. It was five thirty and John had seen neither hide nor hair of another team. Thinking there couldn't be that many hotels in town, he half expected to be the only team there for the dinner.

Wrong again, as it turned out, the New Mexico team was the last of the teams to arrive at the gathering, except for the Arizona team, which didn't come at all. Word had it they were still traveling and wouldn't arrive until the next day. Surprised, John found that the Utah, Nevada and Arizona teams were exactly the same teams that had met in Tucson when the boys were thirteen. Surprised again, after receiving the tournament bracket, he discovered his team would be playing the Arizona team. Not that he was bothered, the coach, as well as his team had wanted another chance to play the boys from Tucson.

Acquaintances were reestablished, both coaches and players as the teams talked about what had happened in Tucson and what had happened during the year in between. Most of the players, coaches and parents had already heard of Ambrose's situation, which became a topic of quiet conversation amongst the adults. It was a night of good times for everyone, telling tales, eating what turned out to be a great meal of chicken and ribs and sharing what baseball was meant to be, a summertime game.

Two o'clock in the morning, John was awakened by the sound of a door slamming, loud talking and even some hollering. The Arizona team had arrived, deciding they weren't too tired from their trip to sleep quite yet and if they weren't ready to sleep, then obviously, no one else should have either. Bottles broke, beds were bounced on, and a door was thrown open so hard it cracked the stucco on the wall behind it, all before sunrise! As a person, John was unhappy and would speak with the hotel manager but as a coach, he hoped the boys in the room right next to the Arizona team, slept too deeply to hear anything.

As the boys gathered to venture out in hopes of finding a breakfast spot, the coach's hopes were shot down. Simply by looking at Kyle and Kris he could see they had gotten little sleep. Rather than fight it, John walked the boys to the Kountry Kitchen where they quickly ate, returned them to the hotel with orders to sleep if they could, as the Arizona team was now asleep so perhaps it would be a wash in the end. After all, the game wasn't until five thirty and there was nothing else to do in Ely.

Arizona wore the same baby blue and navy uniforms they had two years earlier. The same fourteen players made up the roster. Looking across the field though, every one of the New Mexico players felt there was something different about the team they were matched up against.

"They're the same size." John answered the question they were all asking.

John had seen it himself growing up, the Hispanic boys always seemed bigger and they were, when they were younger. Now, most of his team had at least caught up if not passed the Arizona team in size. What had once seemed like not only a great baseball team but also a humongous baseball team now looked quite average in size and really, in several ways.

Judging by their late arrival and propensity to stay up all night, it was obvious to the fellas this team didn't have a great desire to play their best game or probably their best tournament. They had won as thirteen year olds and someone had heard they did again at fourteen. Maybe they didn't care anymore, having reached their goals. This was definitely the time to knock them off.

Ambrose had asked to start the game pitching. From all signs, through the City and State legs of the tournament, he was physically able to make the start. The fact he wanted to pitch proved to John he was mentally ready. John looked down to the bullpen where his assistant Justin watched the bald headed right-hander warm up. He looked good, all things considered but for a moment, John could almost see what should have been. Another fifteen to twenty pounds, a fuller physique maybe more hop in his step. It was a horrible shame what this young man was going through, it made John so angry inside yet he couldn't show any emotion for it. Many months before, when all of this began to take it's course, the twenty four year old had decided he would be strong for all the boys, never letting them see his anger or distress or even his puzzlement. Questions about why God would let this happen to such a good person when there were so many bad people out there. Even himself, why couldn't it be him who was sick? He would have traded places with Ambrose in a heartbeat, no questions asked. Not only so the boy could live the life he deserved but because of John's own mistakes. Surely those mistakes were deserving of punishment more than anything Ambrose could have done. It just wasn't fair but if Ambrose wouldn't say it, neither would he.

Shortly, John composed himself, putting his mind back on the game at hand. Whether the Arizona team was smaller or not, there was no doubt they could play. It would take an entire team effort and a coach on top of his game to pull this one out.

The sun hung gently over the hills West of the field. A few puffy clouds gathered off to the North, pushed there by a soft breeze. The grass on the field was green for the most part but dry, after all it was still part of the desert, bases cut out from an otherwise solid pasture. Ambrose toed the mound as John had won the coin toss and elected to be the home team. Within the confines of the chain link dugout, the coaches and reserves looked on. "Play ball!"

Determination, unlike any John had ever seen before strained in the pitcher's face. Each pitch seemed to be a brush stroke of it's own, adding to a painting which was not yet finished. Strike outs, soft groundouts and can of corn fly balls were all the Arizona team could muster for the first three innings, while the team from Albuquerque did damage to the Arizona starting pitcher. It seemed to John the Arizona coaches remembered what kind of team they were up against from the previous meeting and had chosen to throw what looked to be there number two pitcher. John only assumed this as the best player on the team, from memory and position in the batting order was now playing shortstop. It was a sign of respect but the New Mexico coach hoped it wasn't enough. Six runs through three innings had Roadrunner ahead but it could have and really, should have been worse. Two base running mistakes had cost the team runs, probably two, keeping the total at six when it might have been eight.

In the fourth, Ambrose seemed to tire; giving up three runs but gathered himself to finish strong by striking out the last two hitters of the inning. Knowing he may run out of gas, John had Justin get Kyle ready, just in case but asked Ambrose how he was doing. His still determined face spoke volumes, as did his response. "I'm fine." Not so much the words but the way he spoke them let the coach know he was going back out and the coach would have to pull him off the mound, kicking and screaming. It was exactly what John wanted in a pitcher.

Quickly, John thought things over in his mind, the "what if's" of the game. If Kyle struggled, whom would he turn to? Tim was the obvious answer, knowing he would be unable to pitch the following day but as John had learned a long time ago, *you can't win it if you're not in it.* Which meant, win the game you're playing, no matter what it takes and worry about tomorrow, tomorrow.

Calling Tim over, John let the tall, handsome ace know he would be throwing if necessary and do whatever he needed to get loose. It was then, Tim let John know his arm was bothering him and had been since the day before when the team had killed some time throwing around a football. John was stunned at first, then bothered and before the player could walk away from him, furious. With the attitude he had been displaying throughout the summer, there was no doubt in John's mind this was some sort of ploy by the boy to either get out of pitching as he didn't want to work for his team anymore or worse, an ego driven response meaning Tim only wanted to pitch in the biggest game, not in a "mop up" roll. Either way, it seemed a selfish attitude to have. John wanted to explode, to yell and scream, just rail on the young man. Not here, not now. Instead, gritting his teeth, he walked to the coach's box at third base, mumbling to himself the whole way.

Again, his mind raced, what to do if Kyle didn't throw well, who was next? Before he could gather himself, Brad walked, Bret doubled and the merry go round was on again. Both scored on another double, this one off the bat of Ambrose. The Arizona coaches had seen enough, panicking just a bit, they went to their shortstop. John knew his team might not score too many more runs, particularly if the young man threw as well now as he did in Tucson. Calling his Ambrose from second and the next three hitters he talked with them about making sure to be productive with their at bats. He wanted to make sure the ball was put in play, no strikeouts. Move runners over if making an out. Do the little things. Score Ambrose and the game would be in hand was John's thinking.

Steve grounded out to second base, an out yes, but as his coach had requested it was productive, moving Ambrose over to third. Jason followed with another ground ball, this one to a deep playing shortstop, an out, which should have been productive, but Ambrose froze, not running on the play and not scoring. Of all the players on the team, of all the players he had coached, Ambrose was the last one John thought would make a mistake like that. Just a simple lapse but huge in the scheme of a game. Todd finished the inning by flying out to right field, no more runs, Ambrose didn't score.

A score of eight to three as the sixth inning started. Ambrose had done everything a coach could hope for in getting them to that point. He had battled, worked and demanded something from himself. It was a wonderful performance but a performance that had taken everything out of him. For six batters in the fifth inning, Ambrose fought some more. He managed to get two outs but a single and two walks had loaded the bases and drained him completely. As John made his way to get his pitcher he could see the shoulders slump and the energy leave his body. The closer he got, John could see his pitcher shaking, doing all he could not to breakdown.

"I'm sorry coach." Ambrose said as he handed the ball to John, put his head down and drug himself toward third.

Before handing the ball to Kyle, he took hold of Ambrose by the arm, turning the young man back to face him. "You never have anything to be sorry about. Never." His words were stern but as fatherly as he could make them. He then turned back to Kyle to instruct him.

After getting Kyle straight on what they wanted to do, John walked back toward the dugout, looking at Ambrose as he went. The body language said everything. There was no way to leave Ambrose in the game at that point. He boy had given everything and more, working himself to the point of exhaustion. John walked him off the field.

Those fans who were present, not as large a crowd as John expected, given the lack of entertainment in Ely, clapped loudly for Ambrose. Even the Arizona coaches, very much concerned with only their world clapped for their opponent. Chris and Jon met Ambrose outside the dugout to applaud him and help him to the bench if needed. Jon embraced his friend out of complete love as everyone around watched. As quiet as it was, the ovation was almost deafening.

Turning back to the field, John quickly learned that Kyle had nothing that night, giving up back-to-back doubles, a single and five runs before the coach could get his pitcher out of the game. Kris' pitching was better than Kyle's but the results weren't much better as an error and a miscommunication, which John deemed an error as well, allowed another run to score before the boys from Albuquerque could gather themselves and get off the field.

All the work and extraordinary effort given by their friend had been for naught. Anyone watching could see the wind actually leave the bodies of the boys on the field. John's first inclination was to explode, giving the boys all they could handle after letting Ambrose down but by the time the team gathered outside the dugout it was obvious, nothing the coach could say or do would make them feel worse than they already did. Had they not been strong young men, believing it wasn't right to cry, several of them would have broken down on the spot.

Composing himself, looking into his player's faces, John spoke in a calm, confident voice. "Focus up, go to work and I guarantee you'll remember how much fun this game was when you talk about things in a few years." He smiled, patting Ambrose on the head, "He's here for you, get it back for him now." the coach walked out to coach third. Behind him, he could hear the team come together as they often did. Would it be enough this time?

C.J. answered that question only minutes later, launching a ball way, way out to right-center field, tying the game and bringing the team back to life. Unfortunately, it was only a single lightning strike as the Arizona ace shut down the next three batters. Extra innings was the order of the day it seemed, only it was the team from further West who were up to the task

Kris was unable to keep the Arizona team off the scoreboard in the top of the extra frame. Two runs on three hits gave them an eleven to nine lead. Four batters in the bottom of the eighth and no runs gave them the win. An extremely quiet New Mexico team walked out to shake the winner's hands. Quiet in part because they knew the game had been theirs to win. Quiet in part because it had been two years in coming and they hadn't given their best effort but quiet for the most part because every young man wearing red and white felt as if they had let their friend and leader down. Heads drooped and shoulders slumped as the team packed up their things, emptying the dugout. John pulled his assistant aside asking if there was anything he should say. What was there to say? They all knew what had happened. They all felt badly about it. Maybe this time it was best just to say nothing. The coaches agreed, say nothing, talk about it tomorrow.

A trail of red dragged themselves across the playground of the middle school in the direction of the vans. As he always did, the coach counted heads as they headed out to make sure he had everyone with them. He counted only thirteen. Counting again and having Justin do the same, they came up with thirteen. John turned back to the field to see if one of the boys was just a ways behind, instead he saw a player sitting on the ground, head in his arms, knees pulled to his chest sobbing uncontrollably. It was number sixteen, Ambrose

Quickening his pace, John hurried to his player's side. Kneeling, he put his right arm gently across Ambrose's back. Dusk had arrived, softening the light and cooling the air, the first allowed caused the coach to peer through shadows as Ambrose raised his face, the second contributed to the boy's shivering.

"Do you feel OK?" John asked in a worried tone. Not knowing exactly what he would do if Ambrose's response was "No."

"It's my fault coach!" Ambrose said, saliva stretching across his mouth as he spoke. Sobbing hard again, "My fault we lost."

The young coach calmed himself knowing nothing was physically wrong, and then spoke in a hushed, comforting tone. "No, no, no. It wasn't your fault; it wasn't anybody's fault. You were amazing out there, things just didn't go our way." Tears began to form in his own eyes. "You can't blame yourself. No, no."

Ambrose snapped back almost yelling this time "It is my fault! If I wasn't sick, we'd have won and the team would be..." Wiping the spit from his mouth he tried again. "If I was healthy we'd be making plans for Florida. Because of me the team won't get there!" He sobbed harder, the coach pulling the fifteen year old to him. Under his arms, for the first time since he had been diagnosed, Ambrose questioned things. In a muffled tone, John heard him ask "Why me? Dammit, why me!"

"I don't know Ambrose, I don't know." It was all the coach could think to say, this time tears began to run down his cheeks. So many times he had asked himself and God the same thing. Why, just a half hour or so earlier, in fact. He wished so badly to have an answer at that moment, there simply wasn't one to give. Justin and two of the boys were walking back over from the cars; John waved them off, hoping they would take his hint. They did, stopping and waiting where they were.

Ten minutes or so passed, several parents and small groups passed, looking down at the two young adults embracing under the small tree. Most of the Utah team, playing out of the dugout twenty yards away looked back periodically. John noticed but couldn't have cared less. If Ambrose needed to stay there all night, he would stay with him. For all the strength and courage this boy had shown him and all those around them, he was due to break down. This was it. John knew it and would be there for him all the way through. Ambrose had stopped crying, and then shortly, raised his head, wiping his face on his sleeve. He paid no attention at all to the people or game going on around him. He looked at his coach, then out toward the vans where the team was waiting. Kris and Todd still stood with Justin, waiting as well. Ambrose looked back at his coach as if to say something but stopped, a half laugh snuck out, followed by five or six quick tears. He hugged his coach, grabbed his bag and headed off toward the vans. The two-team mates met him half way then each walked on a side as the three went together to meet the rest of the team. Justin, all of eighteen waited for John. "What did you say?" He figured what had happened but didn't know how he might have responded. He was curious as to what his friend said.

"What do you say?" John answered, looking straight ahead attempting to hold back more tears from himself. "What do you say to a fifteen year old kid who's dying?"

A team poll had decided not to even bother eating that night. It was only eight thirty or so yet everyone was tired. Emotionally drained, most likely. John let them hang around in one another's rooms until ten then insisted they go to their own rooms where they could stay up but make a good decision on what time to actually turn in. Every light was out by ten thirty. Emotions had finally worn them down. In fact, it seemed to John that the emotional drain was more than just a one-day thing it was becoming almost overwhelming. After all, these were just boys, attempting to deal with the most disturbing issue imaginable. Here he was, ten years older and he was struggling to deal with it. He had never had any one close, not even grand parents, pass on. Now he was the father, brother, friend and coach figure to fourteen fifteen year old boys. It was a drain to him so he was certain it was more than that to them.

John told Justin to hang out on the balcony, to talk with Tim's parents or some of the Colorado team, as they were staying at the same hotel. He needed to get away for a short while, to think and try to get himself straight emotionally. He wouldn't be gone long but wanted to make sure someone was there around the team.

Taking one of the vans, John headed east for ten miles, to a man made lake a local had mentioned to him. Sure enough, it was large enough to relax at, while staring up into the sky, wondering about the meaning of life. As a teen, John had enjoyed summer nights, lying in the bed of his pick-up truck with his friend Alex. Sometimes they would have their girlfriends but often it was just the two of them. Late into the night they would discuss life, wondering about space, infinity and what might happen after they died. It had always relaxed him to think about things so big and so undecided that he could forget about everything else. Tonight, at a man made lake, outside of Ely, Nevada, it was the same.

He only stayed an hour, realizing he needed to get back but in that short time, John had counted three shooting stars, not exactly a rare occurrence but also not something seen everyday. As he returned to the hotel he thought to himself that it might be a cool thing to sit out under the stars with these guys, introducing them to something he enjoyed when he was their age.

John found Justin exactly where he'd left him, sitting outside his room on the balcony. His arms draped over a middle bar of the railing, legs dangling off the edge of the walkway. The older coach assumed the same position. There they say, in exactly the same position, talking a little but only a little for two more hours, both men wanting to open up, neither really sure of how to do it. Instead they chose to sit, quietly until John finally yawned, off to bed to prepare for another day of Ely.

Chapter 41

It was after ten in the morning when the majority of the boys began to wake. John would have let them sleep that long anyway but felt it was almost a necessity considering the previous night's events.

Shortly after going to bed, both coaches as well as every player was wakened by a party in the rooms next door. The Arizona team had returned to the hotel themselves and was in the midst of a celebration. The walls shook as they pushed each other against them. Floors bounced and furniture fell as they jumped on the beds. Within minutes, nearly every door on that floor and those beneath it were open to see what kind of horrible problem might cause such a noise.

Seeing it was a group of teens and their coaches, more than one room proceeded to the manager's office to complain. Before long, red lights swirled in the parking lot waiting to escort the team from the premises. Not that having to leave the hotel would really bother the group, having the two motor homes in which to sleep anyway.

What amazed John and many other adults was the fact no arrests had been made, destruction of public property, disturbing the peace or most importantly, public intoxication or contributing to the delinquency of a minor. More than a few beer cans and empty alcohol bottles were left, strewn about the room and broken around the hotel property. John asked the manager if there were any charges filed but found there were none. Amazing.

By the time all the boys were up, it was too late to eat breakfast. Not having found anyplace worth eating a good meal, John and Justin waked down to the gas station where they bought twenty sandwiches, bags of chips and gallons of lemonade and juice. There is no meal quite like a sandwich from a gas station but that's all there was in town. The boys had no problem with it; in fact over the rest of the days in town, it became almost standard eating procedure.

Afternoons would be spent watching HBO and playing video games. It couldn't have any lazier a summer week, a "teenager's dream" to say the least. Sleeping late, eating in bed and playing video games, all while waiting to play baseball. Vacation redefined.

John didn't bring it up but made sure to watch Ambrose. He wanted to make sure the young man's attitude wasn't still down after the night before. After all, the baseball didn't matter compared to everything else. Nothing in his manner led John to believe Ambrose even thought twice about it. He joked and laughed, even eating more than his share for the first time in a while. It must have just been a moment to let off some steam, allow his emotions, which had been held in check so long, so well, to just blow up. It was probably a good thing that it had happened, for Ambrose anyway.

Finally, the late afternoon rolled around. Game time neared. There was a sense around the group, a sense of satisfaction, a comfortable feeling. With one more loss, everything would be done, over. The entire journey, three years together with John and more like eight years together for most of the boys would be finished. All the time in youth sports would have passed and only High School teams remained. Each boy knew as well that at the most, that meant only three more years playing together and that might not happen. Brad was seriously considering only playing football. Steve wasn't sure he wanted to play any more at all. Tim, Ambrose and Kris would play Varsity baseball while the others would play JV. Life was changing, the boys could now see it as well as feel it. For now, they were content to finish out this run, making last as long as they could and enjoying one another just a little longer.

As the sunset, the boys from Roadrunner took the field against a team from Utah. The evening was more than pleasant, warm but not hot. There were no clouds to help the colors of the sunset but it was beautiful just the same.

Maybe it was the feeling of contentment. Perhaps it was the finality of losing. Whatever the case, the boys played relaxed, hard and very well. Kris in particular, launching three home runs, while Tim and C.J. hit one each. The highlight of the evening came when Ambrose, on a two-nothing count, hit his first home run since everything had happened. The accomplishment brought not only his teammates to their feet but also the Utah team and their fans. Staying at the same hotel, the players from both teams as well as the families had gotten to know each other a little. They knew of Ambrose's situation and had taken a liking to the boys from New Mexico. It was a feel good night for all, even the Utah team that took a beating to say the least. When all was said and done, Albuquerque had defeated Utah twenty to nothing.

Another day of gas station food, cable television and video games was interrupted when the coaches, nearing the point of stir crazy, decided to take the two vans and the boys into the nearby mountains. The decision went over like a ton of bricks, as the boys were quite content to just lie around and relax before the game. John worried about lethargy. *A body at rest stays at rest.* There was no way he was going to take a chance of that happening.

A small dirt road turned into two tire width strips of dirt where cars had developed a path over years of heading into the hills. Those two strips disappeared after only a few miles so the coaches, young as they were and knowing the vans were rented, went four wheeling as they neared the peak of the foothills. Swaying to and fro, rattling almost violently, the vans rumbled over the grayish, silt ground of the Nevada mountainside, kicking rocks, out from under them as they went. The ride itself was almost worth leaving the hotel.

The team spent nearly two hours just wandering around, chasing a covey of quail and sitting under arthritic looking pines, talking about anything teenagers talk about. An afternoon waiting to be showered, as huge clouds rolled in allowed the heat to disappear making the temperature more than bearable. Several of the boys walked in a group, picking up and tossing rocks, led by Ambrose. John smiled as he looked at them. More than likely, there was little substance in their conversation, maybe girls or baseball, perhaps something else completely. The moment, however, would stay with one of them, if not all of them as a time they shared in the middle of nowhere. A memory that mattered, bringing a smile years from now, like the song which comes on the radio reminding an adult of a day in their youth, a good day, a pleasant memory. John would remember it and he wasn't really involved.

Todd and the new player, Justin sat under a tree, talking, sharing a drink from a "Big Gulp" cup. At least they pretended to be. John had found a dark stain on the floor of the back seat of one of the vans, where the two boys had sat on the drive from Vegas to Ely. Having played ball most of his life and having friends who "dipped" tobacco, he knew immediately what it was. The boys had played dumb when he asked them about it, so over the past three days, John had kept it in the back of his mind, trying to think of a way to handle it. From the first day he had started coaching, John had done everything he could to be a role model. He didn't drink, smoke or chew tobacco and made it clear that he didn't want his players to do it. Rather than say it again, he had let his two players believe they had gotten away with it, hoping their consciences would get the better of them at some point. After all, he wasn't their parent, it was summer ball, and did he really have the right to discipline them for this type of mistake? It was that moment, standing on a mountain in the middle of the Nevada desert that the young coach realized there was a great deal more to coaching than just on the field. Could he handle it? Did he even want to? There are just some who need adversity to strive. John was one of them.

Driving back to the hotel, Jason rambled on about his few innings on the mound. The other boys, namely Kris, Steve and Brad took shots back at him, friendly shots, reminding Jason how bad he had been. A friendly wager was placed, between Jason and Steve that if given the chance, Jason's E.R.A. would be lower. Jason being the one to make the wager, knowing he would never see the mound anyway. John laughed as he heard the bet being made. Jason, Steve and Brad had made a reputation for making outrageous friendly wagers on most anything. They also like who make rhetorical statements, wondering aloud how much money it might take to get one of them to do something considered by most to be gross or disgusting. How much to eat a handful of worms? How about holding one of the other's jock over your face after a game. Things of this sort. It was the reason John smiled at least this was normal. The coach decided to make it interesting.

"Tell you what." John started. "If we are up by twenty runs or more at any point the rest of this tournament, I'll pitch Jason."

Immediately, three or four "Alrights!" came from the back seat. Jason hesitated, making sure of what he heard. Thinking a moment, he realized there was little, if any chance of being up by twenty in a tournament of this caliber.

"OK, I'm in." The dark skinned boy answered, nodding his head as he did.

"Atta boy Horse!" Kris hollered. The boys called Jason horse as they had learned that his last name meant little horse in one of the Native American languages. No one had ever learned if it was really true but the name had stuck.

As fate would have it, as well as a Colorado team which seemed to want to get home to Denver, a twenty run cushion allowed Jason to throw an inning for his team. The game itself was ugly, not in terms of the Albuquerque team's play but rather the Colorado team's. Mistake after mistake gave Roadrunner more outs to work with. As good teams do, they took advantage, putting crooked numbers on the board in four of the seven innings. Momentum was swinging back toward New Mexico's side, opening the door for an opportunity to sneak into the Championship game and perhaps reaching their baseball lifelong dream of a World Series appearance. Once again, Arizona stood in the way.

The day a father hears that he will have a son; he begins to visualize that boy playing and performing as "the player" in "the game." From the first day that boy puts on a glove and picks up a bat, he sees himself hitting a home run in the bottom of the ninth in the World Series. It's a testosterone thing.

About the age of ten, every one of these boys had thought, more than once about playing in the Little League World Series. They had already missed one opportunity, that being the chance to play on television in that series. Only the twelve-year-old group was televised. Still, they had started thinking about it years before then taking those thoughts to the next level as a group and as friends when they left the field as thirteen year olds. All of that had now come together to be on the line over the next two days.

John had never thought about being in this situation, at least not as a coach. As a boy, he too had dreamt of playing in the "big game" and the World Series. All too soon, the realization that he wouldn't achieve those dreams hit him. When he began coaching, it was only out of a love for the game. Sitting on the balcony of the hotel, long before anyone else was awake, an epiphany struck him. He had taken a part in these boys' life and enjoyed passing on his love for the game as well as his knowledge. More than that, he cherished the fact he could impress upon them some of his values and morals, in turn making a difference in their lives.

More than that, he realized the impact they had on him. How they looked at and up to him. They learned from him as a friend and mentor. He needed that in his life. Now there was a direction. He could teach, coach and continue to help young men in their lives. Teachers aren't made they are born. He had a gift, the ability to pass on knowledge and life lessons. This team, this group of friends had done something for him he could never give back. They had given him purpose.

A warm breeze tickled the toes of his unshod feet. The sun shone brightly as it sat high in the Nevada blue. The smell of late summer, which John loved more than any other scent in the world, was the same in Nevada as it was in New Mexico. The morning gave notice of a good day to come. One of the player's doors open up, one more day as a team.

Chapter 42

While the boys had never minded, both the coaches were tired of gas station sandwiches. John had heard from one of the Utah coaches that a pop up trailer, parked on the sidewalk of Main Street was a pizza place. Rather than spend another lazy day, the coach thought it would be better to take a short walk and sort of "picnic."

Two picnic benches and three round tables, all with umbrellas allowed the team to sit while they enjoyed several types of pizza. The umbrellas provided shade on what was quickly becoming a ninety plus degree-day.

There was a quiet, relaxed feeling surrounding the meal. Any conversation was quiet and in most cases, short. It seemed as if it were better to just be together rather than talk about it. Often times, talking over it can ruin a moment. No one was going to ruin this moment.

Todd and Justin sat close to John. Maybe it was chance, more likely it was guilt. Neither boy talked at all, looking only at their food as they ate it. Rather, they picked at it, moving it around, nibbling but really not eating. Finally, Todd spoke up. It was as if the weight of his crime was pushing him down and he could no longer take it. The words almost jumped from his mouth.

"Coach, we know what that stain on the floor of the van was." He pointed back and forth between Justin and himself. Quietly, he finished. "We did it."

John stopped finished the bite he had just taken, took a sip from his soda then asked, "What do you mean, we did it?" knowing full well what Todd meant.

"We were dipping, and our spitter spilled when the van hit a bump." Todd was firm in his voice but contrite. Justin said nothing and was obviously going to let his teammate do all the talking. John thought it was curious, as it was more than likely that Justin had been the one to buy the tobacco. Not that Todd was manipulated in any way. John knew Todd was struggling in his world and had decided to try all the pitfalls that might be available to young adults. He knew exactly what he was doing. Still, John had hoped Justin would have spoken up as well.

"I figured it was something like that." John's voice was quiet, parent-like. I hope you realize how bad that is for you and now, because you tried to hide it, I will be the one to have to explain and probably pay some sort of penalty to the car place." Both boys looked down at their plates, sheepishly as their coach continued. "Anything you have to hide isn't right or even worth doing. I hope you both realize that."

"You knew all along didn't you?" Todd asked, relief in his voice, as it seemed there would be no punishment.

The coach looked at his player as if he were insulted. "Todd, I have played this game so long and believe it or not, I was a teenager once too. Of course I knew."

The conversation continued a short while longer. John reiterated how disappointed he was and how bad it was for the boys. Still, he would have no consequences, as he didn't feel it was his place. Not that he could do much more to Todd anyway. He was on the bench with an injury so sitting him really meant nothing. Justin was a reserve player as well; so again, there was little recourse to be had.

The relief of getting the guilt off his chest must have given Todd back his appetite as well as his sense of humor. He joked and bounced around like his old self as the others finished their lunch. John wondered if Todd would turn out to be the person he envisioned or just another could have been. He remembered Todd at thirteen, the toughest little player he had ever known, a hard working, and leadership-type player. He had even earned the nickname "Nails" from his coach, as he was as tough as nails, all the potential in the world. Hopefully, he would reach that potential.

Walking back to the hotel, only a few blocks away, John watched his team. They walked with arms over one another's shoulders. They bumped side to side as they were so close to one another, laughing and talking. The shadows under them were short as the afternoon sun stood almost straight overhead, this was their time no matter the outcome later that evening, and this was all about them. It became clear why there was such a calmness about the team, even at fifteen years old, they knew, they felt how special this time was. A gentle gust of wind came up from the west, causing the boys to hold their hats while stirring up a medium sized "dust devil." A hint of evening blew in with that breeze, giving tells that it would be a beautiful evening.

Sure enough, a gentle summer's eve rolled into Ely. A sprinkler hitched then sputtered as it cycled across the grass in the surrounding park. Small, low hanging clouds of dust rose over the cut out bases as a man with a large silver rake smoothed the reddish clay around them. Several of the boys made it habit to not put on their cleats until they were in the dugout, one of many superstitions, namely Brad, Steve and Jason. They continued a conversation, which John thought he remembered starting at lunch, "how much money would it take to…" Over and over the three friends came up with more disgusting ideas to finish that thought. It was a relaxed, genuine conversation reminding John of how comfortable the team was with their situation. Not even the slightest hint of pressure would raise its head around this group. It was friends, team and whatever, in that order.

The two coaches held a conversation as the boys warmed up to their left, along the right field line. Movies, college for Justin and golf were a couple of subjects that came up. John thought back to the very first game he coached with this group. There was tenseness about the boys then; even some anxiety on his part, now there was something else. Confidence? Maybe. Routine? More likely, worn down. That was the only thing the coach worried it might be.

As the boys gathered to take the field, John looked at his watch. The dark, digital lines spelled out the day and time, six o'clock exactly, August 4, 1994. For some unknown reason, the fact it was exactly on the hour struck John as odd. Never before could he remember sending a team onto the field exactly on the hour.

All day, the coach had tried to think of a great speech, something to really make the boys play hard. Something about the previous two games against this team, something about Ambrose. Here was the moment and...he had nothing. Really, he didn't even feel "fired up" himself, just a calm, comfortable feeling.

Pointing across the field, John had only a few words. "How are they going to remember you?" He hesitated, and then went on. "Will they remember the team that gave them everything they could handle in Tucson two years ago, then again two nights ago or just another team they beat three times?" There was no passion in his voice he simply made the statement. While he meant every word and in reality, it did hold some fire, somehow it just didn't seem to come out that way. "You decide." Finishing those words, John held his hand at the bottom of a pile of fourteen hands.

"In it to win it!" He spoke more sternly this time.

"Or get the hell out!" The team retorted as they sprinted out to their positions as they always did. The saying had been a bit calmer two years prior, now both coach and player felt they could use the stronger language and still be classy.

Watching the boys sprint, full out to their spots as they had for twelve games before this and numerous times in the years past, John smiled. It was classic baseball to take the field that way. Few other teams ever did and it often showed in their game. If nothing else would ever be said about John he knew it could never be said that he didn't teach the game the right way.

With Tim's arm supposedly hanging and Ambrose having spent himself in the two team's early match-up, the Albuquerque team had little choice but to send Bret to the mound. John always had a bit of uneasiness when Bret pitched, as he was either great or horrible, at least the coach knew he wouldn't have to wait long to find out.

Pitch number two was ripped to left field where a diving catch produced one out. Pitch five landed some three hundred feet away over the left fielder to where he couldn't catch it. Pitch six landed ten feet further than pitch five and pitch eight landed about twenty feet further than that. At least the coach didn't have to wait long. Eight pitches and they were already down three runs.

As he waited on the mound for Jon to trot out, the young coach looked around at his team. There was no panic, no frustration; just five, fifteen-year-old faces looking back at him. "Worn out," he thought to himself, "they're simply worn out."

Jon battled for the next three innings, giving his team the best effort he had. A short rally in the bottom of the first inning put the score at four to two but things just never quite got going. There was never any quit in the boys, who kept fighting, getting a run or two here and looking as if they might be just one hit away, there were simply no breaks. A sharply hit ball was always right at someone. A close call at a base. In the end it was a case of too little, too late. A final score of fourteen to eight finished the boy's season and for all intents and purposes, their time together as a team.

In answer to the coach's question, "How will this team remember you?" The handshakes and pats on the back signaled that they truly did have a tremendous amount of respect for the team from New Mexico. Even from the coaches, whom John had seen no sign of respect for anyone or anything, there was a sense of respect and rightfully so.

Quietly, almost eerily, the team gathered its equipment; picked up any trash they had left in the dugout and changed their shoes. John had walked down the line with Justin to thank him for all the help and talk a few things over. White uniforms, half buttoned and stained green and brown sat side by side, heads down, allowing the coach only the top of their caps.

John wanted to cry. Justin felt the same. Each boy in that dugout was overcome by emotion, yet nothing came. Nothing was being held back. It just would not come. Not wanting to talk in such an impersonal setting, John quietly picked up a bucket of baseballs and motioned for everyone to follow him. This was a moment the twenty something coach had thought about on many sleepless nights. Tossing and turning he thought of what to say. More than once, he showered for nearly an hour, lost in a trance, thinking about this very moment. Even then, with each step, he tried desperately to think of something, anything to say. Positive, comforting, anything but nothing came to him.

A hundred yards or so from everything else, the field, parents, people walking by the park, a huge, weeping tree, probably a Willow, stood tall. John put the bucket down, and then collapsed on it himself. One by one the boys dragged themselves over as well, laying their own bags down, sitting on them or resting their heads as if the bag were a pillow. Everything seemed so quiet, as if nothing else in the world were even moving. John rubbed his fingers on his chin. He needed to say something.

Slowly, his lip began to quiver, then stop. He tried to speak then changed his mind. It was probably only a few moments but seemed as if it were several minutes before he finally spoke. The words were garbled, choked back by emotions, which had been hidden for months.

"The past three..." It was all John could say before being overcome with tears. Breaking down, he began to sob almost uncontrollably. He couldn't recall anytime in his life when he had cried so hard. Never looking down he watched as each one of the boys lost it as well. All at once, sixteen young men, fourteen players and two coaches wept, holding onto one another physically and emotionally. There was finality to what had transpired. Not only was their season finished, now the inevitable had come true, this was more than likely their last time playing together as well. Certainly, it was the last time John would coach them. Two of the boys went to a different High School. Justin was going to college. Ambrose, well no one even wanted to think about that. Yet it was Ambrose, this was all about Ambrose, all the tears, and every bit of this emotion. This was for him and with him. He had been strong for them for so long, in turn; they had been strong for him. This might have been his last game of baseball. He may never be allowed to play the game he loved so much ever again. What in that was fair? Now it was all coming out. All the love, triumphs and sorrow finally allowed to be shown.

Gathering himself, only a little, John stood, then knelt by each one of the boys, hugging them and thanking them for giving him all they had. The words he had so desperately tried to find had been spoken with his actions. There was nothing to say. The boys knew. They understood. In turn, they hugged one another, continuing to cry, out loud and unashamed as they embraced.

Ambrose, Kyle and Kris' fathers had made a late week trip up to watch what turned out to be the final two games. Having waited a few minutes, allowing the team to have its moment, the three men joined the group under the saddened tree. They too were swept up in a wave of emotion, doing everything they could to comfort their own children as well as the two men who had no one to turn to, those being the coaches who had done so much. More than a half hour went by, as the team composed itself, cried again and finally was ready to move out. It wasn't so much that the boys had finished crying but rather, they had spent every bit of fluid inside of them, there were no more tears.

John called his mom from a pay phone outside the restaurant the team had found for dinner. He always called his mom when a tournament was over. As he spoke, his words were emotionless, and his mom could feel how empty her son was. As he told her the final score, his eyes felt as if they would fill up with tears again but nothing came. It wasn't the loss that brought back the feeling; it was the thought of it ending. Finally, he had found a reason, a direction and now he had to feel this? In a moment's time, he was lost again. There was a feeling of hurt that he could not explain but she could. It was the same feeling she had at that very moment, wanting to be there for him, telling him everything was going to be all right. It was natural to want to do that. He wanted to tell the boys, everything would be all right. Neither adult could do that and be honest. It was a lesson life they both had to teach. Softly, in the tone she had mastered years before, his mom spoke the words he needed to hear, words he would repeat to his players in the days to come.

"I'll be here for you."

Chapter 43

There is nothing in the world that evokes such different emotions than losing. For some it burns inside for days, others for only moments. A few competitors have the ability to leave it on the field, never thinking twice about it, knowing they will have another chance sooner than later. It is the driving force that makes competition all that it is.

There was little, if any emotion shown for the loss itself. It had been nearly two hours, making the time a quarter past ten, since the game had ended, usually more than enough time for even the poorest of losers to get over it and move on. As the boys walked into their hotel rooms undressing, showering or just collapsing on a bed, it was apparent there was no emotion left in any of them. Until, that is, they received word that John wanted then to change, grab something warm to wear and meet in the parking lot. That note brought reactions of wonder, irritation and even a hint of fear. That coming from Sean, the only fourteen year old, when he heard one of the others comment that the coach might be driving them into the middle of the desert to leave them.

All the boys wanted to do was lay in bed and sleep. To sleep meant to forget everything bad that had happened and to put this day behind them. Still, every one of them dressed, quickly in fact, to get out to the coaches. If John wanted them to do something, he must have felt it was important.

Ten minutes after sending the message, John stood outside his van, surrounded by all but one of the players. To no one's surprise, Tim was the lone straggler, having been on the phone with his girlfriend as he had been for the majority of the trip. The coaches had even taken to calling the time of day Tim's standard time as opposed to Mountain Standard Time.

Finally, the tall, slim figure of the fifteen year old emerged from his room and made his way to the group. John pulled the boys in close, explaining that they were going for a short drive, to the man made lake down the highway. There, they could talk; not talk, whatever they wanted but they could do it together one last time.

A collective groan quietly slipped from the group. While he didn't want to admit it, John half expected it as they were still fifteen year olds. What teenager wants to hang out under the stars with a group of boys? Those that did think it was a good idea wouldn't admit it anyway. Into the vans they piled and twelve minutes later, they unloaded onto a dirt parking area under what looked to be ten billion stars.

Looking up, as were most of the fellas, John spoke, "Just give me twenty minutes and we'll head back." they were the last words he spoke for more than four hours.

A couple of the boys had brought blankets from their rooms, while others had on sweat tops. The coaches lay back against the hood of the vans, using the heat from the engines to keep warm. It was a cool night, somewhere in the low fifties but seemed much colder. For all the complaining it took only a few minutes before the group had gathered, laying back, looking up into the sea of endless lights, talking in small groups and as a whole. John smiled. It was as if he were lying in the back of his pick up truck, a teen himself, asking and answering unanswerable questions with his best friend. This was exactly the reason he brought the boys out here.

Conversations ranging from girls to religion carried on all at once. Some of the fellas carried on two and three at the same time.

Memories of baseball, games from two years earlier as well as games John was not even a part of danced over the boys' heads, pictures painted by detailed explanations. There was no need for the coach to even take part; again, this was about the boys, not about him. Even Justin crept down to take part. John stayed back, outside the group, listening. To hear the boys was enough for him.

A shooting star shot through the sky about two in the morning, followed by another a few minutes later. Short, bright, streaks of light as beautiful burning out as those which still had it in them to hang high in the sky, awed the boys and gave new life to old subjects. The conversations seemed to be invigorated as the trails appeared then slowly and quickly at the same time, dimmed to nothingness. Over the next hour and a half, the boys counted six more. John didn't see that many and doubted there were unless there was a meteor shower he didn't know about. It didn't matter anyway. The only thing John could imagine feeling as good as that five-six o'clock hour when everything seems to slow was the majesty of summer's stars. Not only the stars everyone can see but the stars like these, hidden from the world unless you actually take the time to go and find them. Away from the lights of the city, allowing them to peek out from above the false light below.

The time spent was even more amazing than John had imagined, as was its reception. Near four o'clock, boys started nodding off giving notice it was time to go. Standing, gathering themselves then staggering back to the vans, not one of them took their eyes from overhead. Most of them patted their coach on the shoulder, or nodded in approval as the boarded the vehicles but Ambrose stopped, waiting for everyone else to get in before asking his coach for a moment.

"I just wanted you to know coach," The young man spoke between now chattering teeth. "If I die tomorrow, it would be OK because of tonight." John could do nothing but shake his head as if to try and talk him out of admitting his mortality. "No, coach, it's alright, I mean, it would be OK because tonight I saw the most beautiful thing with my best friends. Thank you for that."

All the emotion he had spent earlier that evening had led John to believe he couldn't cry any more, if ever again. Hearing Ambrose say that brought up an entirely new group of tears. Pulling his player near, the coach hugged him, keeping him close as long as he could.

"No Ambrose, thank you."

Chapter 44

The flight back to Albuquerque wasn't leaving Las Vegas until six in the morning the following day. That left an entire day to drive to Vegas then an entire night to do whatever it was teenagers do in a city where anything fun requires a legal I.D.

Most of the drive was consumed by sleep as everyone was still trying to catch up from the star light gathering only hours before. The two van, one car caravan left the city limits of Ely around eleven, arriving in Vegas just after three. Only two stops were necessary along the way, once for the boys who were awake the first half of the drive and once for those awake the second leg of the journey. Both stops required John to test his gambling skills on convenience store slot machines, both times coming up empty much to the chagrin of the boys. They of course, were of the video game generation where each pull should have meant a win of some sort, not a loss and certainly not a loss of their money. John smiled each time hoping there might be a lesson learned.

The second stop also allowed the vans to be refueled. As the coaches stood at the pumps beside the two parents who still remained with the groups, a miserably hot wind howled around them. Having spent such a pleasant week in the foothills had made everyone forget the Hades-like temperature of the city. It must have been over a hundred degrees causing the wind to literally feel like a hair dryer. Thank goodness home was only a night's passing away.

By the time the rental vans had been returned and hotel rooms had been designated, the hour neared five o'clock. Half the fellas wanted to walk the strip again; the others wanted to go the MGM theme park. Ambrose and Kris had no vote as all they wanted was an "all you can eat" shrimp buffet.

Deciding to use his coaching privilege one last time, John chose to take Ambrose and Kris to the nearby hotel their fathers were staying at, drop them off to do their buffet thing, then take everyone else to MGM. The Excalibur was right across the street, which could serve as a quick attraction to quell those who wanted to walk the strip then turn the boys loose at the theme park. Of course, as the boys stood in line to get their tickets, it struck John that his assistant couldn't stay with him in the casino so he had Justin go with the boys. It served two purposes, one for Justin to enjoy himself and two, to keep an eye on the team, satisfaction for all.

Now alone, John thought he might take a shot at rekindling the magic he had only months before. After all, he had nearly a hundred dollars left from his own meal money and no place to spend it. Tomorrow they would be home so, why not?

Five minutes later was why not. Four, twenty-five dollar bets on "the field" at the craps table took all his money and reminded him of how this city was built. For every time a winner walked away, that same person came back, putting more money in that he took out. The house always wins.

Not that it mattered; he hadn't expected to win and really didn't feel like spending his whole evening in the casino. Now however, he had more than two hours to kill before meeting up with the team. He wandered from table to table then from casino to casino, watching real gamblers do their thing. It was fun to watch people win, enjoying themselves, forgetting trouble which might have bothered them. Then he would notice a player who lost. Looking carefully, he could almost see in their faces the overwhelming panic when they lost big money. Maybe they were trying to get out of debt or change their situation and in a moment it was gone. Suddenly, John felt very alone.

As if his life had changed in a single moment. For a while it seemed as if he had finally figured things out, now he wasn't sure. His hands began to shake. His heart raced. Why couldn't he just feel the same all the time?

Sitting down in a rounded booth at one of the buffets, John gathered his composure and began to think. These feelings, this gloom he felt, it wasn't just about him. It was more than just he. What was it? Staring off into nothingness, at least that is what he saw; John began to figure what it was that was bothering him. For his part, he knew he had made his identity baseball many years before, baseball as a player. Now that was gone. OK, he could get past that, even if it took time, he could get past it. What was next? Did he want a job or a career? OK, he could figure that out as well. What was it that bothered him? He nodded to himself. Was he a good person? That was it. How did he view himself?

All his life, John had tried so hard to please everyone. To look right, act right, do the right thing. For the most part, he had. Then in college, and while he was playing ball, maybe he hadn't lived up to his own expectations of what a good person was. Then at once, everything became clear. While he had these feelings about himself, he looked at Ambrose each day, the most angelic person he had ever known, struggling and suffering through his own life. Why did Ambrose have to suffer and there were so many people out there who deserved to have a fate such as this boy's and they were fine, himself included. Not that he had ever purposely hurt anyone nor actually intended to do something wrong but still, why would God do such a thing? Sitting there in a place known as "Sin City" the young man came to understand or at least realize he didn't understand. Did God exist? How could he? To allow something as horrible as this to happen, there couldn't be a God. That's what John had been struggling with. Struggling to understand how something like this could happen, to understand himself and to accept all the things he had done. At once, he was fine. If this is how it is, then so be it. He couldn't change the past; he could only work on the future. Obviously, he would have to do it alone, as there was no help to be found out there, no guidance, no destiny. A new confidence washed over him. Now he could move forward.

Gathering at the front gate of the theme park, in groups of two or three, the team met to return to the hotel. As Las Vegas often does, it had energized the boys to want to stay up and play all night. Already it was ten. The plan was to be up and leaving for the airport by four so John saw no reason to be out any longer. At the same time, he really didn't see any reason for the boys to go to bed either, as they probably would have been up anyway. The decision was easy. Anyone who wanted to sleep could go into one of two rooms, farthest from the others. Those who wanted to stay up could, doing whatever they wanted, including the arcade on the first floor as long as they stayed out of the casino. No one slept.

Around one, John made a trip downstairs to make sure none of the boys had made their way into the casino. He found none. The arcade was empty as well. Hoping they had finally worn down, the coach returned upstairs to find a pizza deliveryman banging on one of the player's room door. He was more than upset.

"Hey, hey! What's going on?" The puzzled coach asked, hoping for a simple answer.

"I just delivered twenty pizzas to this room and got stiffed on a tip!" Spit flew from the man's mouth as he spoke.

Afraid of the response, John thought carefully before asking his next question. "Did they at least pay for the food?"

"Yes, but that's a lot of work to deliver twenty. I deserve a tip!"

John nodded in agreement. He wanted a simple answer he got a simple answer. Entering the room he and Justin shared, John opened an envelope filled with money from the Little League for travel. There was several hundred dollars inside. Returning to the hallway, he tipped the man thirty dollars, which calmed him and sent the man on his way. John then knocked quietly on the door.

Brad opened it a crack, them all the way when he saw who it was. Sure enough, twenty pizza boxes were strewn about the room.

"Twenty pizzas fellas?" The coach asked inquisitively as well as sarcastically.

"Coach, it wasn't our fault!" Jason shouted, his mouth full of pizza. Swallowing, he finished his statement. "We found these coupons," Holding up a handful of buy one, get one coupons he continued. "So we pooled our money, we had just enough for the food. Nothing was left to tip the guy."

John looked around the room thoughtfully. He and his teammates had done the same thing while in college. Not twenty pizzas but basically the same problem.

Taking a slice for himself, the coach replied, "I took care of it. Keep it down and I'll see you in a couple of hours."

As the door shut behind him, John leaned back against it, tilting his head upward. He sighed deeply. His lips pursed like a fish, then broke into a smile as he thought of all the things he had seen this group do over the years. They were good kids.

Laying down in the darkened room on the twin bed next to an already sleeping Justin, John thought back to something he had read. *It's not the destination but the journey.* It was John Wooden, coach of the record setting UCLA basketball teams. That man couldn't have been more right. It was the journey.

Chapter 45

Surgery had been scheduled for Ambrose a week after the team had arrived back in Albuquerque. The doctors had decided the best way to aid in fighting the cancer was not only to remove the tumor in his hip but to cut away some of the hip bone in the process. In doing so, they hoped to prevent any spread to Ambrose's bones and limit the possibility of the cancer spreading to any other part of his body. The procedure would keep Ambrose home from the first week of school but was thought to be a positive step in his cure.

Unable to speak for the others but certain they had similar days, John could say honestly that no hour passed when he didn't think about Ambrose and his surgery. He would have given anything to be able to switch places. All the fellas felt that way.

As it was the final weekend before school starting, several of the fellas slept over or rather stayed over as none of them could sleep, at Brad's house. The following morning they made their way to the hospital to visit their friend. Upon arriving, they were greeted by his parents and several relatives of their friend's.

Good news and bad news was the information they were met with. Bad news in the fact Ambrose was so weakened by everything, he needed to remain in the ICU a day longer, meaning no one could see him. Good news in that the doctors, upon opening his hip, found the tumor to have become detached from the bone, requiring very little else to be done. Rather than taking out a large portion of his hip, all that was necessary was to shave the bone down a tiny bit. A miracle one doctor put it, which brought tears to several mother's eyes. As religious as the family was, many of them said it was a miracle, God's work in reward for Ambrose's faith. Others thought maybe it was due to his love for his friends and playing the game he loved with them that allowed him to overcome the disease. Whatever the case, Ambrose's health was now in a position to come back. At the time, there was no sign of the cancer having spread to any other part of his body.

Of course, hearing such good news led those who were pessimists or simply not knowledgeable in the area of medicine to ask, what next? How long before the cancer would come back? What did this mean?

The short answer to all those questions was unclear but for the moment it was safe to say, Ambrose had a real chance of getting past this.

Tears of joy and hugs of relief circled the room. Phone calls were placed to the rest of the team as well as literally hundreds of friends, spreading the good news. It was amazing how fast the news spread and how good just hearing the news made everyone feel.

Kris's mom called the coaches, having to leave a message for John on his answering machine. Arriving home, John played the message. He could hear in her voice a quiver as she fought back tears. John reached down to push the save button on the machine but missed, accidentally hitting the erase button instead as the tears which had welled up in his eyes made it impossible to see. He collapsed to his knees, wanting to cry again but couldn't make the tears come out. A single drop finally escaped, running down his right cheek then falling to the ground below. It was wonderful news. News, which made the world seem, like a warm place again after a time with a dark cloud hanging overhead. Until that moment, all John had wanted to do was to get home and climb into bed, as it was late afternoon.

Hearing this news, he suddenly felt invigorated, deciding to go for a run and over to visit some friends.

The energy John had received from the news wasn't his alone to have. An entire neighborhood seemed to feel its effects. The fellas, who had seemed to disappear into their homes together, not feeling inspired enough to hang out, now were seen everywhere, Dion's Pizza, the McDonald's parking lot, wherever the teen hang out was, the boys were there again. School had started and with each new year there is always an energy that carries the students for a month or two. This was different. Cliques which didn't normally talk much now inquired to one another as to how they were doing as well as their now in common friend. Football too had begun their season and Brad as a sophomore was going to share time as the starting quarterback. He attributed his success to the inspiration Ambrose had given him, as did the team, which started off the season with three tremendous wins. Everything was golden, the colors seemed brighter and the weather was beautiful. A whole community seemed to take on the life force of this young man. It was amazing and all of this was without the young man even being at school yet.

When that day finally arrived, anyone not acquainted with the situation would have thought a rock star had decided to finish High School. There had been no announcement, as Ambrose just wanted to be another student but as word spread through Eldorado High School both student and teacher went out of their way to seek Ambrose out and pat him on the back. For the first three weeks of school it seemed as if everyday were a holiday.

Ambrose smiled and laughed through all of this, though he really would have preferred none of the fanfare. After all, he was only one person who had accomplished nothing. He hadn't saved anyone's life; he hadn't rid the world of evil. He had simply worked hard to trust in the things he believed in, nothing more, and nothing less. Harder than the hiding of his embarrassment from all the attention was hiding the fact he hurt again. Deep inside he hurt. Maybe it was the cancer; maybe it was his body trying to get right. Not sure of which, he never said a word, not even to his parents. He didn't want anyone to worry about him again. Wake up hurting, go to school, go to bed hurting. Never telling anyone. Always thinking of everyone else.

It was November; a single snowfall had layered the city when Ambrose returned to receive what was supposed to be one final treatment of radiation. It had now been three months and he had told no one of how he felt. Even as the doctor did an outward examination, asking the teen how he felt, Ambrose said nothing. He didn't want anyone to worry but inside he was pretty sure of what was going on.

Looking at the x-rays and results from the tests they had given Ambrose, the doctor saw what the young man was feeling. Clenching his fist, he softly pounded it once on the desk. There was no mistaking what he saw in front of him. How could this be going on inside this kid and him not say anything? The doctor was amazed and impressed all at once. For a moment, he wished he had not become a doctor because of times like this. Having to tell people things they didn't want to hear and things he didn't want to say. Then he thought about being able to meet someone as brave and strong as this young man. That was why he did what he did. Composing himself, the doctor took all the things he needed, walked toward the door to the waiting room where he would talk to Ambrose and his mother and thought of how he would say it. There was only one way.

"The cancer has returned, having spread to your lungs, bones and brain." Taking off his glasses, the doctor continued. "I'm sorry Ambrose."

Beautiful but worn by the past year's events Ambrose's mother broke down, hesitating as if she had any chance of holding back the rush of tears now streaming down her face, turning her red blouse a darker shade as they hit upon her chest. Both the young man and his father moved closer to embrace and attempt to comfort her.

Ambrose's father too, wiped tears from his cheeks, able to hold steady in appearance but falling apart inside. It was the same for Ambrose himself though he shed no tears, knowing for a while this news was coming. Again, he would be strong for those around him.

As quickly as the news had traveled of his well being, the same was true for this turn of events. Faces turned ghostly white and lips quivered upon hearing the news. A group of friends, parents and classmates rushed over to comfort and support the family. Two rows of cars, lined up the entire length of the residential street as well as around the corner to the next street from friends coming to the house.

Again, John received the news over his machine. His reaction was even a surprise to himself. He simply erased the message and began to make himself something to eat. There was no emotion. No anger. No tears. Not so much as a question directed toward the sky. He expected it. All he had seen over the past years, along with his epiphany in Las Vegas allowed him to be cynical and fully expect news like this.

Each day, his bitterness grew inside of him. Why shouldn't it? What kind of a world allows a sixteen-year-old boy, as good a person as there was on the planet to suffer? He had expected this. Over recent weeks, he had begun turning off the radio so no music could brighten his day. If he woke each day expecting something bad to happen and nothing did, then it was a pleasant surprise. This was the news he had been waiting for. Of course this was happening.

The sun was still up outside as the young coach collapsed into his unmade bed. There was solace in that bed. The rest of the world couldn't get to him. The sheets were cool, relaxing him as soon as they touched his uncovered skin. Within moments he was asleep.

Around the neighborhood, many felt the ripple of this stone cast into the pool. Ten boys however, felt it more than anyone. The first time they heard the news, each one of them had thought about the finality of it all. They couldn't help but think about it. Death. It was a real possibility then, after seeing Ambrose the next day or within days, the feeling had passed and once again the ignorance of youth allowed the feeling of invincibility to sneak back in. Every teen feels they are invincible. It's normal and that feeling was only washed away momentarily when the news first came. Now, as they sat in their rooms silently, in front of televisions without really watching, with parents, talking but not really listening there was a realization that life does end and it was just a matter of time before Ambrose would be gone. To a man, this news, this day, was the darkest, most difficult day of their young lives. Music didn't help, games weren't a distraction, and food wasn't appetizing. So many troubles can come into a young person's life. Most of those are trivial in the real world and are gone within days. This, as it should, would stay with them forever and the following days would be somber, reflective and difficult.

A cold wind blew what few leaves remained off a tree outside Kris' window. A symbolic, ironic cover of gray clouds had blanketed the southwestern city for nearly a week. While it was commonplace for the wind to blow in January and February, rarely does it blow in the last two months of the year. Both day and night however, the wind had gusted and often howled brining with it a chill a person could feel deep inside.

Lying on their stomachs, Kris and Kyle worked together on homework. Usually, Ambrose was there with them. Neither spoke, nor looked up from their books, which spoke volumes for their state of mind. As teens often do, more time was spent talking about other subjects than the books in their backpacks. Sports took center stage more often than not, though the subject of girls was quickly gaining speed. Ambrose would get the boys back on track, unless of course it was he who had begun to stray first.

It had been several days now that he was unable to be with them, sick from both inside and out. More and more often, Ambrose was so sick or weak he couldn't even get out of bed. His frame supported no more than one hundred and twenty pounds. Still, if his body allowed, Ambrose would not only attend school but those study sessions at friends' houses as well.

"What do you think is going to happen? Kyle asked, speaking to Kris but not really directing it in his friend's direction.

The question was indistinct, really but Kris knew exactly what Kyle meant. He had been thinking it as well.

"I don't know." Kris mumbled in reply. Inside, he desperately wanted to answer something different, something positive but couldn't

As all the boys had, Kris and Kyle had been in long talks with their parents and parents of friends. The reality of the situation and all the horrible possibilities had been discussed. The doctors had only given him two months to live and already Ambrose was near that. It wasn't the first time one of the fellas had asked another or several others that same question. The answer now was the same.

"Will you keep playing baseball?"

"I've asked myself the same thing." Kris replied. "Sometimes I think I won't or maybe I will but inside won't enjoy it." Looking out the window Kris paused, then continued. "Then I think 'Brose would want me to play, all of us to play and I know I will."

Kyle already knew the answer to his own question. Over a year ago, he had found a fire inside himself to achieve. Not a day had passed in over fourteen months which he didn't do something for baseball. Throw, swing, run or lift weights. To this point it had been for himself. Now he had new motivation. To play as long as he could because his friend could not. No boy in the world, who had ever picked up a ball and bat had ever wanted to play the game as much as Ambrose. If he couldn't, Kyle certainly would. It was a common thread, though none of the boys ever said it aloud. Some part of them, deep inside told them they could and would, find a way to play just a little longer for their friend.

Many of the boys listened to Country music at the time. It was, as all music is, a fad. Country music had come to the height of its popularity in the past few years. One song, now played over and over again by many of the fellas, spoke of a man who lived everyday with a memory, which brought him pain. He talked about what it might have been like to know ahead of time what would happen so he might have avoided that pain or perhaps how his life might be different if he had never lived that time of his life. In the end, the man decides life is better left to chance, for if things had gone differently, yes he wouldn't have to live with the pain but he never would have spent the time or have the memories those times had brought him. He would have missed the dance. Not one boy could honestly say he hadn't thought of both those scenarios. Never having to bear the pain they struggled with now but realizing what they had gained. Any daydreams the boys spent held some form of that sentiment.

More than one afternoon and one boy's room held these thoughts and conversations over the next few weeks. On days when Ambrose was too sick to get to school or homework session, at least one and more often, several of the boys would go over and see him. Never once was a friend turned away or asked to come back. Even if he slept, the boys would wait, talking with his parents or sitting quietly next to him as he slept. Ambrose always wanted to see his friends and they wanted to see him.

Seeing their friend was not always easy, however. The cancer was now eating away at his body, shriveling his arms and legs. Tumors had begun to grow upon his body, several even showing their ugliness upon his head. More than one time a friend would want to look away, as it was hard to see their friend like this. Ambrose always saw it in their eyes, then before anything could be said, he would reassure them that it was still him and it would mean a great deal to him if they would see past the body and see only him. His words always gave strength to those around him as they had from the day he met them.

It would have been so easy for Ambrose to turn away visitors, no one would have thought twice about it. He could have asked, "Why me!" angrily or sorrowfully, and no one would have thought less of him. Still, as he had through the summer, he remained steady, never once worrying about himself in appearance or health. Instead, he made sure those around him were comfortable. His constitution often made the grown men around him question their own character. Though the days were gray, the time spent with Ambrose was not.

The cold winter continued, as if someone was watching, setting the mood for the boys to follow.

One mood, which more than echoed the weather, was John's. Many nights he would lie on the floor, in the dark, looking up at the changing images he saw on the ceiling. On nights when it snowed, soft black puffs dropped silently as the light from across his patio silhouetted their small forms. He listened for the splashing of water and sludge as cars rolled by on the nearby street. Other nights, the same light would cause shadows against the textured background, allowing shapes to come out and then disappear. All the while, he thought about nothing.

Nothing was what he wanted to believe he was thinking about. Everything was more the case. All the terrible decisions he had made from days way back. He thought of the people he had disappointed when he didn't reach his goals. Which ones were his? All the potential in the world, physically, intellectually, artistically. None of that potential reached. Now, he had ten, eleven, twelve young men looking to him for guidance, comfort and reassurance. How could he deal with that? He couldn't even handle his own life, let alone help the boys. The realization of his biggest fear was staring him right in the eye. When would he make another mistake? It had haunted him for years now only this time, he worried his words or actions would lead someone else astray. His thoughts drifted into a dream.

From the very first time a young person steps onto a ball field, they either have a connection with it or they don't. If a connection is made, it never goes away. They are safe there. No matter how well things go or how badly, that person is always safe. Not to say that the game of baseball is always good to that person. The game can treat a person worse than any man or woman, making him or her feel great for a period of time, then snatching it away. Often, it can bring heartbreak and frustration over long periods of time. Then, just as that person is ready to give it up, from nowhere, it comes back, making everything feel good again. Every so often, a person really understands the game and rather than the game taking charge, that person is in control. Sure there are ups and downs but the game never gets away from that person. It is that person that one in a thousand who makes the game everything it is supposed to be.

Though he was in a half conscious state of mind, the words sounded crystal clear to the coach. He could see Ambrose and the fellas playing the game, enjoying every minute. He was there with them, standing off to the side, saying nothing, yet still a part of the whole. Slowly, his thoughts clouded and he could feel himself sobbing.

Waking from his state, John took a minute to gather himself. He remembered what he had dreamt about. Was it good? Bad? Nothing? Confused even more, John picked himself off the floor and climbed into bed. As he had so many nights over the past year, John fell asleep to the same thought. *Let me fall asleep and never wake up, so that Ambrose can.* Selfless or selfish? Either way, morning continued to wake him.

Chapter 46

In a moment's time, everything went black. There was no pain, no suffering and no warning. Feeling for the edge of the couch he had been laying on, Ambrose fell to the ground.

He had been lying on the couch, eyes closed, listening to whatever television show his mother had been watching. It was Tuesday, a quiet, breezy yet uneventful Tuesday. The whole day had been geared, as every Tuesday and Thursday was, toward going to watch the fellas play for the High School.

It had been weeks since Ambrose had been physically able to attend any school but he was lucid, aware and as always, in good spirits. On afternoons such as this, his mother would drive him over to the High School field, where they had cleared an area just outside the fence, down the left field line so a specially rigged van could pull up along side, open a sliding door and allow Ambrose to lay and watch the boys play. Only sophomores, both Tim and Kris had made the Varsity team while the others had made the Junior Varsity. Today, Tim was scheduled to throw. It was a start that would not take place.

As she had been doing, around the three o'clock hour, Ambrose's mother would start the van, get all the moving parts in order, go back inside to carry her son out to the van. Ambrose had lost so much weight; his five foot four mother could easily carry him to and from the garage. Upon returning to the living room, to her horror, she found her son, laying face down on the beige carpet; too weak to push himself back up, two rays of light shown downward through the west facing windows, warming the back of his hairless scalp. He showed no sign of worry or fear. Only his sense of calm kept his mother from the panic she felt about to overcome her. She rushed to his aide.

"Oh baby, are you alright?" She had hoped her voice didn't tremble, giving away her fear.

As she rolled him over, his face, unbelievably, held a smile. Not a smile of joy or laughter but peace. "I'm fine mom, I suddenly couldn't see, then fell off the couch."

In his weakened condition, even a fall so short as two feet could break his brittle bones. He knew it. His mother knew it. This time it was all right.

"I don't think I can go to the game though mom. Do you think the boys will mind?"

His sincerity overwhelmed even his mother. "Of course they won't mind. They want you to be alright." Though her voice didn't tell her secret, tears rolled down her face.

Laying him back on the couch, she gently kissed his forehead. Noticing him wince in pain as she lifted him, she hurried to the kitchen to get his pain medicine.

Standing alone in her kitchen, white tile floor with soft, brown, speckled granite counter tops; Ambrose's mother began to break down. Crying as hard as she ever had before, though without a sound, her knees began to give out. The room so bright, as the afternoon sun shown through the huge bay windows to the back yard began to spin as she began to faint. Her stomach felt sick as she braced herself against the kitchen island.

All at once, she gained hold of herself. Though she knew what was coming, there was no way to let her only baby down. He needed her. Now, after all this time, he needed someone. Not the other way around. There would be time for her grief later. Now she had to be as strong for him as he had for her and all the others in his life.

Wiping her eyes, she composed her body and her thoughts. She took a syringe from the drawer, filled it as the doctors had shown her and returned to her son. He lay still on the couch, just as she had left him. For a brief second, she worried. Had he passed? No, not that, she had so much she wanted to say. To hold him one more time before he left her. That was all she wanted. No, not yet Ambrose.

"Ambrose?" This time there was a hint of panic in her voice.

"Yes mother?" His voice was weak, only above a whisper.

Thank God. He was still with her. Now she could say all the things she needed to. Gently, she began to roll his sleeve back to give him the injection.

"Please mom, no shots. I don't need them anymore." While still a whisper, his voice was calm, steady, as if he knew everything was going to be all right. "Can we..." Ambrose stopped to swallow and regain his thought. "Can we take a bath?"

From birth, water is a religious symbol. Early on, a baptism in or with water signals the beginning of a journey. Perhaps this was the end of a journey. Perhaps this young man could see beyond his surroundings and wanted to end as he began. Perhaps he simply wanted to be cooled and taken care of by his mother once again as he had when he was a baby.

Lifting his limp body, Ambrose's mother carried him off the couch, the hand knitted blanket that had covered him falling to the ground as he went. Gently, she lowered him into the huge oval shaped tub in her bathroom. She helped to pull his legs back so the water could begin to run. Cold at first, then warmer, water rushed out of the faucet, splashing on the porcelain, filling the lowest end of the tub, over the drain first then running slowly up to and around his thin, dry, sore covered legs.

Cupping her right hand to gather water, and then pour it over her son's shoulder, she thought the water felt too cold to be comfortable for Ambrose. He felt nothing. It wasn't the temperature of the water he was concerned with; it was that moment with his mother.

Kneeling beside the tub, she rubbed his shoulders with her hands, alternately scooping handfuls of water to pour gently over them. Taking a washcloth from the towel bar over her, the love of Ambrose's life brushed it against his cheek, then down to his shoulder and over his arm. Neither of them spoke.

Only the occasional sound of soft splashing water could be heard through the house. Particles of dust and lint floated along the white beams of light in the living room and kitchen, a car passed by outside and a robin chirped once to search for company but not a sound came from inside the house. Ten minutes passed.

Her face flushed from the hundreds of tears which had rolled down her face in recent moments, Ambrose's mother sniffled, brushed away a few more, then gathered the strength to speak. For weeks now she had wanted to say these words now slowly coming from inside but she couldn't find the strength the day's event had now brought her.

"Ambrose...baby." She wanted to break down but her mind, now made up, wouldn't let her. Her lips trembled as she started again. "Ambrose, for so long now, you've been strong...for your friends...classmates...and for me." Her eyes looked toward Heaven to give herself a moment and maybe for more.

The boy's mouth opened as if he were going to reply but he spoke no words. His head slowly fell back as the strength in his neck seemed to be giving way. Quickly, his mother climbed to her feet, now sitting on the edge of the tub, so to get behind her son as best she could and support his body for him.

"All this time you've been doing for everyone else, making sure they were alright, making sure they were ready for this." As she continued, the words came easier, her thoughts clearer. It was as if Ambrose's strength, his constitution was now becoming hers. His big brown eyes looked back and up at his mother as she finished.

"It's OK. I'm Ok...your friends they're OK. Were going to make it, thanks to you...all of us are going to be able to move on from this." Now she began to stumble. Her voice remained calm but tears poured down again.

"It's time you...you...you move on. You've stayed as long as you could." The last sentence came quickly as she tried to get it out before breaking. A deep breath allowed her to go on. "Oh my sweet, sweet baby please let yourself move on. I want you to." Her hands trembled only slightly as she caressed his arms and softly dropped her head against the back of his.

Eyes closed, she felt his hand reach up and touch the top of her head as she embraced him with all she had. Without speaking, his touch spoke to his mother, letting her know it was that closure which he needed. To be assured she would be all right without him. Now he could go.

Slowly, his hand moved forward and back down to his side as what little strength remained, finally left him. Softly exhaling, his body relaxing, Ambrose died in his mother's arms.

Chapter 47

Days after the funeral, John received a call from Kyle's mom, a counselor at the High School. In a brief conversation, she asked if he might come in to school and spend some time with the boys.

He had seen several of them and spoken with most of the others, as they had needed someone to talk to, cry on and share with. None of them had ever lost anyone close. Not that John had. Still, he was safe for the boys to open up to. How hard is it for teenagers to open up to begin with. Put on top of that, being boys, not really supposed to show emotion and at the age where parents are hard to talk with. John was the obvious choice.

Not old enough to be a father to them. Not young enough to be a peer. Not far enough removed from that age to still understand what they might be going through. Already he spending time with the boys but of course he would go in.

As the past year's time had taught John, the world is a cruel place, sometimes ironically, often harshly, and occasionally even humorously. What no one knew, not the boys, his parents or friends, John was struggling with this as deeply as anyone. Three years he had spent with Ambrose. They had taught each other and learned from one another. Ambrose had shown John how to lead and at the same time, how to follow. In return, John had helped him to pursue his passion, given a few life lessons and so much more. Between them there was so much more. It was that way with all the fellas on his team but like the players and everyone who had come in contact with Ambrose, the coach had found someone very special and had been drawn to him. It was a gift the boy had been given.

John had never lost anyone close to him. Not like this. A grandfather whom he loved a great deal but only saw twice a year at best had passed away when he was fifteen but the services were in Denver, which John didn't attend. He didn't see his grandfather pass nor did he see him suffer. This was something more, to see what happened to this young man, to see his body wrecked, his physical suffering could have been too much for many people. Now John had to be strong for all these young men when it was difficult to allow anyone to be strong for him. Best to keep it to himself and focus his energy on the fellas, a decision that would haunt him.

The coach arrived at the High School, late morning. Walking in through the glass doors of the administration building, the timing was such that Brett, Brad, Steve and Jason were walking in as well. Shaking hands as they met, the five friends made their way to a room that had been opened up for the group to meet in. The rest of the boys were already there. Tim, Todd, and Jon sat together on one side of a long, cherry wood conference table. C.J., Justin, Kris and Kyle sat in large, black, leather chairs opposite their peers. All those in attendance showed strong faces, as if to say they would break down no more. Tim and Todd were stoic as well. No one could think of anything to say.

Kyle's mom came in, handing the coach an envelope, whispering something in his ear. Shortly, she left the room, shutting the door behind as she left.

Pausing for a moment, John looked at the envelope in his hand. He looked up at the eleven boys in front of him and back to the envelope. After hearing what Kyle's mom had to say, he knew what was in the envelope, he just didn't know how to move next. The boys looked forward, waiting to see what was coming. No one spoke.

Slowly, John opened the envelope, taking from it several pieces of paper. Gently, he unfolded them, revealing in black ink a beautifully penned letter. John looked up at the boys in front of him again. They looked back. No anticipation, no anxiety. They just looked up at their friend.

"Frien..." John started, then had to clear his throat, gather himself and start again. This time he read smoothly.

Friends,

When you read this, I will be gone. I miss you, as I am sure you miss me. Don't be sad though, as I know I am in a better place and am at peace.

I want to thank you for all the times we shared together both on the field and off. We accomplished great things. You need to be proud of that. I know I am. Coach, we couldn't have done it without you. Thank You.

Remember our celebration after winning our first championship. Dancing and singing before State. Our conversation on the lives of Smurfs and the tarantulas and rattlesnake warning in Tucson. Remember, Tim, Kris, Brad and Bret, what it felt like to not win our fourteen-year-old year. Remember Kyle when we held you down to make you say a word you didn't want to say. Remember all the pre-game movies. Remember that Ely doesn't have a McDonald's. All those baseball memories remember them and keep them forever. They are ours.

As he turned the page, John looked up from his reading. Each boy's gaze remained fixed on him, not a dry eye in the group. Small pools had formed on the table in front of those who were leaning forward. None of them wiped their faces. Perhaps it was an act of remembrance, perhaps defiance against their emotions. Whatever the case, they waited to her more. The coach read on.

For me, I will remember most, the night we spent, under the stars by the lake in Nevada. I will remember it because of you. That memory itself causes all the others to come back. We shared everything that night. We shared it together. Please remember that for me.

You are the greatest group of friends any person could ever hope to have. I thank you for that. I hope I gave you as much as you gave me.

Remember, more than anything else, there are NO EXCUSES! You are all too talented with too much potential to let excuses get in the way. Every one of you can do anything you want to in life. All you have to do is go do it.

Tim and Kris, go be baseball players. Brad, make it in football. Todd, C.J., Steve, Kyle, Bret, Jason, Jon and Justin, whatever it is you want to be, you can. I know you can and I will expect it.

Coach, I know you can do it as well. You taught us how to get past the excuses and be the best we can be. Now it's your turn.

I'll be watching, looking out for you guys and somehow, I'll let you know it. I love all of you.

Ambrose

A tear of his own hit the paper before John could fold it and put it back in the envelope. Taking a deep breath, he looked up at the boys who now, wiping their faces, revealed almost determined looks, hidden beneath mournful eyes.

Todd was first, followed by C.J. then Jon to stand and rush to their coach, embracing him. The rest of the room followed, Kris, Kyle and the others and finally Tim to a group embrace, swallowing within it all the tears, love, anger and confusion. For a long while the group stood together in this embrace, until everything that needed to go away finally did.

Epilogue

I stared at the marble block. As I read the words, I felt as I had all those years ago. I felt sad but also inspired. Not so much by the memorial itself but by the young man it stood for. Looking down as a cloud passed in front of the sun, dimming the shine coming off the marble block, I smiled. Those years, those days, those boys. We had grown up together. They took their first steps toward manhood with me. I took my first steps toward adulthood with them. I had been their coach.

The Cottonwood again rustled in the breeze and sprinklers started on the eleven and twelve year old field. As the sun shown through the mist of water in front of me, I looked at my watch. Nearly five o'clock. I had spent an entire day lost in the past, surrounded by strangers, staring at something few, if any, knew anything about. I must have looked as if I had lost my mind.

Only one game was still being played. I sat myself down, this time in the front row, watching not only the ball game in front of me but also the man behind me who lowered the wire that held aloft all those championship flags. As the flags touched down I could see each of the boys' faces flash before my eyes. Tim, Kris and Kyle. All three had gone on to play professional baseball, Tim for the Twins organization, Kris for the Orioles and Kyle for the Cleveland Indians. Tim was a no brainer. He had signed with the University of Miami out of High School but never attended, choosing instead to play pro ball. Kris had gone to college, and then was drafted. Kyle surprised most of us. Not that anyone doubted he would be a success but a pro ball player? No doubt, that one setback, compounded with Ambrose's words, inspired him to outwork anyone around him. He truly reached his potential.

Jason attended one of the military academies, no small feat considering what it takes to get in. Jon tried his hand at modeling, with modest success before deciding to pursue a more stable career. Steve, C.J. Todd and Justin all went to school achieving success there and later with family life, all as they should have. Potential fulfilled.

A teen aged boy walked past me, making his way up the bleachers to sit next to a pretty girl who seemed to be there watching a younger brother. The young man reminded me of Brad and a phone call I received several years after Ambrose's passing.

I had moved to Denver, running away from myself but never too far from what the boys were doing. I knew Brad was attending the University of East Carolina and playing quarterback there. I also knew he was nearing his senior year with little hope of starting as a young prospect had a bead on that job. No shame at all, to get an entire education paid for and be good enough to receive a scholarship at a division one school is a one in several hundred accomplishment. From out of the blue, Brad called me, getting my number from my parents who still resided in Albuquerque. He asked me if I would be disappointed in him if he left the football team to focus on his law degree. I was taken back that he worried that much about what I thought after all that time. Of course, I had no problem with it, telling him so, tears welling up in my eyes as I did. That single question validated my time and really my life. For years I had beaten myself up for mistakes I had made and not reaching my own potential. For one of the boys, one in fact, whom I didn't think had bonded as closely as others, to show me I had made an impact on his life nearly buckled my knees, another success from that group. So many more memories beat at the back of my head to get in, I had to stop and focus on something else.

The hour of day, which I treasured so much, had come. As it did every day of every summer, time seemed to slow down. The heat of the day cooled ever so slightly. A quiet calm eased its way into the Southwestern evening. I nodded to myself. This was good. To be here, living, remembering, but most of all, living, that was good.

The sound of a poorly hit ball, followed by a "Heads up!" brought my eyes back to the game. Looking up, I spied the figure of a ball headed into foul territory, toward the fence, near me. The ball carried over the fence, looking to land just to my left. Reaching out with both hands, I cupped my hands, allowing just enough give for the ball to *smack* loudly against my palms as I caught it.

Spinning the ball in my hand briefly, just to remember one last time, I tossed it back over the fence to the third baseman.

"Pretty good," A man sitting in the bleachers nearby smiled and quipped. "Maybe you ought to give the boys a few pointers."

"Maybe," I smiled back at him, starting my walk out of the park. "And I'm sure they could give me some."